DCOM Networking with Visual J++ 6.0

George M. Doss

Wordware Publishing, Inc.

Library of Congress Cataloging-in-Publication Data

Doss, George M.
    DCOM networking with Visual J++ 6.0 / by George M. Doss.
      p. cm.
    Includes index.
    ISBN 1-55622-655-1 (pbk.)
    1. Electronic data processing--Distributed processing.   2. Object-Oriented programming
(Computer science).   3. DCOM (Computer architecture).   4. Microsoft Visual J++.
I. Title.
QA76.9.D5D67   1998
005.27'62--dc21   98-48781
                                                        CIP

© 1999, Wordware Publishing, Inc.

All Rights Reserved

2320 Los Rios Boulevard
Plano, Texas 75074

Printed in the United States of America

ISBN 1-55622-655-1

10 9 8 7 6 5 4 3 2 1

9811

All inquiries for volume purchases of this book should be addressed to Wordware
Publishing, Inc., at the above address. Telephone inquiries may be made by calling:

(972) 423-0090

This book is dedicated to Minnie Lee Doss, my mother, for who she is and for who she is not.

Contents Summary

Contents

Part II: Administrative Planning Process

Contents

Contents

Acknowledgements

This being my second book with Wordware Publishing, Inc., I would again like to thank the fine people who seek to make the writing process more fun and easier than it should be. I would like to thank in particular Beth Kohler, senior editor; Jim Hill, publisher; Denise McEvoy, interior design; and Alan McCuller, cover design. I would like to thank also the other friendly people there who seemed to have a smile and a hello when I went there to turn in a bit more of the manuscript.

I would like to thank all my former teachers, remembered and forgotten, who gave me this piece of knowledge or that piece of knowledge.

I especially would like to thank Tom Mitchell, a friend and former manager, who first suggested a project management document.

I would like to also thank all those writers of books and articles in this field who gave me an idea or two. Unfortunately, in most cases I do not necessarily remember who gave me what idea.

I would like to thank Thomas Merton for writing his autobiography, *The Seven Storey Mountain*, and the path of life upon which it has sent me.

And finally, I would like to thank people who are never acknowledged at this point—the readers of this book.

Any omissions or technical misinterpretations are mine. *Mea culpa!*

George M. Doss
Plano, TX

Introduction

> *The ability to find an answer is more important*
> *than the ability to know the answer.*

System administrators around the country, and in fact around the world, are seeking to solve their management's desire to have an intranet and also have their companies involved on the Internet (read "World Wide Web") for commercial reasons. They find that their key problem is hardware and software integration. The expected general technical goals of this enterprise network are:

➤ Interoperability
➤ Portability
➤ Reusability

A possible scheme for achieving these goals is the use of the Distributed Component Object Model (DCOM) architecture and its supporting technologies.

DCOM as used throughout this book means Microsoft's commitment to an object-oriented (OO) networking architecture for an intranet with the Internet as an access backbone using Microsoft's technologies (products). The label can be COM or COM+ or any other label. It is the goal of achieving an intranet with Java internetworking or connectivity that is the foundation of this book. While there are many Microsoft products or technologies available for achieving networking, the cornerstone of these technologies for OO architecture is the rapidly evolving Visual J++. Perhaps the other products should not be ignored, but the types of questions and processes raised in this book could also be raised about these products as well.

The guiding definition of DCOM used in writing this book is simple. It harbors many complex design and development issues for the network components and the programming code. The definition is that the Distributed Component Object Model (DCOM) is the theoretical core of an object-oriented architecture that has remote distribution as its end goal.

> **Note:** The above is stated because of Microsoft's dynamic commitment to a tighter Java integration. The technologies or their labels may change, but process and functionality do not change.

Bird's Eye View of Book

The book's first focus is the core essentials of a ten-step process of project management for a collaborative effort in the development of an enterprise network with DCOM architecture and its supporting technologies. Over 250 example questions for a system or network manager show what should be asked to smooth the ups and downs during the network integration process.

The book's second focus is a ten-step technical planning process that parallels the project management process. These steps include defining the network components, network modeling, working with protocols, evaluating service and access servers, and developing technical policies.

The book supplements the process with internetworking basic concepts on DCOM, Visual J++, and an enterprise network infrastructure. A full-blown enterprise network is simply two or more intranets connected through an Internet backbone. Figures show the principles of name context or tree and inheritance (class and hierarchy). An appendix includes a discussion of some Java coding issues for doing internetworking.

The book includes examples of the types of documents and their contents to communicate the status of the project to all shareholders. This documentation includes such documents as the marketing plan, design plan, quality plan, and risk assessment.

The book also looks briefly at two key networking issues—remote access and security. The book closes with summaries of DCOM and metaconcepts for object-oriented design and development synthesis, and a two-sided (administrative and technical) collaborative network integration process. The book has two appendixes for terms and definitions—software and hardware.

Audience

This book is for system administrators and MIS managers who work with enterprise network integration. Any enterprise network integration involves ever-changing goals, issues, and techniques in an environment that has multiple forms of:

➤ Network architecture and configuration
➤ Operating systems
➤ Protocols
➤ Management tools
➤ Application software
➤ Graphical user interfaces (browsers)
➤ User activities, abilities, and needs

Because of the above situations, this book considers the required thought processes for success. The methodology given here enables you, the enterprise network administrator, to plan, coordinate, and evaluate effectively and efficiently your integration processes.

This book is also for people who assist the enterprise network administrator, either in policy or design integration. This would include:

➤ Members of the integration development team
➤ Product vendors
➤ Consultants
➤ Support technicians
➤ Documentation and training groups
➤ Users (internal, customers, or vendors)

Of course, this book is also for anyone who has an interest in the processes for integrating new Internet and intranet technologies for electronic interactive enterprise commerce.

Key Issues

Key issues such as legacy (software and hardware), security, human factors, and connectivity (software and hardware) are discussed. Within the discussion on key issues there are checklists for selecting certain important hardware (gateway, firewall), software (browsers), and applications (e-mail, newsgroups). Security issues are discussed throughout, and there is also a chapter devoted to security.

Focus Is

This book focuses on the system planning, the integration component of creating an enterprise network with DCOM architecture and Java internetworking. Some of the key parameters of the design, development, and implementation should be established in the book. However, no one book can give all the parameters because of local and legacy variables.

Focus Is-Not

This book is <u>not</u> a comprehensive answer to integrating an enterprise network. There is no one way to achieve an enterprise network, but there is a two-sided (administrative and technical) management process that leads to the integration of a successful enterprise network.

There are a plethora of books that detail any one of the components discussed here. For example, there are dozens of books and a multitude of articles on the Internet about TCP/IP networking. This book looks at the key techniques for integration. The focus is the point of integration at the Internet and your intranet(s) to create an enterprise network. This book is an administrative and technical reference guide to selecting the various components in an enterprise network to achieve basic interoperability.

Expectations about the Readers

So there are no surprises as to what is not in this book, here is a list of expectations about the reader:

➤ Reader has a basic knowledge of the technologies (protocols, servers) of the Internet and of an intranet.

➤ An enterprise network is a goal of the reader's corporation.

➤ Reader has a working intranet and needs to know how to integrate the present intranet using the Internet either to connect to another intranet or to connect the reader's corporation with vendors or customers, or a combination of these two architectures.

➤ Reader is a key player in the development of the enterprise network either as the system administrator or in another technical role. However, since a selection process for enterprise network integration is presented here, other types of readers (marketing, training, documentation, and general management) may be interested in certain chapters.

➤ Reader has a basic awareness of what takes place when the enterprise network is implemented.

➤ Reader has a basic familiarity of Internet applications such as e-mail, browsers, and newsgroups.

➤ Reader's enterprise network has a configuration different from any other because of legacy hardware and software, unique corporate goals, and the skill pool of knowledgeable people on Internet and intranet technologies that is available.

➤ Reader can draw upon internal and external technical resources.

Basic Position of the Author

Most authors rarely state their underlying premises as to their position when writing their books. These are the premises in this book:

➤ While there may be no one way to achieve enterprise network integration, there exists a common selection process.

➤ No one person can do enterprise network integration by himself or herself—this means a TEAM!

➤ Enterprise network integration is a logical evolutionary process in networking.

➤ There are two equal parts to project management for enterprise network integration—administrative and technical. The 20 percent rule is used here; 20 percent of this book looks at the administrative aspect, which may be in the end the most critical aspect.

➤ An effort is made to be vendor neutral with the exception of Microsoft's products that support DCOM architecture. A series of checklists were chosen for the reader to evaluate various key components for an enterprise network. The services of a vendor may be better in one part of the country than another.

➤ The reader should use the technical expertise of vendors, not their marketing expertise.

➤ The method of asking questions to lead one to the clarification of scientific and technical truths as used by Socrates (according to Plato) is important to the structure of this book.

➤ When the word "project" is used in the book, you can read it as "enterprise network integration."

➤ The basic project cycle consists of planning, designing, developing, testing, and implementing, with quality control always present. It is recognized there are blurred boundaries in project management. Those boundaries are blurred here. You have to know as a project manager of the enterprise network integration where you are in the cycle and keep the rest of the team on track.

➤ Assistance is given to the reader perhaps on unfamiliar ground in determining the skills people need to achieve enterprise network integration and in evaluating the functionality of applications and hardware for an effective enterprise network.

➤ The end goals are interoperability, portability, and reusability.

➤ Get a definition of customer expectations for

   ➤ Why they want the enterprise network.

   ➤ When they are going to use it.

   ➤ Where they are going to use it.

   ➤ What they want on it.

   ➤ How they are going to use it.

➤ Explain to the customers what part of their expectations is achievable based on

   ➤ Technological developments (what they see on television is not always the present)

   ➤ Budgetary restrictions

   ➤ Time limitations

Key Questions

Here are just a few of the questions that should have some resolution by the last page of the book:

➤ What is an enterprise network? Is there more than one type?

➤ What is an intranet? What makes an intranet different from a network?

➤ What is the Internet? Is it the same as the World Wide Web?

➤ Why does my company need an enterprise network? Do the benefits outweigh the costs?

➤ What is the importance of legacy in developing an enterprise network? What is legacy?

➤ What is the process for determining the architecture of an enterprise?

So you think you need an enterprise network! The concrete selection criteria for the network infrastructure include:

➤ Protocols (HTTP, TCP/IP, POP)

➤ Routers

➤ Servers

➤ Tools (system, management, benchmark)

➤ Gateways

➤ Browsers

➤ E-mail

➤ Access (database, remote)

➤ Applications (software)

➤ Platforms (hardware)

➤ Configuration (client, intranet, Internet)

Security, the Demon Issue

There is the chief demon over all of the above issues—SECURITY!!! The level of security that you want for your enterprise network may be the underpinning of how you develop all of your integration solutions. The chapter on security shows the difference between the security you want and the security you need. There is a basic principle of security—the key to the door keeps the honest man from temptation.

Intranet and Internet Defined

To have a running start at this book, two key questions have to be answered to establish some parameters. It is recognized that the answers given here to the questions can be challenged. These definitions are here to begin a discussion, not end it! If there is not a working knowledge of these core concepts, reading this book is like building your house on sand

and watching high tide come. Two fundamental questions for starting the integration of an enterprise network are:

> How does an enterprise network differ from an intranet?
> How does an enterprise network differ from the Internet?

An *intranet* is a network that has evolved through the integration of standards, protocols, tools, and utilities originally designed for the Internet, in particular, the ones for the World Wide Web. An intranet differs from an enterprise network in that it focuses on the transfer of data from one part of a company to another part. The key characteristics are proprietary data accessed in a closed system by a given set of clients (company employees). An enterprise network's focus can be the sharing of data between two or more companies, or a company sharing its intranet databases with customers or vendors.

The *Internet* was originally designed to transfer data that was important to the defense of the United States and Canada from one location (university, military) to another location in the case of a nuclear war. The focus was not for the improvement of commerce or enterprise.[1] Most of the current Internet data is considered public and is not formally organized for a specific purpose. The successful transfer of data is based on the Transmission Control Protocol/Internet Protocol (TCP/IP).[2] Since the announcement of the "super highway" concept and its use as a justification for the removal of government funding for the financial support of Internet technologies, companies have sought ways to use this architecture for their financial benefit. Out of this desire has evolved the computer system architecture that is referred to here as enterprise network.

Enterprise Network Defined

A <u>simple</u> definition for an *enterprise network* is network architecture created through the integration of two or more intranets using the Internet as the backbone to improve the market share of all parties involved. It

---

1   In 1969 the U.S. Department of Defense created the Advanced Research Projects Agency (ARPA). ARPA created the ARPANET. From this spring flowed the river called the Internet after much trial and tribulation.

2   TCP/IP is a set of 100-plus protocols. Development was started in 1974, but it was not until 1978 that there was a successful public demonstration. TCP/IP is platform independent; however, the UNIX operating system was developed in the same time frame as the protocols, and their histories have become intertwined.

can range from a casual relationship to one of complete merger. An enterprise network can be impacted by all of the latest technological applications and solutions that are directed to intranets and the Internet. This book looks at various technical solutions in the context of financial benefits and restrictions.

There are three basic enterprise network architectures. First, companies connect their intranets together for business-to-business operations using the Internet for connectivity. Second, a company with an intranet wants its customers, vendors, or partners to be connected to that intranet, not just a server, through the Internet. The third is a combination of these two.

Book Outline

Part I: Enterprise Network—What is it?

Chapter 1: Enterprise Network Is and Is-Not

First discussed is the place of the enterprise network in the telecommunications evolutionary chain. Second, very brief thoughts to the place of applications in an enterprise network are given. Next, a blurred vision of an enterprise network is stated. Definitions are given for the technical constructs discussed in detail in the next two chapters. This chapter concludes with a statement about why an enterprise network is more than a network.

Chapter 2: Network Relationship Types

This chapter explains the first of two important technical constructs necessary to the implementation of an integrated enterprise network. The first technical construct is based on types of relationships that define the system structure:

➤ Business-to-business
➤ Business-to-external users (customers, vendors, or partners)
➤ Business-to-business plus external users

These three constructs can be discussed in the context of six aspects. The differences are based on degree, direction, and point of view. These aspects are:

➤ Focus
➤ Culture

➤ Management style
➤ Tools
➤ Communication
➤ Coordination

Chapter 3: Network Relationship Levels

This chapter explains the second of two important technical constructs necessary to the implementation of an integrated enterprise network. This technical construct is based on levels of relationships that make up a network's architecture.

➤ Dating (let's share selective data)
➤ Engagement
➤ Marriage (let's merge)

Network levels of relationships can be discussed in the context of the same six aspects as network relationship types. The differences are based on commitment, direction, and point of view.

Chapter 4: Importance of DCOM

This chapter is a very brief overview of the Distributed Component Object Model (DCOM) architecture. Only essential functionality is considered here. DCOM as used here and throughout this book means Microsoft's commitment to an object-oriented (OO) networking architecture for an intranet with the Internet as an access backbone using Microsoft's technologies (products).

This chapter is a reference to principles and concepts of DCOM as they might be used in designing and developing an object-oriented network. The chapter also discusses a change of paradigm from client/server to object-oriented. The key areas covered are:

➤ Importance of DCOM
➤ Three views of DCOM
➤ Key functions of DCOM
   ➤ Connectivity
   ➤ Language neutrality
   ➤ Location diverseness
   ➤ Performance
   ➤ Platform neutrality
   ➤ Protocol neutrality

- Scalability
- Security
- Traffic management
  - Bandwidth
  - Latency
  - Load balance
- Overviews
  - Core object-oriented programming notions
  - Designing a DCOM system
  - Design issues
  - Interoperability
- Terms and definitions

Chapter 5: Importance of Visual J++ and Java

This chapter looks at the importance of the basic design notions of Visual J++ and Java object-oriented internetworking and some of their impacts on the transition to a network architecture using the object-oriented paradigm. This is a discussion of general object-oriented programming functionality and some of the considerations a network administrator needs to make in the integration process for an enterprise network.

The introduction of Java, a new and dynamic language with a different view of reality, has also generated new thinking on old problems. This is important to anyone interested in enterprise network integration because of the concerns in multi-platforms, multi-environments, multi-protocols, multi-applications, multi-etcs. This chapter does not look at either Visual J++ or Java in detail, but at the questions and issues that have been generated around their introduction as implementation languages of the object-oriented paradigm and internetworking.

This chapter reflects on ten key notions or areas about Java:

- Abilities
- Applet building
- Connectivity
- Business applications
- Security
- Tools
- Paradigm definition

➤ DCOM interaction

➤ Infrastructure overview

➤ Future

Part II: Administrative Planning Process

Chapter 6: Establishing Enterprise Network Parameters

This chapter presents basic information for planning enterprise network integration:

➤ Scope planning and defining

➤ Activity defining and sequencing

➤ Time estimating and scheduling

➤ Resource planning

➤ Cost estimating and budgeting

Chapter 7: Identifying Killer Acts

The best of us sometimes fail in two areas of project management. This chapter focuses on those two areas:

➤ Establishing a quality control process that intertwines within all activities

➤ Documenting what you do and what you have done

For additional details also see:

➤ Skills versus head count—Chapter 9

➤ Communicating—Chapter 11

➤ Time Management—Chapters 12 and 13

➤ Risk Management—Chapter 14

➤ Financial Management—Chapters 15 and 16

Chapter 8: Putting Activities into Logical Sequence

This chapter has ten fundamental questions that you need to answer to develop a logical sequence of activities to achieve effective enterprise network integration. Some additional "sidebar" comments to supplement the questions are given.

Chapter 9: Determining Skill Requirements

The seven topics covered here are:

➤ Questions to assist in defining resources
➤ Required resource data in a nutshell
➤ Procurement—getting outside skill sets
➤ Three important procurement documents
➤ System administrator as project manager
➤ Selecting the team
➤ Picking consultants and vendors

The three procurement documents are:

➤ Business Affiliate Plan
➤ Third-Party Market Agreement
➤ Third-Party Service Agreement

Chapter 10: Forces of Resistance

This chapter is a discussion of a method for solving various types of resistance you may encounter while doing enterprise network integration such as:

➤ God gave us the pencil! Why do I need YOUR computer?
➤ My data is TOO sensitive for other people to see!
➤ I am honest, but I do not trust the other guy!
➤ I do not have one of those!
➤ That is too hard to do!
➤ My way is better than your way!

The method is the use of Return on Investment (ROI). All the above statements are highly emotional charges; however, they all say the same thing—"How can I win in this situation?"

ROI is the positive actions toward perceived benefits. The discussion first looks at financial ends that lead to a successful ROI—an improved bottom line. Then the discussion turns to a series of responses one might give to the above six statements.

Chapter 11: Keeping People Informed

This chapter looks at communications in three phases:

➤ Ensuring your customers—that means everybody else—know the status of the enterprise network integration development

➤ Selecting applications (e-mail and newsgroups) so the users of the enterprise network can electronically interact among themselves

➤ Using a status reporting system because enterprise networking is a process of evolution, not a revolution.

Chapter 12: Time Estimating

This chapter considers three areas to assist you in doing enterprise network integration:

➤ Importance of time estimating

➤ Ten questions to assist in estimating time for your activities

➤ Types of data expected from your time estimations

Chapter 13: Developing the Schedule

This chapter is concerned with two topics:

➤ Questions that assist you in developing a schedule

➤ Data required for a schedule in a nutshell

Chapter 14: Risk Management

The two parts to this chapter are:

➤ Key points in doing risk management

➤ Need for two important risk management documents

Chapter 15: Cost Estimating

This chapter briefly discusses four cost management topics:

➤ Fundamental questions for cost management

➤ Cost estimation data in a nutshell

➤ Additional cost management considerations

➤ Basic cost management documentation

Chapter 16: Budgetary Issues

This chapter looks at three areas related to budgetary issues:

➤ Fundamental questions for resolving budget issues

➤ Budgetary data in a nutshell

➤ Three budgetary management documents

Part III: Technical Planning Process

Chapter 17: Defining Components

This chapter discusses two types of enterprise network components—concrete and abstract. The concrete components are things you can "see." The abstract components are labels for groups of functions of the concrete components. All of these components make up the enterprise network infrastructure.

Chapter 18: Modeling an Enterprise Network

This chapter reviews three types of modeling. These are:

➤ Statistical

➤ Simulation

➤ Extrapolation

Chapter 19: Using Management and Performance Tools

This chapter reviews two types of system tools. These are:

➤ Management

➤ Performance

The chapter does not cover in detail how to use these tools but rather the significance of management and performance tools in integrating your enterprise network.

Chapter 20: Working with Protocols

This chapter looks at some key protocols that are a part of your enterprise integration. The protocols considered here are:

➤ HyperText Transfer Protocol (HTTP)

➤ Multipurpose Internet Mail Extensions (MIME)

➤ Network News Transfer Protocol (NNTP)

➤ Post Office Protocol (POP)

➤ Point-to-Point Protocol (PPP)

➤ Point-to-Point Tunneling Protocol (PPTP)

➤ Reverse Address Resolution Protocol (RARP)

➤ Serial Line Internet Protocol (SLIP)

➤ Simple Mail Transfer Protocol (SMTP)

➤ Transmission Control Protocol/Internet Protocol (TCP/IP)

➤ Address Resolution Protocol (ARP)

➤ File Transfer Protocol (FTP)

➤ Internet Control Message Protocol (ICMP)

➤ Internet Protocol (IP)

➤ Transmission Control Protocol (TCP)

➤ User Datagram Protocol (UDP)

Also included in this chapter are brief discussions on:

➤ Language of protocols

➤ Protocol analysis

➤ Domain Name Service (DNS)

➤ Network File System (NFS)

➤ Managing TCP/IP

➤ Troubleshooting TCP/IP

The chapter closes with a list of some important Request for Comments (RFCs).

Chapter 21: Identifying Interconnectivity Issues

This chapter looks at certain key interconnectivity devices that have an impact on your enterprise network infrastructure. The key devices covered are gateways, bridges, hubs, repeaters, routers, and switches.

Chapter 22: Evaluating Service Servers

A *server* can be defined as any device not on the client side of the network. Perhaps it can be narrowed to two functions—a service or an access. This is similar to defining the human race as women and men. This chapter focuses on the service servers and the next chapter discusses access servers.

There are five "basic" service servers that most users think of as an intranet or the Internet. These service servers are:

➤ Chat

➤ Directory

➤ E-mail

➤ News

➤ Search

A difficulty in defining a service server is there is no simple way to view a service. The basic services can be viewed from one or more of the following four perspectives:

➤ Application
➤ Communications
➤ Database
➤ Storage

The big issue, of course, is legacy software design and technology. There can be significant differences between software written in 1995 and software written today. There can even be configuration issues within a specific version of software.

As a person concerned with integration of an enterprise network you have to resolve legacy and configuration issues in three environments—intranet "A," intranet "B," and the Internet.

This chapter discusses some of the concerns you may have about the five key service servers you probably use and the impact of legacy. This discussion is in the client/server format since that is where most of the technology is at present. However, there is another model—object-oriented (DCOM and Java are discussed in Chapters 4 and 5).

When applicable, associated protocols for a given server are discussed.

Chapter 23: Evaluating Access Servers

This chapter focuses on the access servers, as the last chapter discussed service servers. The word "access" implies a "going into"; however, access servers can involve throughput, input, output, and checking or verification.

There are at least six "basic" access servers in the domain of the network administrator. Access servers usually take their names from the key function they each perform. These key access servers are:

➤ Certification
➤ Firewalls
➤ Gateways
➤ Proxies
➤ Routers
➤ Web server (DCOM)

There are three major issues involved in the implementation of access servers in an enterprise network. They are:

➤ Legacy
➤ Optimization
➤ Security

This chapter discusses some of the implementation and maintenance concerns you may have about these key access servers you probably use. This chapter also discusses optimization.

Chapter 24: Evaluating Browsers

This is probably the most dynamic area of change in all of Internet technology. It is the introduction of a user-friendly graphical user interface and the associated technologies that set the groundwork for the rapid growth of intranets. This chapter looks at evaluating this core software technology and the implications of the use of browsers in your enterprise network.

Note: While it may seem obvious that Internet Explorer would be the browser of choice in DCOM, this is a book on the issues and the questions of the use of other browsers, as legacy software has to be considered.

There are really two browsers against which every other browser is evaluated. Perhaps the two big ones also need to be evaluated. This chapter discusses evaluation criteria. This chapter also discusses why you should examine alternative browsers. For example, have you considered the question, "Do your users' desktops have the memory to handle one of the big two?"

Chapter 25: Developing Integration Standards

This chapter looks at the importance of standards for implementing your enterprise network. The first action is to have a working definition of "standard." For the purpose of the following discussion, *standard* is defined as a property that can be defined, represented, or recorded under specified conditions. A standard is similar to a set of rules for defining a playing field where an exchange can take place, an exchange being, of course, one of data.

Chapter 26: Developing Technical Policies

This chapter looks at the importance of technical policies to give direction to your enterprise network. The first action is to have a working definition of "policy." For the purpose of the following discussion, *policy* is defined as a plan or course of action. While a standard is a set of rules for defining a playing field where an exchange can take place, a policy defines the boundaries of the field and the players. Any policy has three players:

➤ The enforcer—enterprise network administrator
➤ The implementers—technicians
➤ The users

Part IV: Resolving the BIG Issues

Chapter 27: Remote Access

Remote access, while a key aspect of any discussion of security, requires a separate discussion because of the additional issues that are generated. Your enterprise network with remote access is not a wide area network, but a global area network (*cyberagora*). Your users expect to be able to access an enterprise network at anytime and from anywhere in the world.

This chapter looks briefly at three areas:

➤ Key issues
➤ Remote access management
➤ Box of the future (set-top box)

Chapter 28: Security

Since the need for your enterprise network is electronic commerce and it exists in an open architecture, the big issue is not what browser to use or what platforms to use, but how secure the data transactions are. This chapter briefly looks at these security subjects:

➤ Crackers and spoofing
➤ Standards
➤ Policies
➤ Firewalls
➤ Kerberos authentication

➤ Java security highlights

➤ Common access control holes

Part V: Final Thoughts

Chapter 29: DCOM and Metaconcepts

This chapter briefly considers a notation of high-level and fundamental model designing for the synthesis of DCOM and Java internetworking, metalanguages. This notation is valid for the synthesis of components and objects in an objected-oriented paradigm. Two relevant metalanguages are Microsoft's Interface Definition Language and Rational Software Corporation's Unified Modeling Language. They present two environments for developing a synthesis for an enterprise network with DCOM architecture and Java internetworking. This chapter does not give detailed explanations because of legacy environments. These are high-level interpretations based on earlier developments of metaconcepts in the schools of analytical, conceptual, and linguistical philosophies.

Note: A *metalanguage* is the highest level of a language environment. For example, in this book "architecture" could be a concept in a metalanguage.

Chapter 30: Project Management Synthesis

This chapter uses documentation as the synthesizing methodology to demonstrate the project and technical management processes discussed throughout the earlier chapters. A completed documentation set is a statement of administrative and technical network goals and expectations; software and hardware legacy; market realities; and, finally, costs, skills, resources, and time constraints. There are not two sets of documents but one. This chapter is a look at the types of documentation rather than the specific documents.

Appendixes

Appendix A: Software Terms and Definitions

This appendix defines terms that relate to software.

Appendix B: Hardware Terms and Definitions

This appendix defines terms that relate to hardware.

Appendix C: Java Internetworking Code

This appendix is a discussion of some Java coding issues for doing internetworking.

Book Navigation

The book may be read from cover to cover. The table of contents can direct you to points of interests since you may already know what the solutions are going to be in a given area. There is a hope you would read these parts nevertheless, and perhaps there is an idea that can be used here and there. Be not overwhelmed by size or hurdles, for any successful trip of any length begins with the first step.

Part I

Enterprise Network—What is it?

*T*his part of the book first looks at three fundamental views of an enterprise network.

First is a discussion of the enterprise network's place in the telecommunications evolutionary chain and how its place can assist you in developing your own enterprise network.

An explanation of the technical construct-relationship types as it is important to enterprise network integration follows. The types of relationships that make up the system architecture are:

- ➤ Business-to-business
- ➤ Business-to-customers, vendors, or partners (external users)
- ➤ Business-to-business plus external users

Third is an explanation of the technical construct-levels of relationships, as it is important to enterprise network integration. The levels of relationships that make up the system architecture are:

- ➤ Dating (let's share selective data)
- ➤ Engagement
- ➤ Marriage (let's merge)

These viewpoints are based on four fundamental definitions that are the basis of this book. The definitions are for an enterprise network, an intranet, the Internet, and DCOM architecture.

Enterprise Network Definition

An *enterprise network* can be considered network architecture created through the integration of two or more intranets, using the Internet as the backbone, to improve the market share of all parties involved. It can range from a casual relationship to a complete merger. An enterprise network can be impacted by all of the latest technological applications and solutions that are directed to intranets and the Internet.

There are three basic enterprise network architectures. First, companies connect their intranets together for business-to-business operations using the Internet for connectivity. Second, a company with an intranet wants its customers, vendors, or partners to be connected to their intranet, not just a server, through the Internet. Third, there is a combination of the first and second.

Intranet Definition

An *intranet* is a network that has evolved through the integration of standards, protocols, tools, and utilities originally designed for the Internet, in particular the ones for the World Wide Web. An intranet differs from an enterprise network in that it focuses on the transfer of data from one part of a company to another part. The key characteristics are proprietary data accessed in a closed system by a given set of clients (company employees).

Internet Definition

The *Internet* was originally designed to quickly transfer data that was important to the defense of the United States and Canada from one location (university, military location) to another in the case of a nuclear war. The focus was not for the improvement of commerce or enterprise.[1] The data is considered public and is not formally organized for a specific

---

[1]   In 1969 the U.S. Department of Defense created the Advanced Research Projects Agency (ARPA). ARPA created the ARPANET. From this spring flowed the river called the Internet after much trial and tribulation.

purpose. The successful transfer of data is based on the Transmission Control Protocol/Internet Protocol (TCP/IP).[2]

DCOM Defined

This section looks at the importance of DCOM (Distributed Component Object Model), its supporting technologies, and Java internetworking in the defining (modeling) of your enterprise network. The reason for these overviews is that many of the software tools being introduced today that may be used in implementing or enhancing your enterprise network are based on DCOM "standards" or concepts, and Java was designed as a net-centric language.

DCOM, released in 1996, is an evolutionary stage based on the concept of object linking and embedding (OLE) released in 1992. DCOM is an answer to the standards of distributed computing established by the Open Software Foundation (OSF).

Note: For purposes of discussion in this book, the Component Object Model (COM) is defined as the theoretical core of an object-oriented architecture that has distribution as its end goal.

Java is a major language implementation of the object-oriented paradigm. The core of these discussions is on the notion of an object-oriented model (DCOM) and selected Java internetworking capabilities.

2   TCP/IP is a set of 100-plus protocols. Development was started in 1974, but it was not until 1978 that there was a successful public demonstration. TCP/IP is platform independent; however, the UNIX operating system was developed in the same time frame as the protocols, and their histories have become intertwined.

Chapter 1

Enterprise Network Is and Is-Not

Common sense is a very rare sense.

Enterprise Network Defined

An enterprise network, an evolutionary step of the network, uses the protocols, standards, and applications designed for an intranet and the World Wide Web and ultimately the Internet. It is not a theoretical construct. It is not smoke and mirrors. It is a problem that system administrators must resolve for the customers and managers.

An enterprise network is just a step in the evolution of telecommunications that may lead to a place called *cyberagora*, the virtual electronic marketplace. This evolution can be compared to the evolution of housing—tree, cave, tent, hut, cabin, house, and castle. You may ask, "Why include castle last in the evolution?" The castle metaphor defines a way to view the system architecture of an enterprise network. An enterprise network has moats, walls, turrets, and the various parts of the castle—stables, guardhouse, living quarters, administrative rooms, meeting rooms, and kitchen (cannot ignore the support group). This metaphor is expanded on in later chapters. Of course there are many variations on the housing evolution; likewise there are variations on the network and business evolutions. Have you ever thought that English and French castles do not look the same?

Enterprise Network—Team Metaphor

Consider the simplest enterprise network as a team of three players—the Internet and two intranets. Each has its responsibilities and functions. As the coach you ensure these three players win the game—internetworking that is transparent to the users with maximum interoperability. This is the business-to-business model.

The next level has an enterprise network with an intranet, the Internet, and an unlimited number of players (hopefully all have been selected to play in the game). The players are, of course, vendors, customers, or partners (without an intranet). Uninvited players are crackers and hackers. They are the cause for secure access. This is where firewalls become part of the playing field.

The third level of an enterprise network consists of two or more intranets, the Internet, and a plethora of players. This level combines all the issues of the first two levels and more.

Do not give up. There is common ground. I try to keep to the common ground, but I also try to make you aware of peaks and valleys to travel around.

It was said above that each member of the team has its own responsibilities and functions. Let us consider in turn the players—intranet, Internet, and external users.

Basic Features of an Intranet

Let us look at the basic features of an intranet. These features may be similar to functions and services on the Internet.

➤ TCP/IP protocols
➤ Servers usually for specific corporate groups—finance, human resources
➤ Graphical user interface (Internet browser)
➤ Corporate e-mail
➤ Corporate newsgroups (information sharing system)
➤ Accessible databases (some are restricted, such as payroll)
➤ Security level usually requires special ID and a password
➤ Management system
➤ Support group
➤ Remote access (optional, probably selective)
➤ FTP (optional, probably the original transmission protocol)

An *intranet* is a local area network (LAN) or a wide area network (WAN) that uses the technologies developed for the Internet. For example, for an intranet you might have had originally a graphical user interface (GUI), but now you have a browser, for that is the Internet technology now used on your intranet.

Basic Features of an Internet

Let us now look at the parallel features on the Internet:

➤ HTTP (HyperText Transfer Protocol—defines the World Wide Web)
➤ Browsers
➤ E-mail services (Post Office Protocol (POP) plus a number of associated protocols)[3]
➤ Newsgroups
➤ Internet service providers (ISPs)
➤ Search engines

Remember that much of the fundamental development on using the Internet was in academia and its association with the Department of Defense (DOD). I suspect most of the student users did not realize this relationship. The Internet was never free; just the taxpayers paid for it rather than the users. (Get off my soapbox!) This is important to the discussion because there was a strong requirement by the DOD for a reliable and stable electronic data transmission system. The creative functions and applications came from students playing with the system. One result of this playing was the development of the browser called Mosaic. This development evolved into the creation of a company called Netscape.

Request for Comments (RFCs)

Living (real-time) extensions of this book are Request for Comments documents (RFCs). They are dynamic notes on Internet network protocols or services. An example RFC is RFC 1994, "PPP Challenge Handshake Authentication Protocol (CHAP)." Most RFCs are detailed procedures and formats for their implementation. Some deal with

---

3   There is also Simple Mail Transfer Protocol (SMTP).

frequently asked questions, such as RFC 1594, "Answers to Commonly asked 'New Internet User' Questions." All RFCs are considered public domain unless marked otherwise.

RFCs are open for technical review from task forces, individual technical experts, or the RFC editor, as appropriate. Anyone can submit a document for publication as an RFC.

RFCs are accessible on the Web at:

ftp://nic.ddn.mil/rfc/rfcNNNN.txt.

NNNN represents the number of the RFC.

A very important RFC is RFC 1540, "Internet Official Protocol Standards." Once a document is assigned an RFC number and published, that RFC is never revised or reissued with the same number. RFC 1540 is the RFC you use to verify that you have the most recent RFC on a particular protocol.

Age Before HTTP

Too many people confuse the Internet as the World Wide Web. The world before HTTP includes:

➤ FTP (File Transfer Protocol)

➤ Gopher

➤ Veronica

➤ Archie

These tools are important to the development of the Internet but outside the scope of this discussion. The system architecture discussed here is concerned with the system consequences of two protocols—HTTP and TCP/IP.

Between the Internet and an Intranet

There is the world of connectivity and protection in between the Internet and an intranet. Some of the functions are:

➤ Gateway (Web server and associated software)

➤ Firewall (security server and its software)

The third player is the reason for all of this effort. It is the folks with the bucks! If these players are not involved in your electronic business, your company's bottom line can diminish. It is also expected that electronic business can increase the time flow of traditional business. No matter how you like technology, it is the online knowledge level of these people that has the most important impact on the success of your enterprise network. Enterprise network training is outside the scope of this book. There should be a parallel effort to communicate why the enterprise network works as it does. I do not mean what the network configuration is for the e-mail system to run correctly, but why the e-mail has to be configured in a certain way. A good answer usually is security!

This discussion leads to a thought about a situation in European history called the town and gown conflict. The question was who was going to control the street—the merchants or the students. Perhaps today the street can be labeled enterprise network. This is important to you as a system administrator because many security concerns come from the fringe of the gown (lovers of challenges, fondly referred to as hackers) and the seediest of the town (lovers of the malign, crackers.)

Applications

When making the various businesses (financial application) interoperable, a number of questions have to be resolved:

➤ If there are different database formats, should we use the Electronic Data Interchange (EDI) standards?

➤ How can workgroups be organized?

Other chapters detail this question more. The response is heavily dependent on the amount of integration between organizations. For example, is there one financial organization or two with a selective shared database? The word "financial" can be replaced with any number of words such as "human resources," "marketing," "sales," "training," or "technical support."

➤ What type of graphical user interface (GUI) needs to be used?

From a technical view the answer may appear to be simple; however, from a human view this may be a difficult issue. This is one of the most dynamic areas for technological change and there are no universal standards. Certainly battle lines have been drawn between several large corporations that furnish GUIs (browsers). An important component of legacy is the heritage of GUIs.

Vision

Any vision of an enterprise network may be a bit blurred. There are a number of checklists used throughout this book to assist in clarification of what you want in your enterprise network and what you need based on cost/benefit analysis. The vision must be based on:

➤ Type of relationship established

➤ Amount of architectural integration

➤ Degree of EDI compliance (database transparency)

➤ Hardware and software legacy

➤ Expectations of users and management

➤ Technical limitations

➤ Revolution versus evolution

➤ Financial limitations

➤ Resistance to change or to control

➤ Security, security, security

Technical Construct

There are two important technical constructs that have to be defined at the first step of enterprise network integration. The first is the type of relationship:

➤ Business-to-business

➤ Business-to-customers, vendors, or partners

➤ Business-to-business plus external users

The next chapter discusses fully the implications of these different relationships on enterprise network integration.

The second technical construct is the degree of relationship. This is like the levels of the relationship of a couple:

➤ Dating

➤ Engagement

➤ Marriage

It can be stated as:

➤ Selected sharing of data
➤ Workgroups
➤ Merger

Chapter 3 discusses fully the implications of these levels of relationship on enterprise network integration.

Network Plus

An enterprise network is more than a traditional network (LAN, WAN). It has an open business focus and technically:

➤ Uses a new set of protocols.
➤ Blends personal computer and mainframe architectures.
➤ Brings new challenges to old issues such as access security.

Depending upon the network architecture in existence, there has to be an integration of legacy network protocols, standards, and applications in the context of Internet protocols, standards, and applications. Sometimes it becomes necessary to leave in place the old. Sometimes it becomes necessary to modify. The most drastic action may be to delete the old. This book discusses these actions throughout as to when, why, where, what, and how to make the changes required.

DCOM Network Architecture Overview

Because of the legacy of hardware and software that includes a multiplicity of protocols, applications in various versions, platforms, and environments (LANs, WANS, intranets, and the Internet), there has to be some "glue" or something that makes the multiplicity unified. Two possible glues are the Distributed Component Object Model (DCOM) architecture and Java, a language that has three fundamental functions: interoperability, portability, and reusability. First, a brief DCOM overview is discussed (essentials are discussed in a separate chapter), and then a Java networking overview follows (basics are discussed in a separate chapter).

DCOM is a Microsoft solution to the standards and paradigm of an object-oriented distributed network. The goal is to move technology to a plug-and-play environment. The basis of the architecture is to recognize all components of a network's infrastructure (discussed in Chapter 17) as objects. The implication is that both the client and the server are now recognized as receiver and sender, not just as receiver nor just as sender.

DCOM, released in 1996, is an evolutionary stage based on the concept of object linking and embedding (OLE) released in 1992. DCOM is an answer to the standards of distributed computing established by the Open Software Foundation (OSF).

Note: For purposes of discussion in this book, the definition of the Component Object Model (COM) is that it is the theoretical core of an object-oriented architecture that has distribution as its end goal.

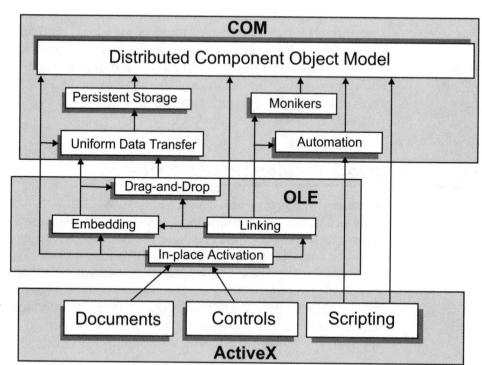

Figure 1-1
Operational flow among ActiveX, OLE, and COM to DCOM

This flow serves as a structure for the design of interfaces. The design of your enterprise network requires you to consider any infrastructure as components. This includes workstations, servers, printers, bridges, firewalls, browsers, e-mail, routers, operating systems, buffers, drivers, and on and on. Part III of this book discusses many of these components.

Besides categorizing the network infrastructure components, the second task is to develop a balanced software architecture. The balance should produce flexibility, interoperability, and reusability. The key design elements are to have horizontal and vertical interfaces, and to have metadata, *metadata* being the self-descriptive data that defines the dynamic data structures of your network. The issue today is that in most networks there is only the vertical interface. The disadvantages do not have to be enumerated because it is the reality of any network administrator.

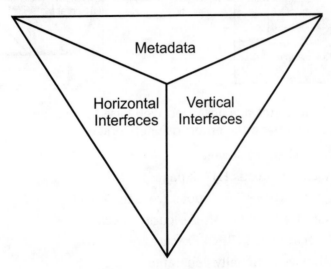

Figure 1-2
A balanced software architecture

DCOM/Java Networking Overview

There are two steps to an object-oriented network. The first is a DCOM architecture that is a distributed object infrastructure using its supporting technologies. The second is a Java environment, which is a multiple-platform, interoperable, and reusable code. The rest of the book discusses some of the details of the development of such network architecture. The figure on the next page is a sketch of such architecture.

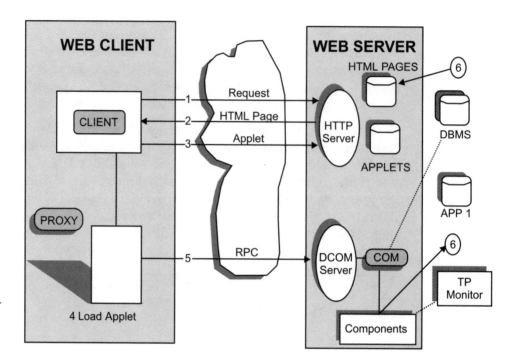

Figure 1-3
Interaction of DCOM, Java, and HTTP

Figure 1-3 illustrates a generalized Web-based client interacting with its Web-based servers on the enterprise network.

1. Request from client to server.
2. Web browser downloads HTML page.
3. Web browser retrieves Java applet from the HTML server.
4. Web browser loads applet after security check.
5. Remote procedure call (RPC) executes.
6. New HTML page optionally generated.

Chapter 2

Network Relationship Types

*Networking is a team effort of people,
hardware, and software.*

*T*his chapter explains the first of two important technical constructs
necessary to the implementation of an integrated enterprise network with
the Distributed Component Object Model (DCOM) architecture and
Microsoft's object technologies. The first technical construct set is based
on relationship types:

➤ Business-to-business

➤ Business-to-external users (customers, vendors, or partners)

➤ Business-to-business plus external users

No matter which construct is involved there should be two guiding
principles:

➤ Stick to business fundamentals

   ➤ User (customer) comes first

   ➤ Activity helps the bottom line in the long term

   ➤ Service, service, service

➤ Keep it simple

   ➤ Point and click

   ➤ Clearly defined and visual functions

   ➤ Easy navigation

Why should you be concerned with an enterprise network, DCOM, and
supporting technologies?

➤ Growth potential is everywhere including in cyberspace

➤ Market timing is critical—the quicker the better

➤ Expect change and the unexpected

These three constructs can be discussed in the context of six aspects. The differences are based on degree, direction, and point of view. These aspects are:

➤ Focus
➤ Culture
➤ Management style
➤ Tools
➤ Communication
➤ Coordination

Overview of Aspects

These aspects are concerned with people. The heart of any network is the people. It is not the applications, the tools, the design, or the architecture; it is the attitudes of the users towards these things.

Focus

Whichever construct is used there should be three common goals, purposes, or focuses. These three are:

➤ Improved relationships
  ➤ Satisfaction
  ➤ Applicability
  ➤ Timeliness
➤ Improved decision making process
  ➤ Quality of information
  ➤ Accessibility of information
➤ Improved bottom line
  ➤ Decreased costs
  ➤ Increased revenues

Culture

There are a number of questions you have to ask about the components of the enterprise network. Do the answers to the questions conflict in nature? If they do, can there be a network solution (read "compromise")? The questions involve the other five aspects, such as the management styles of the components. How can you develop a network where one management style follows the coat and tie manner, while the other follows blue jeans and a hiking shirt? One might want a highly focused and centralized network, while the other wants the use of the latest open-ended technology.

The undercurrent is one of informational issues. What are the input and output informational processes? Who controls the informational processes? How are the informational processes controlled? When is information controlled? Where are the information processes controlled?

Management Style

There has been an evolution in who manages information. The evolution of the computer has caused the change. A simple evolution is:

➤ Pre-computer: functions (heads of functions)

➤ Mainframe: technical specialists

➤ Intranets: functions (teams)

The conflict of management style centers on where each individual is in the evolutionary chain. Most important are the attitudes of the individuals who have high impacts on the design, development, and implementation of the network.

Tools

Any given tool can come in a variety of formats. What may appear to be a simple issue may cause deep personal conflicts. A key tool that may cause personal conflicts is the browser. Is there an obvious answer to the type of browser that may be used? However, a router in a system may not cause personal conflicts, only technical concerns. At what point can a router be considered only hardware or only software or both?

Tools can be discussed in specific terms or in generic terms. Later chapters discuss specific tools. There are at least three sets of conflicting generic tool types:

➤ Heterogeneous versus homogeneous

➤ Discovery versus structured

➤ Creation versus dictated

Communication

Because of recent changes in Internet technologies there are in effect two communication delivery methods—pull and push. *Pull communication* is getting information on request or demand. The challenge is to know how to request information. *Push communication* is getting information in case it is required. The challenge is to know how to focus the amount and what to receive.

Coordination

Network coordination or control can be purpose driven or it can be randomly driven. Coordination can be centralized or distributed. This last type of coordination can be considered in four types:

➤ Central-central (top-to-bottom control)

➤ Central-distributed (client/server control)

➤ Distributed-central (virtual control)

➤ Distributed-distributed (object-oriented control)

Business-to-Business Construct

This construct has gained importance because of the growth of mergers. This construct can be the simple sharing of selected information to a full integration of systems. The levels of relationship of an enterprise network are discussed more in detail in the next chapter.

The following illustration is a basic construct. The next chapter discusses key variations in the construct.

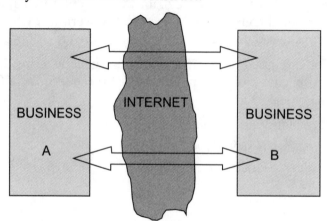

Figure 2-1
Business-to-Business Construct

This construct usually is concerned with management decisions. But as said earlier the other aspects play roles in the design, development, and implementation of the enterprise network. The emphasis is on the word "enterprise." How do two or more companies (corporations) merge their intranets to improve their bottom lines? Perhaps the question can be phrased as "How do they improve the bottom line?"

There are many goals for having a business-to-business enterprise network. Here are some of them:

➤ Shorten the production cycle to decrease costs and increase revenues

➤ Share information that is easily accessible and of high quality

➤ Create an environment where there can be conversations

➤ Provide an environment where teams diverse in ideas and locations can work

➤ Develop a tool set where management and user goals can be successfully achieved

➤ Allow for different coordination styles

Business-to-External Users Construct

This construct has gained importance because of the desire of customers and vendors to shorten the order-delivery cycle. This construct, like the one above, can be the simple sharing of selected information to a full integration of systems.

The following illustration is a basic construct. The next chapter discusses key variations in the construct.

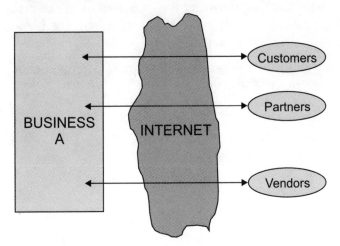

Figure 2-2
*Business-to-
External Users
Construct*

This construct usually is concerned with communication. Another way to read communication is "customer service." As said earlier, the other aspects play their respective roles in the design, development, and implementation of the enterprise network. How does a company assure a secure transaction environment for its external users? This construct was the first model used. Strange as it seems, the best example of this model is how the pornography industry uses the Internet as an environment for its business.

The pornography industry resolved successfully the issues of external users of any legitimate business. Here are some of the goals:

➤ Short order cycle

➤ Secure communications

➤ Clearly defined focus

➤ Simple navigation

➤ A tool set where user goals can be successfully achieved

➤ Easy accessibility to available inventory

The above is not advocating the pornography industry. But it seems the industry that is first into new technologies with the most realistic, straightforward, or practical uses of these technologies is pornography. The key issue of this model is its in-and-out nature as new technologies are being developed. A legitimate business has to look at long-range issues such as maintenance and scalability.

Business-to-Business plus External Users Construct

It is very clear that this construct is a blending of the two above constructs. There has to be a balance between management concerns for a bottom line and customer satisfaction.

The following illustration is a basic construct. The next chapter discusses key variations in the construct.

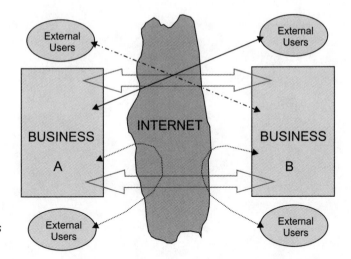

Figure 2-3
Business-to-Business plus External Users Construct

The type of architecture used may probably be evolutionary from simple (server to server) to one (complete integration). The one probably may never happen. In reality, the word "probably" is a condition on the never.

This construct has the biggest challenges. All the "versus" categories given in the discussions above come into play. A short list of challenges is:

➤ Homogeneous culture

➤ Diversity in attitudes towards tools

➤ Management styles range from the individual user to the corporate manager

➤ Ability to communicate in the network ranges from fear of technology to technical sophistication

➤ All four types of coordination interact with each other

➤ Reasons for having the network range from the external users' desire to save money to the external users' desire to protect data

Chapter 3

Network Relationship Levels

Relationships vary as weeds in the garden.

*T*his chapter explains the second of two important technical constructs necessary to the implementation of an integrated enterprise network. This technical construct is based on levels of relationships that make up a network's structure:

➤ Dating (let's share selective data)
➤ Engagement
➤ Marriage (let's merge)

Like the relationship type construct, the relationship level construct has two guiding principles:

➤ Business fundamentals define the implementation focus.
➤ Evolution is simple; revolution is difficult.

The first principle is common to both constructs. The second principle implies that system implementation may best be handled in phases rather than jumping into the middle of an environment that might cause anguish and ultimately divorce.

Why should you be concerned with an evolutionary, enterprise network using DCOM architecture and supporting technologies?

➤ Legacy software and hardware
➤ Commitment to change and compromise
➤ Management tools and techniques

Levels of network integration can be discussed in the context of the same six aspects as network relationship types. The differences are based on commitment, direction, and point of view. These aspects are:

➤ Focus
➤ Culture
➤ Management style
➤ Tools
➤ Communication
➤ Coordination

Overview of Aspects

While dating, the individuals still relate to each other even when holding different goals and cultural values. Each manages its own life without coordinating with the other except on the time and place of their coming together. Engagement requires a greater commitment to common goals and a definite requirement for better communication. Marriage requires:

➤ A commitment to integration to a common culture
➤ A set of agreed-upon goals
➤ An environment of personal communications
➤ An acceptable form of team management
➤ A method for detailed coordination
➤ A set of tools for handling the above aspects

The discussion of the aspects in the last chapter is valid here also. Only one of the aspects will be discussed here to show the method of thinking about this construct.

Tools will be used because this is the area from which the system administrator presents a position of expertise. Some of the answers to the questions below are discussed in Part III of this book.

The methodology used here is an example of a very simple survey. A survey can be a set of questions that when answered result in a focus, a goal, or goals. An analysis of the answers should assist in a decision as to the level of commitment to network integration.

➤ What architecture will be used?
   ➤ Client/server
   ➤ DCOM
   ➤ CORBA

➤ What structure will be used?
  ➤ A single mainframe
  ➤ A single server
  ➤ Distributed data
  ➤ Routing schema
  ➤ Tier design
➤ What software and hardware tools will be used?
  ➤ Management
  ➤ Operating systems
  ➤ Developmental languages
  ➤ Service servers
  ➤ Access servers
  ➤ Web servers
  ➤ Applications
  ➤ Utilities
➤ What advantages are being sought?
  ➤ Customer satisfaction
  ➤ Improved bottom line
  ➤ Ease of use
  ➤ Performance
  ➤ Data flow
  ➤ Maintainability
  ➤ Scalability
➤ What types of transactions will be done?
  ➤ Data
  ➤ Payment
  ➤ Search
  ➤ Order
  ➤ Inventory control
  ➤ Training
➤ What types of experiences have you had with tools?
  ➤ Positive
  ➤ Negative

> What are the limitations or restrictions on building the enterprise network?

> Money

> Time

> People

> Skills

Dating Construct

This construct is in common use today. Its most basic structure is a Web server maintained by a business. Internet protocols are used so that other people (customers, vendors, and even internal users) might interact with the business. The common features are product or service information, an e-mail link, a specific ordering process, and position openings.

The following illustration shows a limited relationship between two businesses. They only share Web servers with a firewall behind the rest of their networks or intranets. All transactions are processed at the server location. The Dating Construct is a minimal commitment; however, it could be short range or the beginning of a long-term commitment.

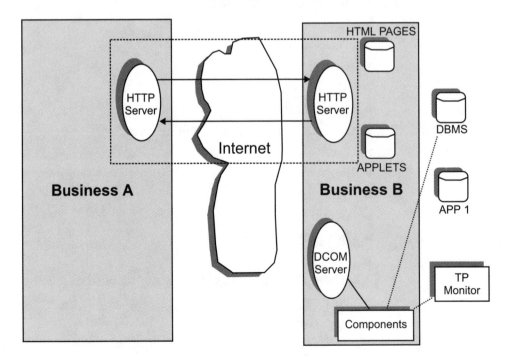

Figure 3-1
Dating Construct

There are specific reasons for having a "dating" enterprise network. Here is a selection:

➤ Fast to implement
➤ Limited commitments
➤ Easy maintenance
➤ Scalability not a concern
➤ Limited tool involvement
➤ Straightforward environment
➤ Low use of technology
➤ Minimal functions

Engagement Construct

This construct has gained importance because of the desire of corporate vendors to shorten the order-delivery cycle. This construct requires a greater commitment to a secure transaction environment. There has to also be a commitment to communicate desires as to design, development, implementation, and maintenance of the network.

The following illustration shows a more committed relationship between two businesses. They not only share Web servers, but, for example, they may share selected database management systems. Transactions are processed at more than one location. The Engagement Construct is a commitment to a wedding. This is more "let us test the waters."

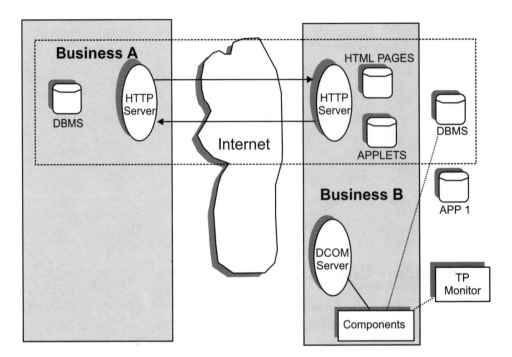

Figure 3-2
Engagement Construct

There are specific reasons for having an "engagement" enterprise network. Here is a selection:

➤ Implementation time frame
➤ High degree of commitment
➤ Maintenance as an ongoing process
➤ Scalability considerations
➤ Some administrative and management tool involvement
➤ Dynamic environment
➤ Some use of intranet technologies
➤ Network functions and business goals determination

Marriage Construct

From a user's viewpoint, the components of a "married" enterprise network are seamless. There is a quotation that comes to mind: "One for all, all for one." This construct can be labeled a virtual corporation or business community. When there is proper integration, the value for all is involved.

The following illustration shows a committed relationship between two businesses. They share everything. Transactions can be processed throughout the enterprise network. This is where DCOM architecture and its supporting technologies come into full play. The Marriage Construct is a commitment to one team. A wedding does not make the marriage; it is the sign of commitment. This construct is an evolution towards the ideal. The success of the marriage is not the sharing of everything but the integrating of everything.

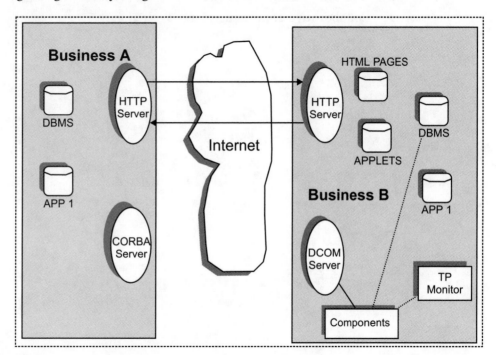

Figure 3-3
Marriage
Construct

This is a commitment to:

➤ Free data flow
➤ Active participation
➤ Community discussions
➤ Common good of all parties

This construct has the biggest challenges. All the challenges of living come into play. A short list of challenges is:

➤ Dynamic implementation
➤ Commitment, commitment, commitment

➤ Maintenance (an ongoing process that requires a team with a variety of experts)
➤ Scalability
➤ Requirement for a tool box or kit
➤ Dynamic environment
➤ High-level use of technology
➤ Changing business and user goals
➤ Collaborative communication

Chapter 4

Importance of DCOM

A paradigm is a twisted view of reality.

*T*his chapter is a very brief overview of the Distributed Component Object Model (DCOM) architecture. Only essential functionality is considered here. DCOM as used here and throughout this book means Microsoft's commitment to an object-oriented (OO) networking architecture for an intranet with the Internet as an access backbone using Microsoft's technologies (products).

The label can be COM or COM+ or any other label. It is the goal of achieving an intranet with Java internetworking or connectivity that is the foundation of this book. While there are many Microsoft products or technologies available for achieving networking, the cornerstone of these technologies for OO architecture is the rapidly evolving Visual J++ (Chapter 5). Perhaps the other products should not be ignored, but the types of questions and processes raised in the rest of the book could also be raised about these products as well.

Note: The above is stated because of Microsoft's dynamic commitment to a tighter Java integration. The technologies or their labels may change, but process and functionality do not change.

This chapter gives broad generalizations to assist in the planning and designing of a network with an object-oriented architecture. The emphasis is on the use of Microsoft products to carry out this task.

This chapter is a reference to principles and concepts of DCOM as they might be used in designing and developing an object-oriented network.

The chapter discusses changing from a client/server paradigm to an object-oriented paradigm. The key areas covered are:

- Importance of DCOM
- Three views of DCOM
- Key functions of DCOM
  - Connectivity
  - Language neutrality
  - Location diverseness
  - Performance
  - Platform neutrality
  - Protocol neutrality
  - Scalability
  - Security
  - Traffic management
    - Bandwidth
    - Latency
    - Load balance
- Overviews
  - Core object-oriented programming notions
  - Designing a DCOM system
  - Design issues
  - Interoperability
- Terms and definitions

There is confusion in reality because the dominant network infrastructure in existence is client/server, and the language of this paradigm is used in the birthing of the new network paradigm of object-oriented. For example, the word "server" is used to name a component or object, but it may have a different meaning based on context. This may be a very simple notion but it can have profound implications in design. Is there a difference between "database" and "Database"? In very early mainframe (IBM) literature James Martin made a distinction between these two concepts. This same action is being played over and over again as people try to explain DCOM. A key concept of OO is inheritance and context. In this book there is a set of figures in Chapter 6, "Establishing Enterprise Network Parameters," that show "trees," which is a blending of these two concepts. The "trees" in Chapter 6 show how the project management process for an enterprise network can be structured so the parts can be considered objects or components rather than a flow.

Note: It is held here that these concepts can be used to design, develop, and implement an object-oriented enterprise network.

Importance of DCOM

As an enterprise network administrator, DCOM can be important to you for two reasons:

➤ It simplifies distributive computing.

➤ It is a developmental standard notation.

A distributed environment blends all differences between operating systems, programming languages, and process locations using an object-oriented paradigm. As a standard notation it resolves differences between software interfaces.

What does this mean to you? Many of the new Internet and intranet technologies are being designed on the concepts of OO architecture. You may have to be less concerned in the future about network configuration management issues. Also, there is now less reliance on the metaphors of the procedural world (paradigm) with their transformation to the object world (paradigm). As a simple example, instead of using a phrase such as "the steps in the process," you may start using a phrase such as "the bridge between objects."

DCOM is an evolved objects technology. What you get in DCOM is a number of Microsoft's efforts. These include:

➤ Dynamic Data Exchange (DDE)

➤ Object Linking and Embedding (OLE)

➤ Component Object Model (COM)

➤ ActiveX

These four technologies give you:

➤ Messaging capabilities among applications

➤ Visual link embedding

➤ Object binding

➤ Internet capabilities

There are a number of reasons for considering a distributed network that is object or component based. Here are just five:

➤ Need to put the latest technologies on the desktop

➤ Requirement to distribute component applications across multiple desktops

➤ Desire to link desktops to the Internet

➤ Necessity to link applications across both public and private intranets

➤ Necessity to establish an "enterprise network" (focus of this book)

Three Views of DCOM

DCOM is really three things in one. It is a specification. It is a standard. It is a practice. No one of these stands alone.

It is a *specification* in that there are documents that specify or state what the theoretical view of DCOM architecture is. See Microsoft's Web site at **http://www.microsoft.com/** for the latest information. Microsoft includes code implementation examples as well in the documentation.

It is a *standard* in that there is documentation that details what enables the specification to be turned into reality. A standard is a set of guidelines for practice. In the simplest terms, there are definitions for an object or a component and how the object or component is called.

It is a *practice* in that it is the act of designing, developing, testing, validating, and implementing a system for the transmission of data among objects in public and private distributed environments. It is a practice with the basic philosophical premise that network architecture should be object-oriented and distributed.

Key Functions of DCOM

This section looks briefly at nine key functions in DCOM. These functions must be considered in any design and development documents. When one moves from a closed architecture of a network to an open architecture of an intranet with Internet access, these functions take on new faces or become concerns that may not have existed before, such as language neutrality. These functions are discussed in an alphabetical list, not by importance. Your environment and your goals determine the priority. These functions are:

➤ Connectivity

➤ Language neutrality

➤ Location diverseness

➤ Performance

➤ Platform neutrality

➤ Protocol neutrality

➤ Scalability

➤ Security

➤ Traffic management

Major impacts on these functions are the legacy hardware, software, databases, and infrastructure. This is important because you probably need to look at outside sources in either implementing or enhancing your enterprise network and you need to understand their correct and incorrect uses of the object-oriented language.

Note: Microsoft does have one of the most aggressive support systems on the Internet. See Microsoft's home page at **http://www.microsoft.com/**.

Connectivity

Connectivity is a concern in an intranet environment because of the fragileness of network connections over local connections. One method DCOM uses in managing single and multiple client connections is by a component reference count. DCOM also has a "pinging" protocol that can manage connections. Also, the directional attribute statement in the interface definition can control the direction of data.

Language Neutrality

One of the issues in developing an intranet is legacy software, especially programming languages. There is a whole series of programming languages that can interact well with DCOM architecture. It is important to recognize the obvious; Microsoft's programming languages have through evolution been designed to work well together. One key result is the ability to use the threading feature more easily.

Location Diverseness

The ability of DCOM to handle location diverseness simplifies the implementation of a distributed application across an intranet. It resolves such issues of having components running on specific workstations or specific locations, or having large components that reduce traffic performance. DCOM architecture can give you the ability to combined related components at the same location or in the same process.

Another advantage of location diverseness is the ability to handle application growth. All components can be put on a single workstation and then distributed as required at a late date. There is a high probability that there may be no code change requirement as determined by basic design.

Performance

An issue not only for the system administrator but also for the end user is performance, with the basic question being, "How fast does 'X' work?" "X" is determined by who you are. It can be how fast a call is made or how fast the workstation closes. An object-oriented remote procedure call (RPC) mechanism is provided to enhance performance. Component design, language interaction, and so forth can impact performance also.

Platform Neutrality

One of the issues of converting to an intranet is legacy hardware. Platform integration is an issue that affects both the client and server sides. The issues include different configurations (software and hardware), interfaces, protocols, and services. Probably the most common approach is the lowest common denominator one, but it is most unsatisfactory in more than one way: overhead and the inability to do performance tuning or optimization. DCOM uses a protocol based on DCE RPC and several platform standards to resolve most, if not all, of the cross-platform development issues.

Note: A DCOM component in Java programming resembles a Java class.

Protocol Neutrality

With the introduction of the HyperText Transfer Protocol (HTTP) suite into a network to assist in its conversion to an intranet, the issues of protocol compatibility and interoperability have come to the forefront. For more details, see Chapter 20, "Working with Protocols."

Scalability

An intranet is never a finished thing unless it is completely deactivated. This means growth or, more precisely, *scalability*, how easily the intranet can grow.

In Windows NT, scalability is supported by symmetric multiprocessing. This is really thread pool management.

Security

The introduction of protocols to create intranets and for Internet access has produced new security issues. For a more detailed discussion of these issues, see Chapter 28, "Security."

Within a distributed environment such as Windows NT, there must be a security system that can distinguish among clients so that any application can perform the correct operations on a component on a particular client or even a group of clients. The common method is to use logins and passwords. DCOM has a function that hides a component's location and its security requirements. You can configure each component's security settings.

Because of some applications, such as the ones for finance, there usually cannot be a single component-wide access control system. This requires the development of special programs to control the various components of the application such as data entry or data rollup viewing. Many can make entries; few can see the results.

Note: This discussion is about DCOM security. When Java internetworking is added to the mix, there are new worms.

Traffic Management

There are three key areas of traffic management: bandwidth, latency, and load balance. Bandwidth and latency are discussed in Chapter 18,

"Modeling an Enterprise Network," and in Chapter 21, "Identifying Interconnectivity Issues."

Bandwidth is the size of parameters passed that affects call completion. *Latency* is the physical distance and number of network elements that impact transmission time. *Load balance* is smoothing out the demands on network components. An example of one of the DCOM solutions to traffic management is the use of the connectionless UDP subset of the TCP/IP protocol suite (Chapter 20, "Working with Protocols").

Core Object-Oriented Programming Notions

While there are notions or concepts that define an object-oriented network, there are also notions to define object-oriented programming. Three of these notions (all originally used in biology) are:

➤ Encapsulation
➤ Inheritance
➤ Polymorphism

Encapsulation is a kind of protective covering for bacteria. In object-oriented programming encapsulation is the implementation to protect the connection between data and code.

Inheritance is a biological reuse of old code such as DNA structures. What the parents are the children become genetically. In programming, it is the method of code reuse so that the functionality of one object can be used by another object.

Polymorphism in biology is the many forms or stages that an organism can undergo. In common English we refer to the stages of a human as baby, child, teenager, and adult. There are, of course, other stages that can be used. In programming polymorphism, it is the writing of code so that it can adapt to new situations.

Designing a DCOM System

Part II of this book details the project management process that is applicable to the designing of a DCOM system. The ten-step process is:

1. Scope planning
2. Scope defining
3. Activity planning
4. Resource planning
5. Activity sequencing
6. Time estimating
7. Cost estimating
8. Schedule developing
9. Cost budgeting
10. System integrating

Part III of this book details the technical management process that is applicable to the designing of a DCOM system. The ten-step process is:

1. Defining infrastructure components
2. Modeling the network
3. Establishing tool requirements
4. Developing protocol infrastructure
5. Identifying interconnectivity issues
6. Evaluating service servers
7. Evaluating access servers
8. Evaluating browsers, or GUIs
9. Developing standards
10. Developing policies

Note: There is an eleventh step for both processes, but it is a part of <u>all</u> of the other ten steps—quality control.

These steps are not necessarily sequential. Some steps run in parallel. Some parts of the steps are done in parallel to other parts within a step. These discussions highlight the activities for the specific consideration of DCOM architecture in the design of an enterprise network. Other functions are system, administration, and code design. These functions are also considered throughout this book.

The design of an object-oriented system using DCOM architecture requires that object-oriented analysis and design be used. This is not a casual statement! The two ten-step processes can be used—and have been used probably many times—in client/server paradigm design and development. You have to consider classes, inheritance, object mapping, and interface definitions.

What is object-oriented analysis and design? There is a three-part answer:

➤ Object-oriented analysis (OOA)—design requirements and overall system architecture requirements

➤ Object-oriented design (OOD)—conversion of system architecture into programming constructs (interfaces, classes, and methods)

➤ Object-oriented programming (OOP)—implementation of programming constructs

This book focuses primarily on the first part of the definition. Appendix C, "Java Internetworking Code," considers very briefly the second part through the use of code examples and related issues. The third part is for local site considerations.

In an objected-oriented system design analysis, there are three major goals. The goals are:

➤ Define the system requirements.

➤ Identify the possible system classes.

➤ Map the system requirements to class attributes and operations.

The result should be a *class diagram* that integrates the system classes into a coherent model. There is a tool that assists in creating an object-oriented design. Rational Software Corporation developed Unified Modeling Language (UML) for this activity. For the latest information on UML, go to Rational's Web site at **http://www.rational.com/uml/index.shtml**.

What is a class diagram? Sometimes referred to incorrectly as an object diagram or object model, it describes classes and their static relationships to other classes in the system. An example of a dynamic relationship is when an object invokes the services of another object.

Design Issues Overview

DCOM architecture is complex; so is client/server. It is a significantly different view of network theory and practice. The client/server is fundamentally a three-part world: client, server, and in-between. It now is also overlaid with tiers. In contrast, DCOM can be a world of objects with any object in a static world defined by its primary function.

System design is concerned first with the legacy infrastructure—all concrete and abstract system components (see Chapter 17, "Defining Components"). The big design goals written in the clouds are interoperability, portability, and reliability. The wind that supports the clouds is software programs.

As a part of the early project definition and the consideration of skills, resources, and time, consider the risks and also consider the opportunities (see Chapter 14, "Risk Management") for impacts on the design and development.

After infrastructure design, perhaps a second problem is the threading environment. The issue may not be major since multithreading is not widespread. The multithreading issue is access concurrency to objects. DCOM does not force system design to be multithreaded. However, the consideration of the nature of the operation of distributed applications is important. One consideration is that on a DCOM server at any one time there may be multiple clients attempting access. With a single thread, the server processes one client at a time. This impacts the goal of system responsiveness.

Terms and Definitions

Here is a brief table of terms relevant to the discussion in this chapter.

Terms	Definitions
Client	A client is any entity capable of requesting a service. See server.
Construction model	A model that describes how services are defined. See implementation.
Context object	A collection of name-value pairs that provides environmental or user-preference information.
Execution model	A model that describes how services are performed. See method.
Implementation	A definition that provides the information needed to create an object and to allow the object to participate in providing an appropriate set of services. See construction model.

Terms	Definitions
Inheritance	The construction that passes the methods of the implementing class from the interface class.
Interface	Describes a set of possible operations that a client may request of an object.
Method	Code that is executed to perform a service. It is an implementation of an operation. See execution model.
Object	An entity that provides one or more services that can be requested by a client.
Object model	A presentation that gives organization to a set of object concepts and terminology.
Object system	An object collection that isolates the service requestors from the service providers within an interface. See object model.
Operation	An identifiable entity that denotes a service that can be requested. It is achieved using the interface inheritance in IDL.
Server	A server is any entity capable of providing a service. See client.
Skeleton	A compiled code piece that builds the server implementation code on the interface. Another name for skeleton is frame.
Stub	A compiled code piece that makes the interface available to a client.
Value	Anything that is an actual parameter in a request.

Chapter 5

Importance of Visual J++ and Java

A baby, a child, a teenager, an adult, and a senior citizen
are labels for any one human being.

One of Microsoft's visions seems to be moving forward for a tighter integration of its products with other product implementations of Java. It is important to understand the key ideas, principles, concepts, standards, and programming techniques that assist in the development of an object-oriented network architecture such as DCOM (COM or COM+ or whatever is the appropriate label at the time of reading this).

This chapter looks at the importance of the basic design notions of Visual J++ and Java object-oriented internetworking and some of their impacts on the transition to a network architecture using the object-oriented paradigm. This is a discussion of general object-oriented programming functionality and some of the considerations a network administrator needs to make in the integration process for an enterprise network.

The introduction of Java, a new and dynamic language with a different view of reality, has also generated new thinking on old problems. This is important to anyone interested in enterprise network integration because of the concerns in multi-platforms, multi-environments, multi-protocols, multi-applications, multi-etcs. This chapter does not look at either Visual J++ or Java in detail, but at the questions and issues that have been generated around their introduction as implementation languages of the object-oriented paradigm and internetworking.

Note: In one version of Microsoft's Visual J++ 6.0 FAQ the statement is made that the "compiler supports all language features in Java including Sun's additions to the language specified in the Java Developers Kit (JDK) 1.1." There are, of course, new additions. Taking the statement as fact means what is written below using the word "Java" could be replaced with "Visual J++ 6.0."

This chapter reflects on ten key notions or areas about Java:

➤ Abilities
➤ Applet building
➤ Connectivity
➤ Security
➤ Business applications
➤ Tools
➤ Paradigm definition
➤ DCOM interaction
➤ Infrastructure overview
➤ Future

The basic question one has to ask is "What is my commitment, legacy hardware and software, to Microsoft's networking products?" If there is a strong yes, then this chapter is for you. If there is a strong no, this chapter is also for you. Any network or system administrator must understand or be aware of the basic concepts for implementing a major technology, an object-oriented programming language.

Key Abilities

The foundational concept of Java as an outgrowth of object technology is that it has three key abilities:

➤ Reusability
➤ Portability
➤ Interoperability

These three abilities are defined as necessary in an object-oriented architecture. This is the keystone, for an enterprise network administrator needs to be aware of Java as an object management tool.

Besides the big three, there are other Java characteristics that are important as a part of justification for moving to Java internetworking. Here are seven more:

➤ Application adaptation is possible because of dynamic network downloading.

➤ Application performance increases.

➤ Design, development, testing, and implementation are simpler because of component-level object programming.

➤ Development time is shorter because of code reuse.

➤ Memory management increases system robustness.

➤ Multithreading produces high performance in GUI functions.

➤ Security improves because the Java runtime system checks for viruses.

There is much hype about Java. The key point to remember about Java is that it was developed as an Internet language. It is a solution to bring unity to a heterogeneous environment held together by a common set of protocols (TCP/IP). Java is a tool with the potential to manage and to control data in a truly worldwide open business environment, *cyberagora*. The goal is to replace existing networks with less costly and more efficient ones. There should be less maintenance and support. A major impact on present networks is the implication that Java can be embedded in anything using a microprocessor. The notion of what is or is not a network becomes blurred with the blink of an eye.

A significant change in networking that Java development is causing is in the view of operating system requirements. The present operating systems are memory grabbers. The idea is that a Java Virtual Machine can be stored in flash ROM with the client or booted from the network. The days of "bigger is better" may turn into "the essential is better."

Besides the operating system view being changed, database handling is changing. The newly developed Distributed Computing Environment (DCE) protocol provides SQL database connectivity. This development results in the creation of three-tier applications for distributed objects.

Perhaps part of the hype—or not—is that Java permits the preservation of an entire legacy system. Certainly new servers have to be used—a Java

Web server and a DCOM-based component server. Over a period of time perhaps it is possible to retain an entire legacy system, but only each involved network administrator can verify this position. The core parameter to this possibility is the customers' expectations.

There appear to be four driving forces behind the introduction of Java into the enterprise network. These four forces are detailed in many places in this book. They are:

➤ Internet marketing (Web site for informing customers about products and services)

➤ Intranet collaborative communication (team effort for pushing corporate information)

➤ Intranet business applications (common business applications such as employee expense reporting)

➤ Internet marketplace (corporate and customer interaction for product and service ordering)

Note: The focus of this book is on the Internet marketplace.

Building an Applet

There are already a number of inexpensive vendor packages available to assist in building a Java applet; however, the most logical action is to use the Applet Wizard in Visual J++. There are two important considerations—building process and package selection criteria. First, here are the basic steps in the building process, not the specific programming process:

1. Plan what action is to happen.
2. Assemble the required parts (sounds, images, links, etc.).
3. Assign actions.
4. Test applet.
5. Compile code.
6. Implement.
7. View with Internet Explorer, a Java-enabled browser.

The simplest code structure for an applet might be similar to this:

```
import java.applet.Applet;
import java.awt.*;

public class MyClass extends Applet
{
        // Code goes here.
}
```

Note: Part II of this book illustrates the project management process in detail. Even small Java developments should be done in the context of this process. The steps reflect the core steps in the smallest of developments, an individual effort.

Second, if there is a requirement for an applet builder, there are certain criteria that are important. There are many criteria that can be considered, such as price, but here are ten important technical criteria:

➤ Can build forms
➤ Can create standalone applications
➤ Can create standard GUIs
➤ Can incorporate external applets
➤ Can publish applets to the Web
➤ Has a graphic editor
➤ Has alignment tools
➤ Has an image-map editor
➤ Has database support capabilities
➤ Has templates available

Java and Connectivity

The place to begin with Java interconnectivity is with the server and the client. The basic example is connecting the client to an instance of the server that is already running. More details on this idea are in Appendix C, "Java Internetworking Code."

Note: Because of browser handling of the restrictions on IP addressing that affect applet connections (security concerns), the client/server connections need to be built as applications.

A focus of any discussion on connectivity is the Microsoft Java Virtual Machine (JVM). It is supposed to remove the problems associated with cross-platforms. That is, there should not be a requirement for different software versions and the consequences of the feature interactivities. A moment for a reality check: While both major browsers do support Java, the doing is not of the same color.

Java applets can only access the file computer system from which they are served. Your computer and the server must be the same for you to read your files. However, databases can be accessed using the Java Database Connectivity (JDBC) class libraries, which provide SQL database connectivity tools. JDBC is located in the base Java class java.sql.*. If your version of Visual J++ (prior to 6.0) does not have it, you can download it from Microsoft.

Note: With the introduction of Visual J++ 6.0 the technical issues and process will probably change significantly; however, one needs to be aware of the basic Java internetworking connectivity process. Also, if one does not have a Microsoft networking environment, one must consider the alternatives.

The key issues are:

➤ Few database drivers for the products are available (need a JDBC to ODBC bridge).

➤ Database access programming is difficult at the least.

➤ Product solutions vary widely.

➤ It is early in the game.

For each qualified negative there is a qualified positive, but in the case of Java there may be far more positives than negatives. Here is a set of qualified positive statements for Java connectivity and its environment:

➤ Applications run anywhere the Java Virtual Machine software is installed. This means any Java-enabled browser, such as the latest versions of Internet Explorer. Applications are downloaded on demand from a Web server.

➤ Client administration and configuration control is done from a central location.

➤ Client data storage is handled from a central file server.

➤ Cost per set connectivity is significantly less than in the traditional connectivity environment.

➤ Java platform independence enables services and interactions to be delivered beyond the firewall.

➤ Seamless connectivity produces a high degree of reliability.

➤ Standard network protocols are used for client/server communications.

Java Security

There have been cries of security breaches since the introduction of Java. However, the important thing is not the breaches (those seem to have been closed) but the general enhancement in awareness about security problems, procedures, policies, solutions, and general ideas that were around long before Java. Chapter 28 discusses security in more detail, but four ideas that hopefully have become a part of any system administrator's knowledge are:

➤ Security weaknesses are cumulative.

➤ A new technology can generate unexpected results.

➤ Firewalls are access control devices that can be breached.

➤ A new technology can generate new types of devious minds.

Java development has addressed some of the key security weak points. There are five security areas Java has sought to improve:

➤ Encryption and signatures

➤ Limited removable storage

➤ Memory protection

➤ Rules enforcement

➤ Runtime verification

Note: With the introduction of Windows Foundation Classes (WFC) in Visual J++ 6.0 many security issues will be resolved. Applications written with WFC and downloaded to a local client machine can only access a declared system.

Java and Business Applications

The development of business applications using Java is a fast-growth industry where an enterprise network administrator can get a nice growth of gray hairs. The key issues are:

➤ Programmers have not yet had time to develop expertise.

➤ Java is not robust.

➤ Design tools are limited.

Note: The actualities of the above three issues are rapidly changing. For the latest in Java development, go to **http://www.microsoft.com/visualj/** or **http://www.microsoft.com/visualjsupport/**.

A major impact of Java is in application version control. Easy deployment of applications across the network environment is possible. This means everyone uses the same versions of word processor, spreadsheet, etc. Individual applications need not be deployed on individual workstations. The key to this possibility is that the enterprise network or an intranet has to have an appearance of being a Web environment. In other words, the network has to use Web enabling protocols.

A part of the solution for Java business application development is have a clearly defined high standard (quality) end goal. Part II of this book speaks to the administrative planning process for enterprise network integration; however, this same planning process is applicable to any Java business application development and design project. Part III speaks to the technical planning side of the design process. Both run in parallel with each other.

Application development productivity increases two to five times over traditional programming development. The development is implemented by an instant rollout over a Web server.

Application usage among clients probably can first be divided into two categories: diversity (number of applications used) and intensity (amount of network resources used). These two categories can then be divided into low and high usage. Examples of these four categories are:

➤ High diversity/high intensity—graphic artists

➤ Low diversity/low intensity—customer service representatives

➤ High diversity/low intensity—office professionals

➤ Low diversity/high intensity—engineers

Note: The most logical group to work with first is the low diversity/low intensity group.

Java Tools

This area is also in the fast-growth mode. The issue is what the tool does for the price. A price range—for discussion only—could be from $100 to $10,000. One can say that is a wide range. If you have been a system administrator for some time, you should have an experiential base in assisting you to define the criteria for your situation.

Note: Microsoft has its Visual Studio that is a comprehensive developmental tool suite. It is growing at a rapid pace. A key component, of course, is Visual J++.

See **http://www.microsoft.com/** for the latest details.

Java tools can be divided into at least five categories:

➤ Authoring and animation
  ➤ Animating objects
  ➤ Scrolling banners
  ➤ "Wizarding" (this is not magic, but a technique for following a step-by-step procedure to achieve a defined goal)
➤ Database connectivity (end-to-end, server-based database solutions)
➤ Developer
  ➤ DCOM
  ➤ JavaScript

> ➤ Microsoft Java Virtual Machine
> ➤ Visual J++
➤ Visual J++ Development Environment
> ➤ Creating an interface
> ➤ Debugging
> ➤ Developing code
> ➤ Managing projects
➤ Miscellaneous
> ➤ Security
> ➤ Services
> ➤ VRML

Selection of the right development tool for the right situation and the right person is very important. There are three key selection criteria:

➤ Experience or skill level of developer
➤ Type of application
➤ Development platform

Skill level can range from a professional object-oriented programmer to an HTML developer to a person with initiative but no practical experience.

Believe it or not, there are development tools available for each of these types.

Paradigm Definition

A *paradigm* is a model or a structure that attempts to organize, define, and solve problems. There are three key criteria for defining a successful paradigm. It appears that Java, as a structure, can be such a paradigm. The criteria are:

➤ Provides a method for analyzing and defining a problem
➤ Allows a solution formulation in its own terms
➤ Provides an implementing language

Infrastructure Overview

There are some basic elements that make up an enterprise network with Java internetworking. Part III of this book has more details on the infrastructure. In particular, see Chapter 17, "Defining Components," Chapter 19, "Using Management and Performance Tools," Chapter 20, "Working with Protocols," Chapter 21, "Identifying Interconnectivity Issues," Chapter 22, "Evaluating Service Servers," and Chapter 23, "Evaluating Access Servers." Part IV of the book looks at remote access and security. Chapter 30 considers project management synthesis that is the integration of the enterprise network with Java internetworking.

Any infrastructure is based on the network's topology. The list given here is not inclusive. This is a beginning point for design discussions; the rest adds to the discussion. The list is not in any particular order:

➤ Legacy system
➤ TCP/IP network, probably with both LAN and WAN interconnectivity
➤ Connecting hardware
  ➤ Bridges
  ➤ Hubs
  ➤ Repeaters
  ➤ Routers
  ➤ Switches
➤ Java Web server
  ➤ Java applets
  ➤ HTML pages
➤ DCOM-based component servers
➤ Distributed application servers
➤ Service servers
  ➤ Chat
  ➤ Directory
  ➤ E-mail
  ➤ News
  ➤ Search
➤ Access servers
  ➤ Certification

- ➤ Firewall
- ➤ Gateway
- ➤ Proxies
- ➤ Clients
  - ➤ Thin
  - ➤ Fat
- ➤ Tools
  - ➤ Administrative
  - ➤ Performance
  - ➤ Validation

Items in the above list can be located in one physical place because of network size. This list also represents the concrete component of the infrastructure. The abstract components are also important and are discussed in Chapter 17, "Defining Components."

One of the changes in the network infrastructure is a return to the notion of "thin client." A *thin client* is a stateless workstation, terminal, or desktop device linked through a network (intranet or Internet) to at least one server. The server handles all the states—operating system, applications, data, etc. This makes the workstation a device with limited management costs and also limits expansion costs. This notion is based on an Internet environment and the use of Java. This notion is further enhanced in the context of an object-oriented architecture. This is a return to a centralized management system but with a better return on investment than in the mainframe period.

Java is effective in the development of the thin client because of its component-based nature. Component-based software has three elements:

- ➤ Components (objects)
- ➤ Containers (assembly of components and objects)
- ➤ Scripts (initiate or direct component interactions)

The most common container is a Java-enabled browser. The browser software that handles the interaction is the Java Virtual Machine (JVM). The key to text or graphic manipulation is that a Java component also carries executable code. Data is thus downloaded along with the code required to work with that data.

JScript is one interpreted language that can handle scripting. JScript's functions include:

➤ Controlling object layering
➤ Creating animated graphical banners
➤ Creating pages that update themselves
➤ Customizing pages for users and browsers
➤ Generating *smart frames* (frames that can be manipulated on the fly)
➤ Managing cookie information

Java and Unified Modeling Language (UML)

Critical to modeling the infrastructure is the Unified Modeling Language (UML). This tool assists in creating an object-oriented design. Rational Software Corporation, along with a number of partners that include Hewlett-Packard, IBM, Microsoft, and Oracle, developed UML for this activity. See Rational Software Corporation's site (**http://www.rational.com/uml/index.shtml**) for information.

UML seeks to use the best engineering practices for developing large and complex system models. It can be used in both software and non-software environments. This means you can model a client as both software and hardware. It is used for specifying, visualizing, constructing, and documenting a system's infrastructure (see Chapters 17, "Defining Components" and 18, "Modeling an Enterprise Network").

A UML model is like a building blueprint. It aids in system definition, system visualization, and system construction. UML assists you in designing an object-oriented system network.

Besides not being a process, UML is not a programming language. Its name says UML is a modeling language. It is also not a tool interface, but a semantic metamodel. A *metamodel* is a high-level abstraction. See Chapter 29, "DCOM and Metaconcepts," for a further discussion of UML.

Java's Future

Everybody should make predictions. It is good for the soul and, if you see the tabloids in the supermarkets, it is also good for the wallet. Here are four emerging Java technologies that may see the shining light of day or the darkest of nights:

➤ Components

➤ Operating systems

➤ Java workstations

➤ Net computers (a merging of the three above)

There is a dark cloud in the future—the notion for the need for 100 percent pure Java. The problem is in the courts as this is written. This book represents one of the positions held in this discussion, but this book is not an argument for one position or other. (There is a companion book to this one titled *CORBA Networking with Java*.) The position taken in this book is that to achieve the core ideals of Java, there have to be standards. Just as it was agreed upon to have the order of the colors on traffic lights be top to bottom—red, yellow, and green (because of color-blind drivers)—so do there need to be rules on the cybernetic superhighway.

Part II
Administrative Planning Process

This part of the book looks at ten fundamental steps in the administrative planning process to implement an enterprise network. These steps logically raise questions that you have to answer in the administrative planning, designing, developing, and implementing phases of your enterprise network. Some questions may be answered with a simple "not applicable."

This part is in contrast to the next part, which is concerned with the technical planning process. The technical planning process for an enterprise network involves: modeling, performance, optimization, tools, traffic, interconnectivity, servers (access and service), and standards.

The administrative planning process steps are common to any successful project management. However, the focus is specific to enterprise network implementation. They are given here to assist you because you are probably working under a short deadline. As the system administrator you want to ensure that all your bases are covered.

Each step is covered in a separate chapter. The steps are:

➤ Establishing parameters for an enterprise network
➤ Defining quality and documentation controls
➤ Sequencing activities
➤ Determining skill requirements
➤ Handling resistance
➤ Developing a communications policy
➤ Estimating time requirements
➤ Developing a schedule
➤ Defining a risk management policy
➤ Establishing cost factors
➤ Developing a budget

Some of the steps happen in parallel, while some have to have a significant portion done before moving to another step. You may have a single overall budget figure given to you, but before detailing the budget you need most if not all of the cost factor defined.

Internet Resources—Sources

Beyond the discussions given in this book, there are many Internet resources that give alternate solutions to the issues concerned with the design, development, and implementation of an intranet and the access to the Internet, the core to any enterprise network. Two important differences need to be established. The first is how you integrate two or more intranets. The second is how you transmit secure data from one intranet to another, and how data is made secure from a remote access point, the access point being a customer, a vendor, or an internal intranet user.

Note: Because of the dynamic nature of the Internet, these addresses may not be valid.

The BSGnet site (**http://www.bsgnet.com**) gives you the opportunity to make better-informed decisions in the design of an intranet with Internet access. It has questionnaires, checklists, and matrices.

IntraNut (**http://www.internut.com**) is a weekly netzine (net + magazine). It covers many topics, including applications, budgeting, designing, security, and tools.

David Strom (**http://www.strom.com/pubwork/internet.html**) has developed a collection of sites that can further your knowledge on intranet design, development, and implementation. The site includes Strom's white paper on "Creating Private Intranets: Challenges and Prospects for IS" (1995 viewpoint).

Intranet Design Magazine (**http://www.innergy.com**) is biweekly and includes analysis and "how-to" for intranet development. Innergy, Inc. produces it.

Internet Resources—White Papers

Microsoft's Intranet Strategy, "Creating Business Solutions Using Intranets and the Internet," (**http://www.microsoft.com/cio/articles/intranet-strategy.htm**) covers, of course, Microsoft's products and how they are positioned for intranet implementation.

Hummingbird Communications' white paper, "Implementation of Internet and Web Technologies in Organizational Information Systems," is an overview of Internet technologies (**http://www.hummingbird.com/whites/internet.html**).

International Data Corporation's white paper on the results of its research on Return on Investment (ROI) is "The Intranet: Slashing Cost of Business" (**http://www.netscape.com/comprod/announce/roi.html**).

Note: This is only an example list. There is no implied statement that these are the best Internet resources, only some the author considered supplemental ideas. Be aware that the addresses may not be valid.

Chapter 6

Establishing Enterprise Network Parameters

A parameter has two sides:
internal and external.

While this book is not about the project planning process per se, this part of the book reflects on the key ideas of the process. The project planning process uses the environment for evaluating the technical checklists for integrating the components of an enterprise network with DCOM architecture and its supporting technologies. For example, when you go to select a Web server and integrate it into your enterprise network, some or all of the items discussed below play a part in your selection.

Scope Planning in a Nutshell

One of the first actions you must take is to establish the goals and performance expectations of your network enterprise. Second, you must determine how the individual components or objects (protocols, firewall, servers, e-mail, browsers, etc.) fit into the overall objectives. You should have as a minimum the following data:

➤ Network parameters and performance expectations

➤ Performance benchmarks

➤ Validation system parameters

➤ Start and end date of integration completion

➤ Criteria for establishing time lines

➤ Criteria for identifying skill requirements

➤ Basic team list

> ➤ People with technical skills (network, intranet, Internet)
> ➤ Marketing people
> ➤ People with project management skills
> ➤ Representatives for external users

➤ General cost requirements (How much can you spend or expect to spend?)

➤ General budgetary requirements (Who is going to pay for the costs?)

➤ Historical and marketing data (important in shaping enterprise network goals)

➤ User or customer expectations (should be on the team, not looking in from the outside)

➤ Criteria for selecting resources

➤ Criteria for communications (training, documentation, status reporting)

➤ Standards for risk management

The following figure shows scope planning in the form of a hierarchy or a naming tree. Scope planning also can be considered an object of the class network integrating (see Figure 6-10).

Figure 6-1
Scope Planning hierarchy

The list is not by priority. The priority can change. Notice the use of the words "criteria" and "standards" in the above list. This is like having the bricks for your castle.

Scope Defining in a Nutshell

Scope defining is taking the standards and criteria above and putting some flesh on the bones. It is the time to get a "firm" first commitment from all the parties involved. Notice it is firm, not final, commitment. Your enterprise network evolves. It is not complete on day one. This is important so that user expectations are not set in stone or concrete.

The scope definition should have as a minimum:

➤ Firm start and end dates for basic usage

➤ Key integration milestone dates (some databases will be available day one, others on day *x*)

➤ Clear definition of your responsibilities as network administrator

➤ Basic definitions of responsibilities

➤ Integration methodology (single browser or multiple browsers)

➤ Chart of relationships and brief link descriptions tied to responsibility definitions

➤ List of realistic manageable enterprise network services

➤ List of cost estimates by human, materials, and time (budgetary considerations come later)

➤ Descriptions of the quality control and verification systems used in the planning, design, development, and implementation phases of the enterprise network

➤ List of resource estimates by human and material (how to get these resources is detailed later)

➤ Communication policy that includes who sends information, what kind of information is sent, when information is sent, who receives what types of information, and, of course, what types of communication are used and why

➤ Threat (security) policy that illustrates how types of threats are handled; this includes from a simple "nothing will be done with a minimal threat" to a complex statement on how to handle very dangerous threats

The framework of scope planning determines a detailed scope definition. The blueprint of the castle should now have at least the moat, walls, room types, etc. The plan must be a useful and usable size.

The following figure shows scope defining in the form of a hierarchy or a naming tree. Scope defining also can be considered an object of the class network integrating (see Figure 6-10).

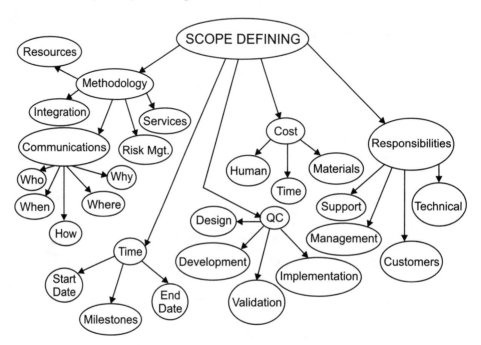

Figure 6-2
Scope Defining hierarchy

Activity Defining in a Nutshell

When you have the details, definitions, and descriptions of the actions for your enterprise network, you should clearly define the activities required to complete basic integration based on established goals.

While writing this book, certain actions were defined up front. The key activities required in drafting this book were:

➤ Methodology for writing the chapters
➤ Use of a spell checker and a grammar checker

➤ Use of old resources and acquisition of new ones

➤ Use of prior written documents

➤ Methodology for printing the book for review based on publisher's guidelines

Your activities when defined give as a minimum:

➤ Firm start and end actions

➤ Clear definition of the activities

➤ Basic definitions of actions of support team members

➤ Design, development, control, and implementation activities

➤ Flow chart of activities (think critical path)

➤ List of realistic manageable activities

➤ List of specific milestone activities with their importance to enterprise network integration as determined by the criteria for establishing these milestones

➤ List of cost estimates associated with each function, application, or service that is going to be on your enterprise network

➤ Activities for the quality control and verification systems used in the planning, design, development, and implementation phases of the enterprise network

➤ List of resource estimates associated with each function, application, or service

➤ Activities for handling the established communications policy

➤ Actions to ensure a realistic security policy can be implemented when necessary

The following figure shows activity defining in the form of a hierarchy or a naming tree. Activity defining also can be considered an object of the class network integrating (see Figure 6-10).

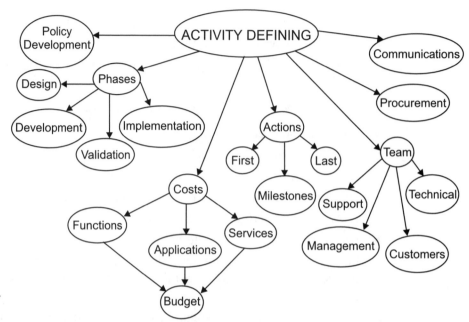

Figure 6-3
*Activity Defining
hierarchy*

The blueprint of the castle should now have at least the types of rooms, walls, and moat you are going to have. The activity definitions can be several pages in length or a large flow chart.

Resource Planning in a Nutshell

A number of technical checklists for various components of your enterprise network are included later in the book. There are other resource considerations, but they are outside this book's range. For example, do you have resources to train the enterprise network user to function at an expected defined level of expertise? Select an e-mail system that is not user friendly and see what happens. You probably have already had this problem when you implemented your intranet.

Your resource definition should include as a minimum:

➤ Firm resource requirements and how not having them may impact your network implementation

➤ Policy for how resource utilization for the enterprise network is determined

➤ Policy on who determines resource requirements

➤ Policy on when resources are required

➤ Policy on how resource requirements are to be handled

➤ Chart on how resources are linked together (a certain function or service requires associated equipment and materials)

➤ Procedure for turning an unavailable resource into an opportunity

The following figure shows resource planning in the form of a hierarchy or a naming tree. Resource planning also can be considered an object of the class network integrating (see Figure 6-10).

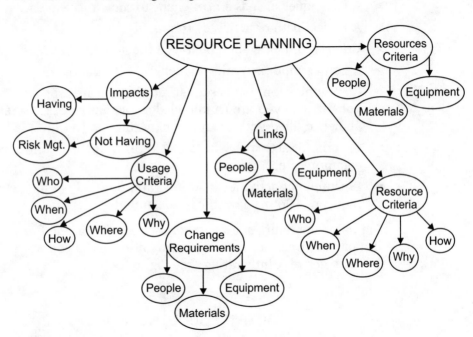

Figure 6-4
Resource Planning hierarchy

You should have not only a working blueprint for your castle, but a list of castle builders, equipment, and materials to build the castle. Real world—you must be able to find alternative vendors that can furnish the components for your enterprise network.

Activity Sequencing in a Nutshell

When you have sequenced your activities to implement enterprise network integration, you should have a clear statement as to order of activities and their relationships to each other as to time, people, equipment, materials, and cost. The usual presentation is a flow chart. Here is a list of actions or things you should have at this point:

➤ Quality control and verification activities scheduled throughout

➤ A technique, such as a flow chart, to show the sequence of the activities

➤ A critical path of activities (optional)

➤ Criteria for being able to change the activity sequence if necessary

➤ Resource input activities sequenced with the operational activities

➤ Communication points sequenced that ensure all parties involved know where you are (A knowledgeable audience is better than an audience filled with unknown expectations.)

➤ Criteria for activities where the status of quality control can be communicated

➤ Procurement activities identified appropriately in the activity sequence (Got to have those consultants!)

The following figure shows activity sequencing in the form of a hierarchy or a naming tree. Activity sequencing also can be considered an object of the class network integrating (see Figure 6-10).

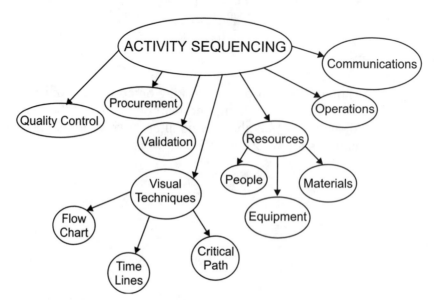

Figure 6-5
*Activity
Sequencing
hierarchy*

At this point in your castle building you should know when the parts of the castle are going to be constructed. The start date is when the contract is signed, while the end date is the move-in day. As you would not build the second floor before the first floor, you have to consider the activity sequence.

Time Estimating in a Nutshell

Time management experts or software tools should be used to develop time estimates. This activity can use historical data for establishing benchmarks. Pessimism is better than optimism in doing time estimates.

Here are some of the types of information you need when you finish your time estimates:

➤ Criteria for formulating time estimates

➤ Procedure for associating time estimates with people, and equipment and people acquisition

➤ Methodology for validating time estimates based on the defined goals for enterprise network integration

➤ Criteria for establishing time measures

➤ Criteria for associating cost and time estimates and potential changes

➤ Quality control and validation time estimates (suggested 20 percent of your project)

➤ Time estimates based on <u>skill types and levels</u> rather than on head count involved

The following figure shows time estimating in the form of a hierarchy or a naming tree. Time estimating also can be considered an object of the class network integrating (see Figure 6-10).

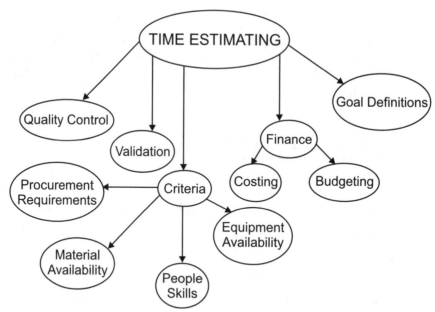

Figure 6-6
*Time Estimating
hierarchy*

Cost Estimating in a Nutshell

Cost management software tools should be used to develop cost estimates. This activity can use historical data for establishing benchmarks. Pessimism is better than optimism in doing cost estimates. This activity is discussed in more detail in a later chapter covering costs and budgets.

Here are some key points of cost estimating:

➤ Criteria for formulating cost estimates

➤ Procedure for associating cost estimates with people, and equipment and people acquisition

➤ Methodology for validating cost estimates based on the enterprise network definition

➤ Criteria for establishing cost measures

➤ Criteria for associating cost and time estimates and potential changes

➤ Quality control and validation cost estimates (suggested 10 to 20 percent of your project to implement enterprise integration)

➤ Cost estimates based on skill types and levels rather than on numbers of people involved

The following figure shows cost estimating in the form of a hierarchy or a naming tree. Cost estimating also can be considered an object of the class network integrating (see Figure 6-10).

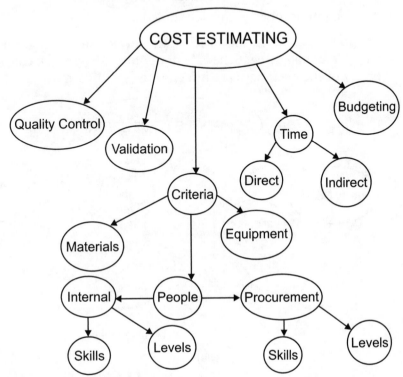

Figure 6-7
Cost Estimating hierarchy

Schedule Developing in a Nutshell

Time management software tools can be used to develop schedules. This is where fixed time and ordered activities are combined. A schedule can be as simple as a calendar with activities inserted on milestone days to an elaborate flow chart with dates placed on directional arrows.

Your schedule should include as a minimum:

➤ Time line (calendar, flow chart)
➤ Time line for acquiring skills, equipment, and materials
➤ Schedule based on the enterprise network scope definition
➤ Schedule for quality control and verification
➤ Schedule for notifying everyone of significant changes

➤ Time allocated for risk management

➤ Criteria for being able to change the schedule if necessary

➤ A consistent and coherent set of time lines

➤ Communications points scheduled

The following figure shows schedule developing in the form of a hierarchy or a naming tree. Schedule developing also can be considered an object of the class network integrating (see Figure 6-10).

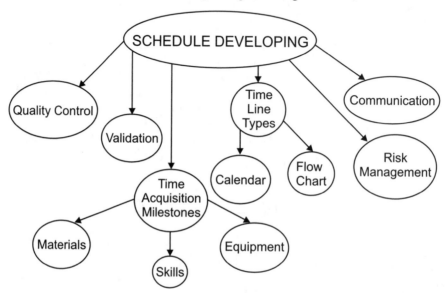

Figure 6-8
*Schedule
Developing
hierarchy*

At this point in your castle building you should know when the parts of the castle are going to be constructed. The start date is when the contract is signed, while the end date is the move-in day. All that is left is the budgetary plan. Another way of looking at this action is this is where you close the mortgage with the bank.

Cost Budgeting in a Nutshell

Budgeting is taking cost estimates and entering them into a formal financial structure. A budget is to cost as a schedule is to time. At the end of the cost budgeting you should at least have the following:

➤ A budget or budgets that are consistent to the enterprise network's scope definition

> Links between the enterprise network's budget and any support budgets (These are the budgets of the folks with the bucks.)
> Separate budget lines for quality control and verification (optional)
> Procedure for handling the payments for outside resources
> Procedure for making changes and updates to the budget reporting system as relevant to any enterprise network integration
> Either a separate budget line for risk management or an identified component of another budget line

The following figure shows cost budgeting in the form of a hierarchy or a naming tree. Cost budgeting also can be considered an object of the class network integrating (see Figure 6-10).

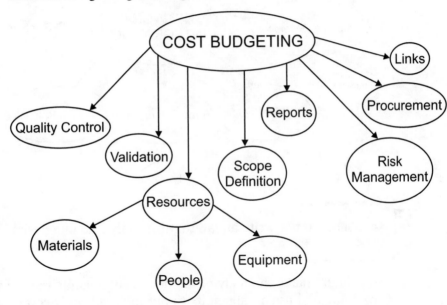

Figure 6-9
Cost Budgeting hierarchy

Enterprise Network Integration Plan in a Nutshell

Project plan development is when you take the results of the prior nine activities and integrate them into a consistent and coherent document. Establish chapter (section) one as the (executive) summary and a chapter (section) for each delimiter. Have an appendix to supplement the data in the document's body.

The following figure shows network integrating in the form of a hierarchy or a naming tree. Network integrating can be considered an object of the class project management.

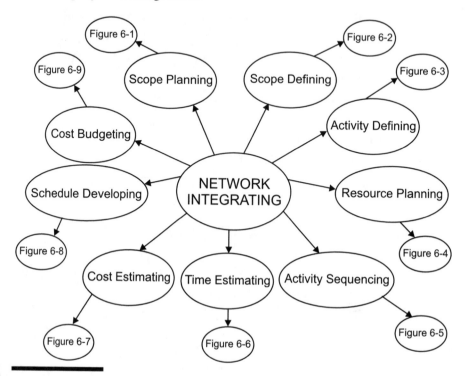

Figure 6-10
Network Integrating hierarchy

 Caution: Do not write a plan that is so large no one desires to read or use it.

You should make the body of the document a summation of where you are going and use an appendix to put in details only certain people want to read. For example, for each procedure that is required to handle a specific technical issue, such as building a firewall, just include it in an appendix.

The recommended components are:

➤ Summary
➤ Scope definition
➤ Activity sequence (a flow chart)
➤ Resources defined
➤ Time estimates
➤ Schedule (a flow chart with activities and time lines)
➤ Cost estimates
➤ Budget
➤ Appendix

 Caution: All deliverables, milestones, and metrics should be identified, negotiated, and approved by all functions or the project should NOT go forward!

The body of your plan should be a summation of activities. The appendices should hold the <u>details</u> of the activities, costs, resources, and procedures. It should be updated as required. The updates should have version numbers and dates.

Any changes that modify function, content, or date should be processed through a change management process. This process should be included as an appendix unless it is a standard of the company or corporation. It then should be noted that the standard change process is being used.

Chapter 7

Identifying Killer Acts

Any activity has its own hidden agenda.

There are many activities that can play the role of killer if you do not pay attention to them. All of them are discussed in this book at least once and perhaps, in some cases, more times than you like. The killer acts that are discussed in other chapters include:

➤ Defining the goals and objectives of your enterprise network integration (version 1.0)

➤ Defining the people involved in the integration

➤ Establishing milestones

➤ Establishing cost and budgetary parameters

➤ Determining skill levels to get the job completed on time and under budget (Fantasizing is healthy!)

➤ Developing risk management criteria

➤ Determining the impact of the use of outside resources (procurement management)

All the above are probably done almost at a subconscious level by any good system administrator. However, the best of us sometimes fail in two areas. The focus of this chapter is on those two areas:

➤ Establishing a quality control process that is intertwined with all activities

➤ Documenting what you will do and what you have done

For additional details, also see:

➤ Skills versus head count—Chapter 9

➤ Communicating—Chapter 11

➤ Time management—Chapters 12 and 13

➤ Risk management—Chapter 14

➤ Financial management—Chapters 15 and 16

Quality Control in a Nutshell

Here are three questions you need to answer so the dark things in the night do not attack your enterprise network integration:

➤ Have the quality standards been made consistent?

➤ Has a quality control system been established?

➤ Have verification activities been formulated?

Benchmarks of the quality and performance of the network should be established at your earliest planning sessions, not after the network is completed. What are the realistic expectations of your customer(s) for enterprise network integration? Get it in writing. You should be as specific as possible about expectations. Everyone will be happier when the integration is completed.

Benchmarks should be clearly formulated in the definition of the goals and objectives of the enterprise network, the use of DCOM architectural standards, and the amount of internetworking. The use of external appropriate benchmarks or standards for project activities and for evaluation of the end goal would make your enterprise network[1] more valid to the world. This can be significant to your customers and perhaps to yourself.

The forefront of defining integrating activities should be quality control. Do you know of a project that was completed without a change? You must have activities that show how you handle change. You must establish benchmark actions at the beginning of the project for validating the end network.

Note: These points are not negotiable.

When you plan your resources you have to look at all the resource types and in particular how the resources impact the quality of your enterprise

---

[1] Requests for Comment (RFCs) are noted throughout this book. The standards found in many of the RFCs can assist in validating your enterprise network integration implementation.

network. If a new skill requirement is identified halfway into the project cycle, has a process been defined that can handle this issue? What skills are required to do adequate controlling and verifying of a network integration segment and the status of the project?

Across any activity sequence there must be quality control activities. Are there also validation activities in the activity sequence? Never say you will do all of the quality control at the end.

Time estimating can be at certain moments more of an art than a science. There are many time management software packages available to assist in doing your enterprise network integration. Doing time estimates for quality control can be the trickiest. A specific amount of time should be allocated for quality control. You should set a benchmark of, say, 20 percent. This percentage is based on the estimated time for the project. This task should be at the beginning of the planning phase.

A specific cost estimate should be established for quality control. You should set a benchmark of, say, 10 to 20 percent. This percentage is based on the estimated total cost for the project. This task should be among the first tasks of your integration planning.

Within any schedule the quality control and verification milestones should be clearly defined. The quality control time line may be defined as a separate time line; however, when and where quality control flows into the main project cycle must be stated.

It is recommended to have at least two lines in your budget for quality control. The lines are controlling and verification. You may want to divide these two lines into salaries, equipment, and materials.

Selected Documentation Content

The list of documents is not comprehensive nor is it expected that you would use all of them. However, they are here to assist you in identifying the types of data you may want to develop for the history and benchmarks of your integration of an enterprise network. In some cases you may be expected to give input for others who desire to have the documents. Or you may be asked by others to give input about these documents so you can function effectively as a system administrator.

Market Analysis Report

This report documents and verifies market opportunities. It can be global in nature or segmented for localized conditions. This report should be an agreement of the viability of enterprise network integration using DCOM architecture and its supporting technologies. The report should include how your enterprise network is to be introduced into the marketplace.

The report is the justification for the features, services, and applications for enterprise network integration. This input can be based on such things as customer needs, market opportunities, competition, new governmental regulations, product surveys, and (inferred) commitments for special functionality. The report should include adequate descriptions of the input so the network administrator has sufficient information to make design decisions. The report should also include revenue gains. The counter to this is a statement on revenue losses if this activity is not taken.

A life cycle statement identifies the various stages of this version of the network's market cycle such as introduction, growth, maturity, and replacement. It explains impacts on existing products by the introduction of the enterprise network integration.

Business Justification

This document is the general rationale for making the financial investment. Some of the following questions should be answered to develop the initial justification:

➤ What is the business (nonprofit) opportunity?
➤ What is the financial (revenue) opportunity?
➤ What are the musts to be successful?
➤ When must the integration be completed?
➤ What are the impacts on your intranet?
➤ How does this enterprise network integration affect already-established market policies and strategies?

The Business Justification may include:

➤ Market need
➤ Concept (as compared to definition)
➤ Required functions and characteristics
➤ Impact on products
➤ Distribution strategy

➤ Competition data

➤ Return on Investment (ROI)

➤ Market window

Commercial Specification

This specification is an evolution of the Business Justification and identifies the market need. The specification gives adequate requirement and limitation data for the design and development group(s). There should be design flexibility to achieve expectations. The Commercial Specification describes the expected "what" for enterprise network integration.

The Commercial Specification describes in <u>detail</u> the enterprise network integration requirements and the targeted market. The key to a successful network would include:

➤ Market historical background

➤ Application of the enterprise network

➤ Life cycle

➤ Portfolio information

➤ Key performance requirements and features

➤ Target costs versus revenues

➤ Market window

➤ Success criteria for the enterprise network

➤ Special interfaces

➤ Design constraints

➤ Enterprise network maintenance

➤ Enterprise support requirements

➤ Standards

➤ Usage of the enterprise network

➤ Distribution methods

➤ Customer verification plans

➤ Customer participation

This is a suggested unordered list. A one-page spreadsheet for a very large project can be effective and successful, but it is very rare. I have heard of three people who did such a spreadsheet, but they were very intelligent and had a strong knowledge of the specific market.

Organization Chart

There should be an organizational chart of the team, which includes a description of major project responsibilities. The detail should be included in an appendix. There must be a detailed statement of the network administrator's responsibilities. All other responsibility statements should be linked to this description. The format of the chart should be at your discretion or in accordance with corporate policy.

Enterprise Network Proposal

This proposal is a formal response to the Commercial Specification that <u>describes</u> the requirements for an enterprise network.

This proposal may include the following information:

➤ Commercial Specification compliance
➤ Definition of preliminary functions
➤ Hardware requirements
➤ Installation requirements
➤ Maintenance requirements
➤ Software strategy
➤ Target costs based on preliminary development definition
➤ Software requirements
➤ Summary of commercial information
➤ Testing requirements
➤ Verification requirements

Enterprise Network Specification

This specification is also a formal response to the Commercial Specification that <u>specifies</u> the requirements for an enterprise network.

This specification may include the following types of information:

➤ Updates to the Enterprise Network Proposal
➤ Enterprise network definition from a user and external viewpoint
➤ Enterprise network definition from a technology (hardware and software) element point
➤ Enterprise network estimated costs
➤ Enterprise network introduction strategy

> ➤ Enterprise network operational description
> ➤ Specific testing requirements
> ➤ Standards requirements

There should be a section on possible noncompliance which describes deviations from the Commercial Specification. It should be determined if noncompliance is permanent or temporary. When the noncompliance is permanent, the changes should be noted in a basic plan for an enterprise network through the change management process.

Content Agreement

This agreement is the written "contract" between the development group and the marketing group as to the content and functions of the network. This should include the following:

> ➤ Start and end dates for completion of the enterprise network integration
> ➤ Software features and requirements
> ➤ Hardware requirements (availability status)
> ➤ How end users use the enterprise network

Schedule

The schedule can be as elaborate as required to implement your enterprise network. It should be usable. An example of a schedule is a flow chart with milestones and times. There could also be links to key players and groups and their responsibilities to the implementation of the enterprise network integration. A schedule should include the quality control milestones and the verification milestones.

Design and Development Plan

This plan drives the Enterprise Network Integration Plan that captures all major design and development deliverables and milestones for management tracking and reporting.

The document may include the following items (if applicable):

> ➤ Enterprise network goals
> ➤ Enterprise network definition
> ➤ Enterprise network software structure description

➤ Enterprise network hardware structure description
➤ Enterprise network user definition
➤ Enterprise network market (summary from Enterprise Network Specification)
➤ Risk assessment
➤ Responsibilities defined
➤ Resources defined
➤ Enterprise network milestones
➤ Verification dates

Initial Budget Estimate

This document provides a view of the expected development costs. The estimate is usually based on the preliminary Enterprise Network Specification. The document gives estimates for direct labor as well as capital and expense requirements. Remember, the indirect costs should be considered as important as direct costs.

This document is updated in the Enterprise Network Integration Cost Update.

Initial Funding Requirements

This document is for monitoring and reporting enterprise network integration costs at each major phase of implementation. There should be comparisons to the original funding document used to establish financial targets and expected milestones and deliverables.

This document can also be included in the Enterprise Network Integration Cost Update.

Enterprise Network Integration Cost Update

This document updates initial enterprise network integration cost estimates at each major key phase of implementation with comparison to the Initial Budget Estimate. The concern here is how the costs (actual expenditures) and revenues go into the budget (the financial plan). The costs are usually reported on a monthly basis.

Quality Plan

This plan defines the role of quality control in <u>all</u> phases of the enterprise network integration process. It also defines the deliverables, functions, and specific activities required of quality control to ensure successful completion. Quality procedures that are specific to enterprise network integration should also be identified in an appendix.

There should be a set of quality metrics that defines the various measures by which the quality of a new application is measured, attained, and controlled. This is also included in the project plan with the quality procedures.

The Quality Plan also summarizes the staff, resources, and equipment required by quality control to perform specific activities and to support a new application.

The Quality Plan should be updated before each major phase review to reflect changes.

Trial (Beta) Strategy

This strategy identifies the software and hardware elements in the enterprise network that are a part of the trial, and the trial's location. Also, the when and by whom should be included in the strategy. This provides a clear identification of the testing requirements plus the extent of the resources and capabilities to trial.

Field Introduction Requirements

This document reflects the strategy and detailed plans to verify conformance to specification and functionality as defined in the Enterprise Network Specification. This document should be concerned with such events as how the customers become users of the enterprise network.

Enterprise Network Support Plan

This plan ensures that the enterprise network is supportable in a market environment. This plan should include a process for customer support.

Customer Documentation Strategy

This strategic document provides how timely and quality enterprise network documentation becomes available. There really is a triad in quality: control, documentation, and training.

This document contains a strategy of activities, schedules, and estimates that develops into a plan. The strategy is developed out of a set of negotiations among the product management group, the marketing group, and the development group. The strategy might include the following:

➤ Key activities
➤ Schedule
➤ Manpower requirements
➤ Cost estimates
➤ Production process

Training Strategy

This document can have two components: internal requirements and customer requirements (external). The Training Strategy should show how training is to be designed, developed, implemented, and verified. The emphasis should be based on the customer's needs and expectations.

The strategy might include the following:

➤ Key activities
➤ Schedule
➤ Manpower requirements
➤ Cost estimates
➤ Implementation process

Communications Plan

This plan should include as a minimum:

➤ People doing the reporting
➤ People who receive the reports
➤ Types of reports to be sent
➤ When reports are sent (specific dates or after an event occurs)
➤ How reports are sent

The Communications Plan should have a global component as well as "local" communications processes. You may wish to create a local form which your developers use to communicate to each other on status.

Business Justification Update

This document assures the current view of the implementation of the enterprise network integration performance meets previous commitments and management expectations. The update may have a one or more year view of:

➤ Revenues
➤ Maintenance costs
➤ Investment
➤ Return on Investment (ROI)
➤ Customer impact

Risk Assessment

It is important that any Risk Assessment consider both threats and opportunities. The Risk Assessment should be reviewed by all the components of the team. The review should at the least involve representatives from each component (your group, marketing, and enterprise network users). A Risk Assessment should be done at least at every major phase of integration.

The assessment should be against established thresholds. An example of a threshold is that no action is taken until a certain number of errors are found.

Business Affiliate Plan

This plan provides information when the enterprise network is to be developed by a third-party developer, such as a DCOM vendor or developer. The plan can consist of the following:

➤ Explanation for the need for a third-party developer
➤ How the third party doing the development qualifies
➤ What part the third party plays in the marketing program
➤ Training requirements
➤ Documentation requirements
➤ Quality control system description

Third-Party Market Agreement

This agreement provides the plans where the enterprise network is to be developed by a third-party developer. This agreement may include:

➤ Product content

➤ Delivery schedules

➤ Marketing strategy

➤ Verification strategy

➤ Documentation strategy

➤ Training strategy

Third-Party Service Plan

It provides how the enterprise network is to be serviced by a third-party developer. The question is "Will the third party do customer service?" The plan may include details on:

➤ Customer training

➤ Customer documentation

➤ Diagnostic tools

➤ Support process

Note: Do not forget ongoing maintenance for the software internetworking resulting from the implementation of DCOM architecture if there is a lack of internal programming expertise.

Chapter 8

Putting Activities into Logical Sequence

A sequence may be a bit forward and a bit backwards.

This chapter looks at the three key types of questions about activities that you need to do to reach your goal of a successful implementation of an enterprise network with a DCOM architecture and its supporting technologies. The three sets of questions center around the core project management activities, the core design considerations of DCOM architecture, and the Java approach to a distributed architecture.

Below are examples of beginning questions to establish parameters and a sequence priority. There is a set of comments to aid in establishing a basic Java approach to networking within DCOM architecture.

Sequencing activities is the determination of a logical order of activities that can be used in developing a realistic and achievable schedule. There are available automated project management software tools to aid in the sequencing. The tools also let you establish a schedule. Developing a schedule is when you combine time estimates and sequenced (ordered) activities. To establish a basic sequence, all you need is a pencil, index cards, and tape. For example, you could write your activities on index cards and then stick them to the wall until a logical order and associations are made. This is inexpensive but very effective.

The basic question is "What is the best type of activity sequencing so that it communicates the quickest, cheapest, and most effective form of enterprise network integration?"

Fundamental Project Management Questions

Below are some fundamental project management questions you need to answer in developing your enterprise network integration plan:

What are the funders' expected milestones?

In any activity sequence there are always the same two doors: The front door is the start date, and the back door is the end date. The rest of the activities are a walk through the chosen castle. The importance of this sequence is that you see all the rooms in the shortest distance.

What resources are required to be successful?

This question has three important prongs: Who are the people involved? What people and activities need special equipment? What materials are required? The concern here is to determine the relationships of the project activities. One way to link the activities is critical; major but not critical; and minor.

How can the scope definition for implementing the enterprise network be used in developing the schedule?

In developing the activity sequence, use the scope standards, descriptions, and definitions formulated during scope definition. The parameters of the project should be a major factor in developing the sequence.

Have delays been considered in the schedule?

When setting up a schedule, specify that the activity is completed from *x* day to *y* day or from *x* period to *y* period. Users need to be aware when their expectation might be fulfilled.

How do cost estimates affect the schedule?

Costs should be divided over all the phases (planning, designing, developing, controlling, verifying, and implementing) of the enterprise network integration. Never take from the quality controlling activities to seemingly improve another part of the schedule. This type of action has a way of biting you in places where it hurts.

Has time been scheduled for quality validation?

Quality control activities need to be established throughout the schedule. There should be validation activities in the activity sequence. Never say all of the quality control will be done at the end.

How do resource estimates affect the schedule?

You should have a procedure that ensures the resources are available when an activity is scheduled. It is important to define critical resources just like defining a critical path of action. A key component of a critical path is the flag when resources must be available. Remember that resources can be skills, equipment, or materials.

Does the schedule have time allocations for communicating progress?

There should be a communications activity sequence. There may be one sequence for the coordinating committee. There may be different sequences as the integration evolves. There should be key activities during the project to evaluate the success of the communications system.

Have potential threats and opportunities been identified for schedule changes?

There should be activities in the sequence that evaluate potential threats and opportunities. You need to consider that a given configuration, such as a Web server, may take longer than expected.

Are there any internal or external procurement policies or standards that affect the schedule?

You need to be aware of all procurement policies and procedures that impact the integration end date. A project may be stopped or heavily impacted because a policy or a procedure was not followed.

General Activity Sequencing in a Nutshell

At the end of this activity, you should have a clear statement as to order of activities and their relationships to each other as to time, people, equipment, materials, and cost. The usual presentation is a flow chart. Here is some of the information you should have as a result of this activity:

Part II

➤ Quality control and verification activities

➤ A technique, such as a flow chart, to show the sequence of the activities

➤ Resource input activities sequenced with the operational activities

➤ Sequential communications points

➤ Quality control activities that can be communicated to all parties concerned

Fundamental DCOM Design Questions

When one is considering the use of DCOM architecture and its supporting technologies (see Chapter 5), one must consider the design implications for the use of Microsoft products, vendor support products, and the hardware that will support these products. More so the focus of the questions asked should relate to the object-oriented paradigm and Java internetworking. However, the beginning activity questions should be asked and answered in relation to the object core concepts. The below list is not a sequential one, so one should, so to speak, do "parallel processing." All of these concepts need to be related to the legacy system environment and the expected outcomes not only in parallel but also in a dynamic interplay.

➤ Analysis process: OO analysis versus system analysis

➤ Architecture—Specification—Implementation

➤ Contextual forces: benefits and consequences

➤ Granularity level

➤ Hierarchical pattern: class and inheritance

➤ Interfaces: horizontal, vertical, and metadata

➤ Parallel operations

➤ System versus application level

➤ Type management

What type of analysis should be used and what are the results on the system design?

The result of a system analysis is different from an OO analysis. For example, in a system analysis a result might be that the system has *x* number of computers with a certain type of operating system. In an OO analysis, these same computers at a minimum would be defined as one or more DCOM components and the benefits and consequences to the system design. There are flaws in both types of analyses. An analysis used in and of itself can produce serious misinformation when used across systems enterprises.

What needs to be evaluated when considering the interplay of the DCOM architecture, Microsoft Interface Definition Language (MIDL), and the support technologies such as Visual J++?

> The evaluation of the DCOM architecture includes details on data flow, definitions, abstractions, standards support, etc. The MIDL specifications include the formal definitions and compiling specifications. Implementation considers architecture constraints enforced by compiler checking.

What is the impact of considering contextual forces as to their benefits and consequences?

> A basic principle of risk management is that every action has a positive (benefit) and a negative (consequence). A part of the design process is to establish points where design considerations can resolve problems within a specific context. A major contextual force is DCOM components.

To what level of granularity must the design be to achieve expected outcomes?

> Granularity is concerned with the patterns within the system model. A pattern is a statement of intent with a concrete solution. Granularity is to take a pattern-based solution and augment another pattern-based solution. The finest level of granularity is when there cannot be another solution. Granularity is to refine a notion about a DCOM interface such as number of methods and parameters.

What is the core level technology of DCOM that exists to achieve the expected system outcome?

> While DCOM is a solid desktop environment, does it handle the distribution of DCOM components required for the designed network? Are the vendor support products available in the critical areas of network design?

What is expected from an analysis that considers horizontal, vertical, and metadata interfaces?

> The issue is that most systems only have a vertical interface. To achieve balanced software architecture there also needs to be a horizontal interface and metadata. *Metadata* is the self-descriptive data that defines the dynamic data structures of the system network.

What is the impact of a three-tier architecture using DCOM?

Microsoft Transaction Server's impact has to be considered at each of the three tiers: client, business-rules, and database server. What in-process components have to be designed in particular to resolve issues at the business-rules tier?

What is the impact of using Visual J++ versus Visual Basic to build DCOM-based components?

When there is a goal to make the transition from a client/server paradigm network, there are two fundamental questions that have to be asked. First, what will be the OO architecture? The answer here is DCOM. Second, will there be Java internetworking? A related question is, to what degree will Java be used? If the answer is significantly less than 100 percent, then there is an opportunity to use both Visual J++ and Visual Basic.

What are the expectations from system-level and application-level modeling?

There is a need for both external and internal modes that reflect the system and application levels. The system level focuses on interoperability. The application handles the mapping between the external and internal models.

How is type management handled in DCOM architecture for network design?

Type management is the act of evaluating an object with different sets of definitions. A programmer could be considered as three independent objects: programmer (general function), manager (level in organization), and tester (specific function). These three could be related into one object (person). A programmer and a manager could be related (inheritance) to employee, but not contractor. Employee could then be related to worker. This is a very simple example of type management.

DCOM Design Activity Sequencing in a Nutshell

At the end of this activity, you should have a statement as to the order of DCOM model concepts and their relationships to each other for object definition for the enterprise network model. The usual presentation is dependent upon the resolution format. Here is some of the information you should have as a result of this activity:

➤ DCOM component definitions

➤ Interface (horizontal, vertical, and metadata) definitions

➤ Type management model

➤ System and application (external and internal models)

➤ Hierarchical pattern model that should be mapped to Java classes

Fundamental Java Approach Questions

According to Sun Microsystems' first white paper on Java, the language has 10 major characteristics, actually 11 if you count simple. The list here is alphabetical, not by order of importance; that is a judgment call. The big 10 are:

➤ Architecture-neutral

➤ Distributed

➤ Dynamic language

➤ High performance

➤ Interpreted and compiled

➤ Multithreaded

➤ Object-oriented

➤ Portable

➤ Robust

➤ Secure

Because of local considerations, any one of these characteristics may be more dominant in the design approach than the others. However, at the beginning of the design approach each of these characteristics has to be considered an equal partner.

What has to be changed in the legacy intranet that assists in an architectural-neutral environment?

While Java should work on any platform, hardware or software, there are exceptions. The legacy hardware has to be verified that it meets the minimum capabilities to process Java applets and, more importantly, Java-developed applications. As to software, it should be noted that the two major browsers handle Java applets differently.

What are the basic goals for having a distributed network?

One way to determine the Java design approach is to consider the network's sophistication and complexity. The highest level of sophistication is the use of an enterprise-class application (DCOM being the choice of architecture). The lowest level is the interactivity of Web pages and applications (client-side plug-in would be the choice).

What can be achieved with Java's dynamic execution?

Programming-wise, Java permits the complete use of the capabilities of the OO paradigm concepts. From a non-programmer's view, this means the real use of plug-and-play software modules.

What is required to change the legacy system to achieve the highest level of performance that a Java environment can achieve for the upgraded system?

Java as an interpretation of bytecode objects may be acceptable. However, Java permits a runtime translation of the bytecode into native machine code. This permits the implementation of Web applications into small programs that are fast.

What does the interpretative characteristic of Java mean for the design of an enterprise network?

Java is compiled and interpreted. It is first compiled into a platform-independent binary bytecode format. Second, Java is interpreted by a platform-specific Java runtime environment. This means when a Java runtime environment is installed on any computer (whether it is a PC or something else), the compiled Java program runs on it. This has major implications for an environment that has multiple versions of the same applications.

What is required of the enterprise network to make full use of the capabilities of multithreading?

Multithreading permits a form of parallel executions. This means a superior interactive response for the client. The dark cloud in a clear sky is that if the operating system does not support parallel threads, the capabilities cannot be achieved.

What has to be identified in the system infrastructure to use Java's object orientation?

Simple answer that has a complex process. The requirement is to identify <u>all</u> concrete and abstract components in the system infrastructure. The Java and object-oriented paradigms require a change of view that an object is only a receiver or a sender as in the client/server paradigm. For example, a client within the OO paradigm can be a receiver and a sender. The infrastructure components have to be decomposed into logical, intuitive, and distinct objects so the Java hierarchy of system objects can be realized.

What has to be identified in the system to ensure full Java portability?

Java uses the IEEE standards for data types. A requirement is to identify each computer's operating system and application as to how these standards are addressed. When Java portability is implemented, this action eliminates maintenance, redundant implementation, and testing.

What is required to achieve robustness and thus a higher level of reliability?

The client sees the end result of a robust application—reliability and stability. The programmer sees data checking at compile time rather than at run time, better memory management, an elimination of normal corruption, and correct method invocations.

What has to be done to the system to ensure full Java security features?

Java security is linked with safety and trust. The key to Java and the other two features is a security policy that is enforced consistently while at the same time recognizing the balanced needs of both users and the system administration.

Java Approach Activity Sequencing in a Nutshell

At the end of this activity, you should have a clear view as to the requirements of the Java programming approach and its relationship to user expectations. The usual presentation is a checklist of three columns: Java attributes, specific results, and priority level of the specific results according to user expectations. Here is some of the information you should have as a result of this activity:

➤ Java attributes and the requirements to achieve full use of the attributes

➤ A determination as to the use of a Java requirement (full, partial, or none)

➤ A resource statement to achieve full Java implementation

➤ A priority listing of Java implementation by attribute or characteristic

➤ A statement as to the place of quality control

Chapter 9

Determining Skill Requirements

*Because I know one word in a language,
does that mean I have the skill to speak it?*

Resource planning determines the people (skills), equipment, and materials that ensure that all deliverables are within defined milestones. The usual thought at this time is, We need six people for the project. What does that really mean? I (the author) think I have the skills of a particular type of writer; however, I do not consider myself a writer of plays. A programmer is a programmer is not a logical equation. The planning of skill types and skill levels is more important than "body" count. If you cannot find a given skill, can you substitute with another skill type? It is amazing how many times this question is answered in the positive.

Resource planning could be called resource planning and defining. The answers from the following questions should assist you in developing details as to the required skills, equipment, and materials for enterprise network integration using DCOM architecture with its associated inter-networking. For the word "resource" used in the questions throughout this chapter, replace it three times with the words "skills," "equipment," and "materials." For example, using the basic context question, you get these questions:

➤ Who defines the skill types and levels for the project?

➤ Who defines the equipment requirements?

➤ Who defines the materials requirements?

The "who" in the above questions can be either individuals or a team.

This chapter has seven discussions on resource defining and the impact on procurement. *Procurement* is the act of going outside of your company to get people, services, or equipment. The topics covered here are:

➤ Questions to assist in defining resources
➤ Required resource data in a nutshell
➤ Procurement—getting outside skill sets
➤ Three important procurement documents
➤ System administrator as project manager
➤ Selecting the team
➤ Picking consultants and vendors

Questions to Assist in Defining Resources

This section has questions that may help you decide what skills and other resources you need to achieve effective enterprise network integration, the impact of DCOM architecture, and the skill levels required for its software programming.

Who defines the resource requirements? Do there have to be teams that consider skills, equipment, and materials?

In the first round of planning resources there could be three or more teams doing the planning; however, there needs to be a team that ensures consistency.

How have resources been related to each other?

One type of link is a given person with given skills must have given equipment and materials for a specified time. Why is this important? You may have to lease a special piece of equipment for a given period.

Have the enterprise network scope definitions been used to plan resource estimates?

The basis for defining the resources should be the defined scope of the integration. One of the considerations should be special requirements. The parameters formulated in scope definition can also be used to state what is not to be used. Occasionally in talking with a vendor, there may be discussion that the vendor's product, application, or utility does not have the function set required. A product might have most of the required functions but not the set. You need to consider the available functions in DCOM support technologies.

What are the impacts of the milestones on the resource estimates?

> An important linkage to time is the available skill level involved. Perhaps an expert in a given area can do the activity in a third of the time as a novice. If the skill level is not available, how does the time for training impact the project schedule? What are the expected and realistic experiences for a programmer who can use DCOM supporting technologies?

What are the effects of the cost parameters on resource estimates?

> Is it better to pay $100 an hour to an expert or $50 an hour to a novice? Are the people involved in integration full time or part time? It can be surprising how many different categories resources can be divided into that can impact cost.

What is the control system to handle resources and any changes?

> If a new skill requirement is identified halfway into the project cycle, has a process been defined that can handle this issue? Skills are required to do adequate controlling and verifying of the development, and the status of the project needs to be identified.

Have resources been closely related to cost estimates? Have skill types and levels rather than head count been defined?

> The broadest question is "Have the resources (skills, equipment, and materials) been related to all the delimiters?" For example, you can ask, "Since I do not have a given skill, do I have a threat or an opportunity?" Perhaps not having a given skill gives you a new perspective on how to accomplish the project more easily. Remember the old Russian proverb, "Necessity is the mother of invention."

What documents are required to handle resources?

> It should be determined who is responsible for handling communications. It can be several people. It must identify the skills and equipment required to have a stable communications system. Determine to whom resource requirements need to be communicated.

What is (are) the range(s) for having an inadequate resource(s)?

> Determine the minimal skill level requirements. Perhaps some activities a novice can do, while other activities need an expert. Remember that a lack of a skill can be turned into an opportunity.

What procurement policies have to be followed? Has it been determined the impact of outside policies on the project?

> Remember that any large company—it can be true for small companies also—may have three different procedures for contracting outside people, for leasing equipment, and for buying materials. You need to define project activities that ensure these procedures are followed.

Required Resource Data in a Nutshell

As a result of this activity you should have a set of detailed definitions and descriptions that shows what resources are required to complete the product by the end date. The resources are divided into three categories: skill types and levels, equipment, and materials. In the list below the word "resource" is used; however, any of the three categories can be used as a replacement.

Your resource definitions should have as a minimum:

➤ Firm resource requirements and how not having them may impact the achievement of enterprise network integration

➤ Policy for how resources are determined

➤ Policy on who determines resource requirements

➤ Policy on when resources are required

➤ Policy on how to handle changes in resource requirements

➤ Chart on how resources are linked

➤ Chart on resource requirements

➤ Procedure for turning an unavailable resource into an opportunity

Procurement—Getting Outside Skill Sets

You may realize that you have to hire people with special skills outside of your organization; this is the activity of procurement. This can involve policies or practices such as:

➤ "You must have three bids."

➤ "You must run an advertisement."

➤ "You must follow federal guidelines on gender, race, age, etc."

Even if you are a business of one, federal and state guidelines can be very important to you.

Your company's procurement policy or policies may have a significant impact on your selection of components for your enterprise network, network architecture, and use of programming languages.

Has a contracting (outsourcing) system been established if required for humans, equipment, and materials?

If outside resources are required, then a system must be formulated to procure these resources. The best thing to do is formulate a system even if at the moment no outside sources are perceived as required. Are there required guidelines to be followed for outsourcing? What is the impact on the end date if these guidelines are followed? Have you considered all the appropriate guidelines, policies, and practices for procuring people and materials? If you ignore these guidelines, they can come up and grab you.

There are many types of policies that can impact the procuring of human resources and materials. You may say, "I am in a small company and we do not have to worry about any procurement procedures." Do you know the maximum number of people that can be in a company before federal guidelines take effect? When you have the need for outside resources, you should have activities to determine if there are procedures you must follow.

Sometimes resource planning takes a larger than expected team to work on just acquiring resources. For example, building a new airplane requires a large procurement team. Remember that any large company— small companies too—may have three different types of procedures for contracting outside people, for leasing equipment, and for buying materials. Have you defined activities that ensure these procedures are followed?

In sequencing activities you should always consider what tasks are needed to do procurement. You need to be aware of all procurement policies and procedures that impact the end date. Your enterprise network integration may be hampered because a policy or a procedure was not followed.

Your time estimates can be seriously impacted when there is a delay in acquiring any required skills, equipment, or materials. It is better to be pessimistic than optimistic on time estimates in the area of procurement.

Your cost estimates can be seriously impacted when there is a delay in acquiring any required skills, equipment, or materials. It is a good idea to be pessimistic rather than optimistic on cost estimates in the area of procurement.

The schedule should have the flexibility to handle the procurement of outside resources (skills, equipment, and materials). There should be in the schedule time to work within the procedures required to do any procurement.

One of the difficult budgetary issues is the paying of contractors. Not only is where in the budget the expenditure appears important, but also when the expenditure is paid. If you have set up your budget to meet certain financial milestones, a late payment can have an impact on status reports.

Three Important Procurement Documents

Business Affiliate Plan

This plan provides information when the network component or application is to be developed by a third-party developer. The plan can consist of the following:

➤ Explanation for the need for a third-party developer
➤ How the third party doing the development qualifies
➤ What part the third party plays in the marketing program training requirements
➤ Documentation requirements
➤ Quality control system description

Third-Party Market Agreement

This agreement provides the plans for where and when the network application or component is to be developed by a third-party developer. This agreement may include:

➤ Product content
➤ Delivery schedules
➤ Marketing strategy
➤ Verification strategy

> ➤ Documentation strategy
> ➤ Training strategy

Third-Party Service Plan

This document provides how the network is to be serviced by a third-party developer. The question is, "Can the third party do customer service?" The plan may include details on:

> ➤ Customer training
> ➤ Customer documentation
> ➤ Diagnostic tools
> ➤ Support process

System Administrator as Project Manager

Besides having the obvious abilities to turn water into wine and walk on water, what are the core qualifications of the system administrator (project manager) for implementing enterprise network integration? Here is a list without commentary:

> ➤ Decisive
> ➤ Technologically aware
> ➤ Not afraid of change
> ➤ Comfortable with details
> ➤ Accepts customers as a part of the effort
> ➤ An organizer
> ➤ Recognizes the difference between "smoke and mirrors" and the "real stuff"
> ➤ Can see how the parts fit into the whole
> ➤ Can seize the moment (the opportunity)
> ➤ Proven ability to accomplish
> ➤ Can quarterback the team

Selecting the Team

The secret of success for creating a team is finding the correct size and mixture. Do not attempt to do everything discussed in this book with three people. It is not head count that is important but skill interplay. Here are characteristics of team members:

➤ Technologically comfortable, but able to recognize this is a business effort, not a place for hacking (the comfort zone is in degrees because besides information service personnel, there should be representatives from human resources, marketing, training, documentation, and the customer base)

➤ Accepts change

➤ Comfortable with details

➤ Accepts customers as a part of the effort

➤ Able to work within an organization

➤ Proven ability to accomplish

➤ Can be a player on a team

➤ Specialist, not generalist

Picking Consultants and Vendors

The first act of many system administrators in this situation would be to get consultants or bring in local network vendors. Before getting the consultants or vendors, establish criteria for selection. This is the type of information you should get from them before they grace your doors:

➤ References from where they have done similar work

➤ Development, design, maintenance, and support levels available

➤ Security solution knowledge level

➤ Resumes with emphasis on Internet and intranet experiences

➤ Rates

Once they have passed this hurdle, call them and state some issue that you think you are going to have and ask for their ideas and suggestions. Do the same thing with all candidates so you can evaluate their solutions and your comfort zone.

Chapter 10

Forces of Resistance

Resistance is a serious folly.

This chapter discusses a method for solving various types of resistance you may encounter while doing enterprise network integration such as:

> God gave us the pencil! Why do I need YOUR computer?

> My data is TOO sensitive for other people to see!

> I am honest, but I do not trust the other guy!

> I do not have one of those!

> That is too hard to do!

> My way is better than your way!

This method is the use of Return on Investment (ROI). All the above statements are highly emotional; however, they all say the same thing: "How can I win in this situation?"

ROI is the positive actions toward perceived benefits. The discussion first looks at financial ends that lead to a successful ROI—an improved bottom line. The discussion then turns to a series of responses one might give to the above six statements.

Successful ROI Goals

An ROI goal list can be very short or it might be long. The following is long for the single purpose of generating ideas. These items are like headlines, not the articles. The order is alphabetical by the first word of the goal, not by importance. Importance is a local issue.

> Common environment
>> Applications with version control

- ➤ Core training environment
- ➤ Common tools
- ➤ Ease of use
- ➤ One browser
- ➤ Remote access
- ➤ Streamlined processes
- ➤ Decentralized working environment (offices)
- ➤ Enhanced productivity
- ➤ Information efficiencies
  - ➤ Easier access
  - ➤ Faster access
  - ➤ Increase in accuracy
  - ➤ Increase in availability
  - ➤ Increase in communication
  - ➤ Increase in resources
  - ➤ Increase in timeliness
  - ➤ Just-in-time
  - ➤ More marketing data
  - ➤ More technical sources
  - ➤ Quicker data transfer
- ➤ Opportunities for
  - ➤ New roles
  - ➤ New skills or enhancements
- ➤ Reductions in
  - ➤ Documentation costs
  - ➤ Duplicative resources
  - ➤ Mailing costs
  - ➤ Ordering time
  - ➤ Printing costs
  - ➤ Search effort time
  - ➤ Software distribution
  - ➤ Support costs
  - ➤ Telephone support costs

Ten Common Rules for Handling Resistance

A list of ten seems a standard. The method here is to use the list above to respond to particular issues, but you need to do the following actions all the time to even further reduce the concerns.

1. Respect your most valuable assets—the people.
2. Keep the users focused.
3. Keep a smile when you least want to have one.
4. Encourage participation.
5. Develop initial support and keep building on it daily.
6. Have a plan and let everybody else know the details.
7. Set realistic goals.
8. Control the technology; do not let it control you.
9. Sustain momentum.
10. Use the planning process given in the other chapters in this section.

God gave us the pencil! Why do I need YOUR computer?

The person who says this kind of statement is fearful of the technology and its impact on their job status. This is the place to emphasize ease of use and access, commonality, availability of training, and the opportunities for more informational resources.

- Common environment
  - Common tools
  - Ease of use
  - Remote access
  - Streamlined processes
- Decentralized working environment (offices)
- Enhanced productivity
- Information efficiencies
  - Easier access
  - Faster access
  - Increase in accuracy
  - Increase in availability

- ➤ Increase in communication
- ➤ Increase in resources
- ➤ Increase in timeliness
- ➤ Just-in-time
- ➤ More marketing data
- ➤ More technical sources
- ➤ Quicker data transfer
- ➤ Reductions in
  - ➤ Documentation costs
  - ➤ Printing costs
  - ➤ Search effort time
  - ➤ Telephone support costs

My data is TOO sensitive for other people to see!

This person thinks their job is protected because of the information that they hold and do not share. You should emphasize their importance in the improved and enhanced information processes that come with the new system.

- ➤ Common environment
  - ➤ Applications with version control
  - ➤ Common tools
  - ➤ One browser
  - ➤ Streamlined processes
- ➤ Information efficiencies
  - ➤ Increase in accuracy
  - ➤ Increase in communication
  - ➤ Increase in resources
- ➤ Reductions in
  - ➤ Documentation costs
  - ➤ Duplicative resources
  - ➤ Printing costs
  - ➤ Search effort time
  - ➤ Support costs

I am honest, but I do not trust the other guy!

Honesty may not be the issue this person has in mind, so emphasize controls and the common environment. Also speak about a more efficient environment for communication.

➤ Common environment
  ➤ Applications with version control
  ➤ Core training environment
  ➤ Common tools
  ➤ One browser
  ➤ Streamlined processes
➤ Information efficiencies
  ➤ Increase in accuracy
  ➤ Increase in availability
  ➤ Increase in communication
  ➤ Increase in resources
  ➤ Increase in timeliness
  ➤ Just-in-time
  ➤ More marketing data
  ➤ More technical sources

I do not have one of those!

Emphasize what is available to users—applications, tools, and utilities. Show that this person has an opportunity for a new awareness in information and in productivity.

➤ Common environment
  ➤ Applications with version control
  ➤ Common tools
  ➤ Ease of use
  ➤ One browser
  ➤ Remote access
  ➤ Streamlined processes
➤ Decentralized working environment (offices)

➤ Information efficiencies
  ➤ Easier access
  ➤ Faster access
  ➤ Increase in accuracy
  ➤ Increase in availability
  ➤ Increase in communication
  ➤ Increase in resources
  ➤ Increase in timeliness
  ➤ Just-in-time
  ➤ More marketing data
  ➤ More technical sources
  ➤ Quicker data transfer
➤ Opportunities for
  ➤ New roles
  ➤ New skills or enhancements

That is too hard to do!

The words are easy, easier, and training. You need to emphasize the common environment.

➤ Common environment
  ➤ Core training environment
  ➤ Common tools
  ➤ Ease of use
  ➤ One browser
  ➤ Remote access
  ➤ Streamlined processes
➤ Decentralized working environment (offices)
➤ Information efficiencies
  ➤ Easier access
  ➤ Faster access
  ➤ Increase in accuracy
  ➤ Increase in availability
  ➤ Increase in communication

- ➤ Increase in resources
- ➤ Increase in timeliness
- ➤ Just-in-time
- ➤ More marketing data
- ➤ More technical sources
- ➤ Quicker data transfer
- ➤ Opportunities for
  - ➤ New roles
  - ➤ New skills or enhancements
- ➤ Reductions in search effort time

My way is better than your way!

Ask this person to be a part of the design process. Since the person knows the best path, they can give advice as part of a concerned team for a better company.

- ➤ Common environment
  - ➤ Applications with version control
  - ➤ Core training environment
  - ➤ Common tools
  - ➤ One browser
  - ➤ Remote access
  - ➤ Streamlined processes
- ➤ Decentralized working environment (offices)
- ➤ Information efficiencies
  - ➤ Easier access
  - ➤ Faster access
  - ➤ Increase in accuracy
  - ➤ Increase in availability
  - ➤ Increase in communication
  - ➤ Increase in resources
  - ➤ Increase in timeliness

Chapter 11

Keeping People Informed

> *Shakespeare would not have been able*
> *to write a play if Caesar had read the message.*

This chapter looks at communications in three phases:

➤ Ensuring your customers—that means everybody else—know the status of the enterprise network integration development.

➤ Selecting applications (e-mail and newsgroups) so the users of the enterprise network can electronically interact among themselves.

➤ Using a status reporting system because enterprise networking is a process of evolution, not a revolution.

First Phase

Communications and Integration

Part of your enterprise network integration is to keep all parties informed. This section looks at questions you should ask so you can establish some parameters on your customers' expectations. People do watch television commercials and they do think "If they have that, I can also!"

The first question you need to ask is "Has the reporting and change systems report structure been defined?" The second question is "Is there a consistent and coherent communications system available?" The rest of the questions flow from these two.

Since you have already given some thoughts to your integration issue, these ideas are probably obvious. I would like to make them a part of the record. (I have been watching too many court cases!)

Someone may say, "The answer is use electronic mail." You use a Mac and I use a PC. Is this a problem? Of course it is. The solution to this point is fundamental to platform integration on your enterprise network, in particular internetworking for portability.

Another person who wants to be supportive says, "I have a fax machine." You mean you do not have one? This is another problem. The solution is fundamental to what kind of peripheral equipment is going to be on the enterprise network.

In disgust, another helpful soul says, "Let us use the telephone!" You mean you do not have conferencing? The solution is basic to the type of services that are going to be on the enterprise network.

The generic answer is that more than one form of communicating must be used.

In this age of global corporations, there is one more communications issue you need to consider: Do not forget bilingual situations!

All the above issues are a part of why you as the system administrator need to formulate a communications system so you can give and receive information for integrating your enterprise network. Here are a few key pointers:

➤ There may be a different list for those who see progress status and those who see change.

➤ The communication should be simple.

➤ The form or forms of communications should be available to everyone.

➤ There may be different word processors or even different versions of a single word processor.

Some of the activities for achieving enterprise network integration may appear the simplest thing in world and actually be very difficult. People have different word processors and platforms. Some people do not have fax abilities. Some people seem to be unable to talk on the telephone. People cannot seem to get together for a conference.

A number of questions on communications should be asked and answered as to the level of resources required for enterprise network integration. Here are three good questions:

➤ Who is responsible for handling communications?

➤ What skills and equipment are required to have a stable communications system?

➤ To whom do resource requirements need to be communicated?

You need to consider various types of activity sequences for communicating information on the status of your enterprise network integration. Here are three important guidelines to follow:

➤ There may be one sequence for the coordinating committee.

➤ There may be different sequences as the project cycle evolves.

➤ There should be key activities along the sequence to evaluate the success of the communications system.

Your time estimates for activities should be formulated to show when and how long it should take to communicate with people. Do not forget the number and length of conferences. Six people in a room for an hour is six person hours! It should not be shown as one hour. What does this idea communicate? You should not have conferences unless something really has to be said. Do not set up meetings for every Wednesday morning. Just make a statement to keep Wednesday mornings available for a meeting when required.

Two activities in enterprise network integration is establishing cost and discussing financial impacts on the budget. One of your issues is to establish the criteria to who sees what and when they see it. Remember that this is a continuous process. It starts on day one and goes until you leave the position of system administrator.

A schedule is a set of ordered activities defined in the context of time. One set of these ordered activities is communications reports. The schedule should reflect the types of reports (status, change), who does the reports, and the form (e-mail, conference, or fax) of these reports.

One final comment on the communications process: It is important to have knowledge of the procedures for communicating with the appropriate people who post expenses to a budget when you are in a corporate environment. Expenditures can be posted to the wrong line in a corporate budget related to an activity and can take more than several months to correct. As the system administrator, you need to know the details of how reporting is done for your enterprise network.

Communications Plan

As a summary you probably need a document that can be labeled as a communication plan. The Communications Plan should include as a minimum:

➤ People doing the reporting
➤ People who receive the reports
➤ Types of reports sent
➤ When reports are sent
➤ Methods on how reports are sent

The Communications Plan should have a global component as well as "local" communications processes, such as the method by which programmers communicate to each other on status.

Second Phase

Select applications (e-mail and newsgroups) so the users of the enterprise network can electronically interact among themselves. It is also effective to send a regularly scheduled e-mail to all users on the status of the system. Use the ideas from the first phase as required.

Third Phase

Use a status reporting system because enterprise networking is an evolutionary process, not a revolution. Use the ideas from the first phase as required. This phase goes on after implementation unless a decision is reached not to maintain or update the network.

Chapter 12

Time Estimating

Time is both benign and malign.

Time is one of the two important components of a schedule. Scheduling is discussed in the next chapter.

This chapter considers four areas to assist you in doing enterprise network integration with DCOM architecture and its supporting technologies:

➤ Importance of time estimating

➤ Ten questions to assist in estimating time for your activities

➤ Types of data expected from your time estimations

➤ Brief discussion of the time estimation process

Importance of Time Estimating

Time estimating should be done in parallel to activity sequencing and cost estimating (see Chapter 15). To meet identified measurable goals, each major activity should have a defined time estimate. People who are familiar with the activities should do the estimating. It may be important to get outsiders to do these time estimates too (vendors should have benchmarks for how long it takes to configure their product).

The first place a project fails is because of time estimates. The usual failure is the estimates are too optimistic. A key to good estimates is to have a precise definition of the skill types and levels available.

The start and end dates of the project should not be agreed upon in fixed terms until this process is completed. It is good to have outside experts do the estimates because of their experience and because they are not emotionally involved in the project. Time management is a critical process of the project process.

Ten Helpful Time Estimation Questions

The answers to the questions below should be based on your goals and objectives for enterprise network integration and the activities to achieve them. Think in plus and minus terms. Think in terms of an optimistic date and a pessimistic date for an activity. The final completion should be a range of days rather than a particular day. You still have an absolute date at the end of the range, but at least it is the pessimistic date.

Who determines the time estimation that is used to establish the schedule?

> Before getting too deeply into the time estimates there should have been some criteria or standards established as to how to do the time estimates. One should not accept a comment such as "Oh, I think this activity might take so many days." This is not an effective statement unless there is a reason or reasons behind it. A more comfortable statement is "I estimate the action will take this much time for these reasons."

Who should have inputs into or be notified of the time estimates?

> When a time estimate has been distributed and is changed, there should be a list of those to be notified. Why has the phrase "been distributed" been used in the prior statement? It can happen that even during this process the agreed-upon time estimates are changed without notifying the concerned parties.

What is the complete duration of the project (include "update" time)?

> Take all the time estimates if given in duration and determine if there is an overestimate so the end date cannot be achieved. This is done even if the customer has given an absolute fixed date. For example, the customer has stated the enterprise network must be ready because there is going to be a rollout that starts on a given date. A fundamental question is to ask what has to be demonstrated at the rollout.

What are the time increments (days, months) to be used?

> You can simply have a time line in calendar days with an activity sequence flow chart. There are software programs available to assist in developing time estimates. Remember that there are many ways

to present time estimates. Use one that is effective for the team. An example of an ineffective presentation is when a "project manager" uses software that no one else can use. How successful can the project be?

What is the financial impact of expanding or shortening the implementation of the integration?

All time estimates should have an associated cost. The costs do not have to be detailed to everyone. However, those responsible for cost estimates and budgetary planning should be involved. You may ask, "Why should every time estimate have a cost estimate?" A set of activities may cost more than they appear as a whole.

What is the impact of the quality control and assurance processes on the project?

A specific amount of time should be allocated for quality control. You should set a benchmark of, say, 20 percent. This is a percentage of the estimated time for the enterprise network integration. This task should be a part of your original planning.

What are the impacts of the resources on the project?

"Can four people be used instead of two and do the work in half the time?" is an invalid question. The question should be concerned with skill types and levels. A better question would be "Can one expert do the work of two novices in half the time?"

How are time estimates to be communicated to all?

Time activities should be formulated to show when and how long it would take to communicate with people. Do not forget the number and length of conferences.

How will changes in the time estimates affect the integration's outcome?

You should have time allocated for risk management in each of the key phases of the implementation of the enterprise network. If you have no threats to the project in a given phase, you have generated an opportunity!

What are the impacts of any procurement policies or requirements on your time estimates?

Your time estimates can be seriously impacted when there is a delay in acquiring any required skills, equipment, or materials. It is better to be pessimistic than optimistic on time estimates in the area of procurement.

Data Expected from Time Estimating

Time management experts or software tools should be used to develop time estimates. This is a process that can use historical data for establishing benchmarks. Pessimism is better than optimism in doing time estimates.

Here are some of the types of information you need when you have finished this process:

➤ Criteria for formulating time estimates

➤ Procedure for associating time estimates with people, and equipment and people acquisition

➤ Methodology for validating time estimates as to the project scope definition

➤ Criteria for establishing time measures

➤ Criteria for associating cost and time estimates and potential changes

➤ Quality control and validation time estimates (suggested 20 percent of project)

➤ Time estimates based on skill types and levels rather than on head count involved

➤ Policy on notifying team members of time changes to the project

➤ Specific time estimates for handling risks (threats and opportunities)

➤ Time estimates that reflect the harsh reality of procurement

Brief Overview of the Time Estimation Process

The two basic questions that start the time estimation process are:

➤ Have the project milestones been made consistent?

➤ Has an agreement been reached by which milestones can be updated?

The first draft of milestones can be based on a specific calendar date, a number of days from when another milestone has been accomplished, or when a specific event is completed. Time should not be considered as a single "measure." Perhaps a mixture is more practical than saying on day 21 an event will be completed. The important date is the "drop dead" date of the customer.

The milestones as formulated in your planning sessions should be made firm. Many people think of time in working days, but there are many other forms of scheduling. Only two dates are important: start and finish. Of these two, the finish date is the most important.

A simple action of defining events is to draw a block with the start date at the top of a piece of paper. You draw another box with the end date at the bottom of the page. In between these two boxes list all milestone activities and the estimated workdays to complete. Add the workdays of the milestone activities. Is the sum less than the workdays between the start and end dates? If the answer is yes, then you are okay. If the answer is no, then you have a problem in change management.

Resource planning is concerned with three prongs: skill types and levels, equipment, and materials. An important linkage to time is the available skill level involved. Perhaps an expert in a given area can do the activity in a third of the time as a novice. If the skill level is not available, how does the time for training impact your time estimates?

When ordering activities one can use one timing format or a mixture of timing formats. Have you ever considered when setting up a time estimate that you say that the activity will be completed from x day to y day?

The end result of time estimating is the schedule. How has the schedule been defined? You can simply have a time line in calendar days with an activity sequence flow chart.

Cost estimates should reflect time estimates. The cost estimates should reflect the type of time measure used. If the time estimate formula uses plus or minus measures, then cost estimates should reflect this type of formula also.

Use time management techniques and tools to validate your time estimates. Use "what if" scenarios to assist in verification of time estimates. Use time measures that reflect the situation of the project.

Chapter 13

Developing the Schedule

One name for a timely <u>commitment</u> is a schedule.

*T*he schedule can be as elaborate as required. It should be usable. An example of a schedule is a flow chart with milestones and times. There could also be links to team members and their responsibilities for enterprise network integration. A schedule should include the quality control milestones and the verification milestones.

This process requires analyzing the milestone interrelationships. The sequence and duration of activities (primary and secondary) also need to be considered. The impact of resource requirements is equally important.

Developing a schedule is to estimating time as ordering a set of activities is to defining a set of activities. It is an ordering of activities along a time line.

Developing a schedule is the establishment of a <u>realistic</u> and <u>achievable</u> schedule. These are two important criteria. They should be used so all parties involved in the enterprise network integration project have manageable expectations.

There are available automated project management software tools to develop this type of schedule. Some of the software is very inexpensive, while other software can be very expensive. However, a pencil can be as effective as an ink pen and costs much less. There are a number of manual methods that can be used. For example, you could write the activities on index cards and then stick them to the wall until a logical order and associations are made. This is cheap but very effective.

This chapter is concerned with two topics:

➤ Questions that assist you in developing a schedule

➤ Data required for a schedule in a nutshell

Ten Questions to Assist in Scheduling

To answer the ten fundamental questions below for the development of a schedule you need the following:

➤ Defined enterprise network scope

➤ Defined and ordered (put into a logical sequence) activities

➤ Defined resources, including any special requirements and the time estimates for procuring them

➤ Defined key time milestones

The results of this activity should be an ordered set of activities organized around time. The sequence could be based on calendar time or on a critical path where the completion of a given event or set of events is important to the enterprise network integration cycle.

The core question (which can be referred to as the *metaquestion*) of this activity is, "What is the best way of presenting integration activities with a time line so that it communicates clearly the expected outcomes?"

Have the who, what, where, and how been clearly defined and placed in the schedule?

> This is the activity that also includes the when. The environmental expectations should be fully defined at this point except for budgetary considerations.

Have the key people who can have an impact on or approve the schedule been identified?

> In the schedule it should be defined when people come into and leave the integration of the enterprise network. You come into the project at the start date and leave at the end date. (Read "you are stuck.")

Have the start and end times been confirmed? Have expected deliverables been identified?

> The dates for the scope definition are start and end. Other key milestones should be when the customers expect to be given a status report of the network enterprise integration.

Are the key scheduled milestones realistic?

> Use time management techniques and tools to validate the schedule. Use "what if" scenarios to assist in verification of time estimates. Use time measures that reflect the situation of the integration.

How are the budgetary procedures going to affect the schedule?

> The activities leading up to and then making changes to the budget should be in the schedule. One of the activities of the schedule is to report on the status of the budget. This may be done at a high level of management, but this activity should be defined.

Have the quality control events been included at appropriate points?

> Within any schedule the quality control and verification milestones should be clearly defined. The quality control time line may be defined as a separate time line; however, when and where quality control flows into the main part of the integration project must be stated.

Are historical data available to determine adequate resources?

> Sometimes the use of historical data can be important in establishing a schedule. For example, you may have kept records on how long it took to do the configuration for various applications in your intranet. These figures can be used as benchmarks. A better set of figures, of course, would specify the skill level required to do the configurations.

How will the schedule and its changes be given to the customers?

> A customer is anyone else. The schedule should reflect when you or your designates communicate status or significant changes. Marketing may have a program that they forgot to tell you about and they have used your original dates in the schedule to establish their actions. One day may not make a difference, but ten days may.

What are the known key constraints to doing enterprise network integration? How can the formulated schedule impact the outcome of integration?

> The schedule should have activities that assess the project's status at key milestones and determine if there are potential opportunities and threats.

Can resources be acquired on time?

> The schedule should have the flexibility to handle the procurement of outside resources (skills, equipment, and materials). There should be in the schedule time to work within the procedures required to do any procurement.

Schedule Data in a Nutshell

Time management software tools can be used to develop schedules. This is an activity where fixed time and order activities are combined. A schedule can be anything from a calendar with activities inserted to an elaborate flow chart with dates placed on the directional arrows.

Here are some of the types of data you need when you have finished developing the schedule:

➤ Time line (calendar, flow chart)
➤ Time line for acquiring skills, equipment, and materials
➤ Schedule based on the scope definition
➤ Critical path (optional)
➤ Schedule for quality control and verification
➤ Schedule for notifying the team members of changes
➤ Time allocated for risk management (threats and opportunities)
➤ Criteria for being able to change the schedule if necessary
➤ A consistent and coherent set of time lines
➤ Communications points scheduled

At this point in your castle building you should know when the parts of the castle are going to be constructed. The start date is when the contract is signed, while the end date is move-in day. All that is left in the planning phase of building the castle is the budgetary plan. Another way of looking at this action is this is when you close the mortgage with the bank.

Chapter 14

Risk Management

A risk can be a victory or a loss.

Most people think of risks only as a threat to the goals. What if you find a new product that can ease your enterprise network integration by ten-fold? (Let us do some dreaming!) Is this a risk? It is just like finding out the configuration for a product is going to take twice as long. You say no! Have you considered the implication of the new product on your whole project? Do you have to set new expectations? Do you now have the opportunity (read "requirement") to add additional functionality and services to your enterprise network?

This chapter only has brief thoughts, but important ones, on risk management. The two parts to this chapter are:

➤ Key points in doing risk management
➤ Need for two important risk management documents

Risk Management in a Nutshell

To establish a risk management process you need to ask yourself two core questions: Do you have a list of assumptions and guidelines for handling potential threats and opportunities? Are there identified fixed points in the project cycle for assessing risks?

When planning the scope of your enterprise network integration you have to think in terms that a risk is a threat. But you can be one of those unique people who see a way to turn a situation into an opportunity. Perhaps it takes six months to develop a product, and then someone has invented a utility that cuts the time in half or less. Does this affect the integration? Of course it does! As an example, just think of the new Web home page creating utilities. Are they as simple as the vendors say?

When you define the scope of integration you should establish how to handle threats and opportunities. Unfortunately, in risk management most people think of only the threats to the project. What if someone comes up with an idea that a component of a hardware product or a software application can be omitted and still achieve the customer's expectations? This is an opportunity! A pebble thrown into the sea could become a tidal wave. This is a nice metaphor but not physical reality. Perhaps you get the point anyway.

There should be defined activities for handling threats. There should also be activities that handle opportunities if they arise. A simple activity rule would be: "Until a threat (an opportunity) reaches a certain risk level (your definition), no action shall be taken."

Risk assessment is important to planning resources. You need to determine the minimum skill level requirements. Notice head count requirement was not used. Perhaps a novice can do some activities, while an expert is needed for other activities. Remember, a lack of a skill can be turned into an opportunity.

You should order the key tasks required in your enterprise network integration so that you can evaluate potential threats and opportunities. A minimum recommendation is at least one risk review during each phase of the implementation of integration. Quality control should always be on the outlook for risks.

You should set aside time for risk management during each key phase of your enterprise network integration. If you have no threats to the project in a given phase, you have generated an opportunity!

You should have cost estimates for risk management in each key phase of integration. If you have no threats to the project in a given phase, you have generated an opportunity!

The schedule (activities plus time) should have at each key milestone an activity that assesses the project's status and determines if there are potential threats and opportunities. How can the formulated schedule impact the outcome of the project? Time analysis is a major component in risk management.

In your budget there should be factored in an amount for risk management. The most logical line is the one to allocate moneys for contractors. Another line to consider, if one is established, is for quality control and verification. Your product may need more testing than you estimated.

Documenting Risks

Remember that risks come in two forms—threats and opportunities. Both should be equally documented. Given here are examples of two important risk management documents:

➤ Business Justification

➤ Risk Assessment

Business Justification

The reason for having an enterprise network with DCOM architecture and its supporting technologies is to improve your company's bottom line and make more effective financial relationships with either another company or your venders or customers. In this light you are doing a business justification, and sharing it with others is necessary, perhaps for your survival or at least your good health! The Business Justification assures the current view of the enterprise network integration performance meets previous commitments and management expectations. The document may have a one or more year view of:

➤ Revenues

➤ Maintenance costs

➤ Investment

➤ Return on Investment (ROI)

➤ Customer impact

Risk Assessment

It is important that any Risk Assessment consider both threats and opportunities. All involved parties should review the Risk Assessment. There should be, at the least, representatives from each component. Perhaps only one or two key vendors should do the review for all the others. A Risk Assessment should be done at least at every major phase of enterprise network integration.

The assessment should be against established thresholds. An example of a threshold is that no action is taken until a certain number of errors are found.

Chapter 15

Cost Estimating

Bad cost estimates impact the budget, the financial plan.

Cost estimating is like time estimating in many ways. One of the difficulties of cost estimating is hidden expenses. For example, travel costs can be allocated in many different budgets without reflecting direct costs to any project. Hidden expenses happen frequently in a large corporation. This can also be seen in a company of less than 20 people.

Cost estimating should be done in parallel to activity sequencing and time estimating. Each major activity to meet identified <u>measurable</u> goals should have a defined cost estimate. People who are familiar with the integration or particular types of Internet or intranet configuration activities should do the estimating. It may be important to get outsiders (vendors) to assist in doing these cost estimates.

Cost estimates are also done in the context of the scope enterprise network integration goals and resource plan. Cost estimating considers both tangibles and intangibles. A tangible cost is using known rates (hourly, weekly, or monthly) for the services of people involved in the project. A related intangible cost is the impact of the skill levels of the same people. A novice might cost more in the long run than an expert. It is very important to evaluate tangible costs against potential intangible costs.

Cost management has software tools that parallel time management tools. Good project management has both tools.

This chapter is a whirlwind through the world of cost management. Four topics are discussed here:

➤ Fundamental questions for cost management
➤ Cost estimation data in a nutshell

155

➤ Additional cost management considerations

➤ Basic cost management documentation

Fundamental Questions for Cost Management

Questions for cost estimating should be based on identified benchmarks (a measurable activity) when possible. Questions need to reflect the handling of actual specific expenses (costs) against the planned costs (budget).

The questions given below try to reflect the realities of corporate America. Also, the questions may be helpful in sorting the differences between cost issues and budgetary issues. Budgetary issues are discussed in more detail in the next chapter.

How does the chart of accounts, if one uses such an item, affect the cost estimating process?

> A chart of accounts can be organized in many ways. Each line in the budget can be numbered or labeled. The important idea is that cost estimating should reflect the structure of the chart of accounts. The budget structure is just one of many items that impact how enterprise network integration is viewed.

Who is going to fund the integration activities?

> Is there a reporting system that links the appropriate people to the enterprise network integration costs and to the people with budgetary control? You should always think of linkages in terms of cost estimates and budgets that should reflect these costs. Some people may confuse your daily intranet or Internet costs as being a part of the integration process.

How do cost estimates reflect final network integration expectations?

> Ensure the total of the estimates is not greater than the customer's cost expectations. Identify what can be done as to functionality and service expectations within cost constraints. Sometimes it is better to have half an apple than none.

To what degree is the firmness of the defined time estimates?

> Cost estimates should reflect time estimates. The cost estimates should reflect the type of time measure used. If the time estimate formula uses plus or minus measures, then cost estimates should reflect this type of formula also.

What are the key inputs (resources, duration) to be considered?

All cost estimates should have associated time estimates. The time estimates do not have to be detailed to everyone. However, those responsible for time estimates and budgetary planning should be involved. You may ask, "Why should every cost estimate have a time estimate?" A set of activities may require more expenditures than they appear as a whole.

What are the impacts of the benchmarks and validation process on the integration cost?

A specific amount of cost should be allocated for quality control. You should set a benchmark of 10 to 20 percent. This percentage is of the estimated total cost for the project. This task should be among the first tasks of the cost estimating.

Should resources be internal only?

Cost estimates should reflect skill levels rather than head count. When cost estimating use the basic categories of resources: skills, equipment, and materials.

What are the costs for informing people about the status of the enterprise network integration?

There are two basic parts to any communications system: cost status and budget status. Criteria should be established as to who sees what and when they see it.

Do the known costs outweigh the known or potential threats or opportunities?

You should have cost estimates for risk management in each of the major phases of your enterprise network integration. If you have no threats to integration in a given phase, you have generated an opportunity!

What are the hourly or daily rates for outside services?

Your cost estimates can be seriously impacted when there is a delay in acquiring any required skills, equipment, or materials. It is a good idea to be pessimistic rather than optimistic on cost estimates in the area of procurement.

Cost Estimation Data in a Nutshell

Cost management software tools should be used to develop cost estimates. There also is the need to use historical data for establishing benchmarks.

Here are some of the types of data you need when you have finished your cost estimates:

➤ Criteria for formulating cost estimates

➤ Procedure for associating cost estimates with people, and equipment and people acquisition

➤ Methodology for validating cost estimates according to the goals of your enterprise network integration goals and objectives

➤ Criteria for establishing cost measures

➤ Criteria for associating cost and time estimates and potential changes

➤ Quality control and validation cost estimates (suggested 10 to 20 percent of total cost estimates)

➤ Cost estimates based on skill types and levels rather than head count

➤ Policy on notifying others of cost changes to the integration process

➤ Specific cost estimates for handling risks (threats and opportunities)

➤ Cost estimates that reflect the methodical nature of procurement

Cost Management Considerations

There are two questions that you must answer yes to before continuing:

➤ Have the project cost definitions been made consistent?

➤ Has a list for cost responsibility been formulated?

Your scope plan must be clear on funding because it can become very complex. It can become a key factor in getting your project terminated. There should be clear definitions and understandings of the funding policies and invoicing practices of the doers and the receivers. It is possible in a large corporation to have multiple layers of funders. Those at a high level of funding are sometimes surprised how "their" moneys are being used. It is important to ask, "Are all levels of funding authority in agreement with this project?"

In defining your costs there are available a number of software packages that can assist in this task. Because the opportunity might rise up and shake your hand, you should consider ways to improve costs. All types of costs should be considered: human (actual and potential), materials, and time. Costs can also be divided into design, development, production, and most importantly, quality and verification controls.

An important costing activity is determining how the budget issues are handled. You use cost estimates to formulate budgetary plans. A *budget* is a plan where costs are organized into debits and credits.

Resource planning requires that you consider seriously skill types and skills required for success. Is it better to pay $100 an hour to an expert or $50 an hour to a novice? Are the people involved in the project full time or part time? It can be surprising how many different categories resources can be divided into that can impact cost.

As you order your activities for the enterprise network integration process, the availability of funding should be used. Have costs been divided over all key phases of the integration process? Never take from the quality control activities to seemingly improve another part of the schedule. This type of action has a way of biting you in places where it hurts.

All time estimates should have associated cost estimates. The time and cost estimates do not have to be detailed to everyone. However, those responsible for time and cost estimates and budgetary planning should be involved. You may ask, "Why should every time estimate have a cost estimate?" A set of activities may require more time than expected or cost more than the total of the individual items.

An integral part of a schedule is defining the activities involved in cost management. This may be done at a high level of management, but this activity should be defined.

Cost estimates can go into one budget line or many. The usual case is at least three budget lines. The resources of the project can be divided into salaries, equipment, and materials. You probably also need a separate line for vendor or consulting costs.

Basic Cost Management Documentation

You could have any number of documents based on sound cost management principles. Recognize that good cost management probably is a blending component of any management process. Here are three examples of related documents:

➤ Project Cost Update
➤ Initial Budget Estimate
➤ Initial Funding Requirements

Project Cost Update

This document updates initial project cost estimates at each major phase of your enterprise network integration in comparison to the Initial Budget Estimate. The concern here is how the costs (actual expenditures) and revenues go into the budget (the financial plan). The costs are usually reported on a monthly basis.

Initial Budget Estimate

This document provides a view of the expected development costs. The estimate is usually based on the scope definition of the enterprise network integration. The document gives estimates for direct labor as well as capital and expense requirements. Remember that the indirect costs should be considered as important as direct costs.

This document is updated in the Project Cost Update.

Initial Funding Requirements

This document is for monitoring and reporting project costs at each major phase of integration. There should be comparisons to the original funding document used to establish financial targets and expected milestones and deliverables.

This document can also be included in the Project Cost Update.

Chapter 16

Budgetary Issues

*A budget is a financial plan that is
impacted by wayward cost estimates.*

This chapter advocates a separate budget for the enterprise network
integration project. This budget could become important historical and
benchmark data. It is recommended that any upgrades to your enterprise
network be included in your operations budget.

Your budget costs specify the cost estimates as to individuals, equipment,
materials, and activities. The results of this process should be entries in
the budgets of the approving management authorities within a
corporation.

Cost budgeting is to cost estimating as schedule developing is to time
estimating. A similar relationship is activity sequencing to activity defining. Budgeting takes cost estimates and groups and consolidates them
into a formal structure (the budget). Remember that a budget is a plan of
expenditures and revenues for a given period, usually a year in length for
a company. Your enterprise network integration budget is specific to the
length of time it takes you to do the implementation. Upgrading your
enterprise network should be a part of your operational budget.

This chapter discusses three areas related to budgetary issues:

➤ Fundamental questions for resolving budget issues

➤ Budgetary data in a nutshell

➤ Three budgetary management documents

Fundamental Questions for Resolving Budget Issues

A *budget* is an itemized plan of revenues and expenditures for a given period. The period here is the length of the implementation of the original integration goals. Your enterprise network integration budget can be linked to other budgets and is important to define those linkages. The answers to the questions should be relevant to the integration budget and these other budget links.

To answer these questions the responses from cost estimating (in the previous chapter) should be used. The fundamental question of this activity is "How do I organize enterprise network integration costs into a formal structure?"

In whose budget (chart of accounts) do the cost estimates go?

> You need to know the organizational structure of the budget where the cost estimates are going. It is possible to have several different types of budgets. There must be one consistent and coherent integration budget that adheres to the defined goals and objectives.

How are various budgets interrelated?

> The important links are the cost estimates to budget lines. It is also important that budget expenditures and revenues reflect the time line of the integration cycle.

How many budgets are affected by this integration project?

> The scope definition is important for the budgeting activity. It can be used as a basis for structuring the cost estimates. The scope definition may point to a special line in the budget. Some corporate budget structures are very elaborate, to say the least. Remember the "rollup" principle. Your enterprise network integration may be entered in your manager's budget as a single line or multiple lines. You need to be aware of the type of rollup so you can explain variances in budgets.

What is the defined duration of the integration project? Is more than one corporate budget cycle involved?

> A project budget is the duration of the project cycle. If there are other budgets to be considered, you must define the project budget's impacts on them. More and more projects seem to be defined to less than a year. Also, there is a tendency for a project's start and end dates to fall in the same calendar year.

How are integration cost estimates allocated?

> Cost estimates can go into one budget line or many. The usual case is at least three budget lines. The resources of the project can be divided into salaries, equipment, and materials.

Has the quality process been cost estimated and budgeted?

> It is recommended to have at least two budget lines for quality. The lines are control and verification. You may also wish to divide these two lines into salaries, equipment, and materials.

How are internal and external resources budgeted?

> The buying of equipment for the integration may go in a budget line separate from leasing the equipment. The salaries of corporate employees would certainly go on a different line than contractors' salaries. An important question is "Are the other corporate budget lines associated with an employee's compensation included in the project's budget?"

How and to whom is financial information given?

> There may be special requirements in a budget for such items as postage and shipping expenditures. It is important to have knowledge of the procedures for communicating with the appropriate people who post expenses to a budget when you are in a corporate environment. It is likely to happen more than once that some expenditures get posted to the wrong line in a corporate budget related to a project. Usually this takes more than several months to correct.

Have potential threats and opportunities been factored into the budgetary process?

> In one or more budget lines there should be factored in an amount for risk management. The most logical line is the allocation of moneys for contractors. Another line to consider, if one is established, is for quality control and verification. Your integration may need more testing than you estimated.

What are the impacts on the budgetary process for outsourcing activities?

> One of the difficult budgetary issues is the paying of contractors. Not only where in the budget the expenditure appears important, but also when the expenditure is paid. If you have to set up your budget to meet certain financial milestones, a late payment can have an impact on the project status. You need two change notices for the following situation. You stated you were going to spend a certain

amount on contractors in the first quarter of the year (corporate budget). However, the expenditure did not appear in the budget until the second quarter because of the procurement procedures.

Budgetary Data in a Nutshell

The budgeting activity is to take cost estimates and enter them into a formal financial structure. A budget is to cost as a schedule is to time. At the end of the cost budgeting activity you should at least have the following:

➤ A budget or budgets that are consistent with the enterprise network integration's goals and objectives

➤ Links between the enterprise network integration's budget and any other budgets that have been defined

➤ Procedure for handling the enterprise network integration's budget cycle when it impacts another budget over several of its cycles

➤ Statement on which budget lines are impacted (this is for all involved budgets)

➤ Separate budget lines for quality control and verification (optional)

➤ Procedure for handling the payments for outside resources

➤ Procedure for making changes and updates to the budget reporting system as relevant to the project

➤ A separate budget line for risk management or an identified component of another budget line

Three Budgetary Management Documents

Given below are three budgetary documents that can assist you in controlling your budget for enterprise network integration. Actually they would be useful all the time. Recognize that good budgetary management is the end result of good cost management. These documents are for both cost and budgetary management. Remember, costs are the actual expenditures. The budget is the formal structure for accounting for the costs.

➤ Project Cost Update
➤ Initial Budget Estimate
➤ Initial Funding Requirements

Project Cost Update

This document updates initial project cost estimates at each major phase of your enterprise network integration in comparison to the Initial Budget Estimate. The concern here is how the costs (actual expenditures) and revenues go into the budget (the financial plan). The costs are usually reported on a monthly basis.

Initial Budget Estimate

This document provides a view of the expected development costs. The estimate is usually based on the scope definition of the enterprise network integration. The document gives estimates for direct labor as well as capital and expense requirements. Remember that the indirect costs should be considered as important as direct costs.

This document is updated in the Project Cost Update.

Initial Funding Requirements

This document monitors and reports project costs at each major phase of integration. There should be comparisons to the original funding document used to establish financial targets and expected milestones and deliverables.

This document can also be included in the Project Cost Update.

Part III
Technical Planning Process

This part of the book looks at ten fundamental steps in the technical planning process to implement an enterprise network with DCOM architecture and Java internetworking. These steps logically raise questions that you have to answer in the technical planning, designing, developing, and implementing phases of your enterprise network. Some questions may be answered with a simple "not applicable."

This part is in contrast to the previous one, which is concerned with the administrative planning process. The administrative planning process for an enterprise network involves identifying activities, defining skill and people requirements, estimating time requirements, establishing schedules, handling people issues, establishing risk parameters, making cost estimates, and creating a budget.

The technical planning process steps are the project management steps for an enterprise network implementation. They are given here to assist you because you are probably working under a short deadline. As the system administrator you want to ensure that all your bases are covered.

Each step is covered in a separate chapter. The steps are:

➤ Defining components

➤ Modeling an enterprise network

➤ Using management and performance tools

➤ Working with protocols

➤ Identifying interconnectivity issues

➤ Evaluating service servers

➤ Evaluating access servers

➤ Evaluating browsers

➤ Developing integration standards

➤ Developing a technical policy

Some of the steps happen in parallel, while some have to have a significant portion done before moving to another step. Developing a technical policy would be outlined based on the nine areas above. However, it would be completed after all the areas have been defined.

The Internet can be searched for further information. Some of the words that you can use are:

➤ Enterprise network

➤ Network

➤ RFC

➤ Servers

➤ Browsers (better, look at **www.microsoft.com** and **www.netscape.com**)

➤ Protocols (perhaps better is network protocols)

➤ Performance tools

Besides doing word searches, take a look at vendor sites. You can get comparison data. If there is no data, look for a telephone number or an e-mail address.

If you use the steps in this part of the book and the previous part of the book, your common set of issues should be covered. However, there is always the iceberg in the fog. If you try to keep people aware, you are likely to have enough lifeboats just in case the iceberg does strike during the dance.

Chapter 17

Defining Components

Components are visible and invisible, but all are important.

Throughout the administrative planning process (Part II), you have to consider the components of your enterprise network. The components come in two flavors—concrete and abstract. Knowing what the enterprise components are and their places in the enterprise network is key to modeling, determining what tools you need, establishing protocols that implement integration, identifying interconnectivity issues, and establishing the roles of the service and access servers. All of the components make up the infrastructure, the enterprise network.

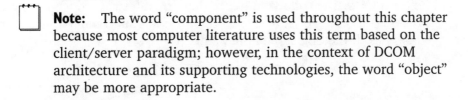

Note: The word "component" is used throughout this chapter because most computer literature uses this term based on the client/server paradigm; however, in the context of DCOM architecture and its supporting technologies, the word "object" may be more appropriate.

Concrete Components

Concrete components or objects give structure to the enterprise network. They are things you can see either with your eyes or with graphical user interfaces (management tools).

The most important component is the people. These are the users (internal and external, customers, vendors), technicians (support, development, maintenance), administrative support (training, documentation, procurement, finance, etc.), facilities, and you. Without people, there is no need for an enterprise network. An associated component is the organization. The organization has its policies, goals, practices, locations, and financial sources.

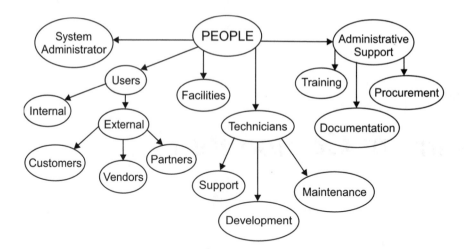

Figure 17-1
People class hierarchy

The primary components or objects of the hardware structure can be categorized as hosts, central processing units (CPUs), intermediate nodes, and peripheral nodes.

Besides using the Java class notion to describe these components, an object-naming notation may be used to assist in visualizing the hardware structure and in developing the Java code structure. A parallel process is used in developing a hierarchical naming tree and a class. An object can be defined using a hierarchical naming tree that is a logical sequence of object names. The following figure demonstrates this concept. The process is a breakdown from the highest compound name down to the lowest level, the object's simple name.

Concrete Infrastructure

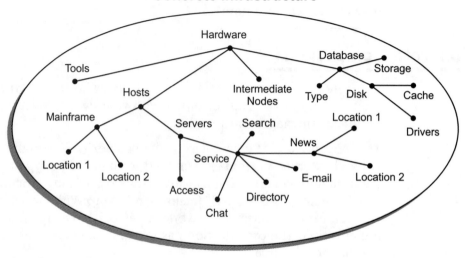

Figure 17-2
Hardware object naming tree

Software components would include databases, memory, disk, tools, graphic user interfaces, applications, server software, protocols, system kernel, and code (source and executable). While software and hardware logically belong to a higher object—concrete infrastructure—for ease of discussion and perhaps for practice, another naming tree demonstrates the hierarchy of an object called software.

Concrete Infrastructure

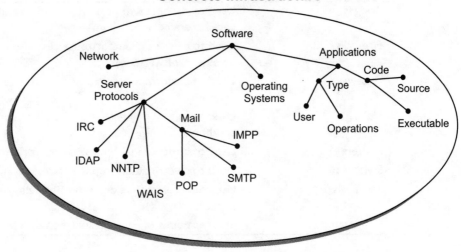

Figure 17-3
Software object naming tree

Note: The figures demonstrate an example technique more so than an actual naming tree or a Java class model. It, however, changes the visual paradigm from the client/server mode.

The following lists are arbitrary. They should assist you in more easily visualizing your infrastructure and in clarifying the previous figures.

Hosts	
Mainframe	The central processing unit (CPU) of a computer system
Servers	Components in a distributed environment that act for a set of clients as functions such as access or as a service such as a newsgroup

CPUs	
Mainframes	The central processing units that do not include remote devices or peripherals
Operating systems	The basic software that defines the fundamental operations of a computer such as inputs and outputs

Intermediate Nodes	
Bridges	Used to connect two or more networks and forwards packet data between them
Firewalls	Used to prevent unauthorized access into a network; may be either software or hardware
Gateways	Used to perform format translation from one system to another
Hubs	Used as central points to move data from one network to another
Routers	Used to direct the path flows of network traffic
Switches	Used to divert data from one network to another
Terminals	Used as access points or to transfer data—modems, printers
Workstations	Used as points of data manipulation by a person

Peripheral Nodes	
Faxes	Facsimile devices used to forward images of printed matter from one location to another
Printers	Devices that produce printed matter

Applications	
Operations	Used to do the basic functions of the computer
User	Used to extend the abilities of the user such as word processors or spreadsheets

Code	
Executable	State of a programming language that does the operations
Source	State of a programming language as written

Databases—Proprietary and Public	
Buffer size	Space to store data so it can be transmitted smoothly through the network
Cache	CPU fast storage buffer
Number of users	Includes people, servers, and peripherals

Disk	
Cache	Disk fast storage buffer
Controller speed	Speed limitations of device that move data from a network
Drivers	Software used to define specific functions between two network components such as a workstation and a printer
Load balance	Process of defining adequate flow of data traffic

Graphical User Interface	
Server	The visual component that permits the user to see a structured view of data
System	The visual component that permits an administrator to see a structured view of data flow

Memory	
Cache type	Memory fast storage
Size	Virtual RAM or ROM bandwidth
Speed	Degree of effective accessibility

Protocols	
Intranet	Protocols such as Ethernet and Token Ring overlaid with TCP/IP
Internet	TCP/IP suite
System	Protocols based on LAN or WAN traffic

III

Part

Server Protocols	
Chat	Internet Relay Chat (IRC)
Directory	Lightweight Directory Access Protocol (LDAP)
E-mail	Post Office Protocol (POP), Simple Mail Transfer Protocol (SMTP), Internet Message Access Protocol (IMAP)
News	Network News Transfer Protocol (NNTP)
Search	Z39.50 Standard—Wide Area Information Server (WAIS)

Tools	
Blueprints	Network maps—process flows, detailed wiring routes, equipment locations, structure representations, and geographical views
Equipment diagrams	Used for performance tuning and design refinements
Inventories	Used for resource accountability—hardware (spares control) and software (version control)
Management	GUIs to identify bottlenecks and assist in real-time maintenance. Aid in cleaner configurations.
Performance analyzers	GUIs to tighten vendor specifications as to operational performance standards
Policies (disaster, security)	Standards for expected network failure rates and recovery times for various failure types
Process flow charts	Either in electronic or in written format. Ability to meter data movement (traffic levels and types) from any two points in the network
Protocol analyzers	GUIs to establish the effectiveness of protocol configurations and to determine if traffic is within stated standards
Wiring route map	Documentation to adhere to TIA/EIA standards

Abstract Components

Abstract components are the functionalism (purposes, utilities, and flows) of the enterprise network. They are things you cannot see either with your eyes or with graphical user interfaces (management tools). The concrete cannot stand alone without the abstract and the abstract cannot stand alone without the concrete. The abstract components are the results of trying to describe the concrete capabilities.

Within the administrative planning process you can have a question such as "How complex is it to maintain the database?" With this technique you can see how many basic questions you can develop to ask vendors, users, and your development team. To assist you further, there are two dozen abstractions to go with the concrete items given above.

A naming tree for the network's abstract objects is more difficult to develop because of the individual interpretations of any abstraction. The following figure gives one possibility. You should try to develop your own naming tree before doing a detail analysis of this figure. There is no correct answer. What is important is that you create a visual presentation to represent what is in the mind's eye.

Abstract Infrastructure

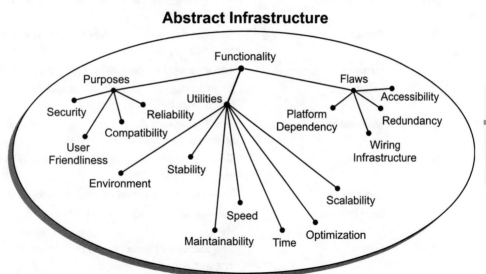

Figure 17-4
Functionality object naming tree

Abstraction	Definition
Accessibility	To what degree a user can use a network or the process for entering a network
Compatibility	To what degree the network components interact successfully with each other
Complexity	To what degree the network system architecture has been developed—two computers connected is simple; 100 computers, both mainframe and personal, is complex
Cost	Amount to be paid to maintain and use a network—visual and hidden

Abstraction	Definition
Design	The plan of the system—purposeful or haphazard
Environment	The conditions or circumstances of the network
Flaws	Things in the system that are not a part of the design plan
Functionality	The amount of functions or abilities within a network
Interoperability	To what degree the various network components work with each other successfully
Integration	Process of organizing the various components to act as one
Maintainability	To what degree maintenance updating is required to ensure user requirements of the network
Optimization	To what degree the components comply to the ultimate capabilities
Platform dependency	To what degree the network components require a particular software or hardware environment
Purpose	The goal of the network as defined by the users
Reliability	To what degree the various components continue to function at the required level
Redundancy	To what degree duplicate components are required to ensure a continuous flow of data
Scalability	To what degree a network can be added to without a major change in design
Security	To what degree network data is protected
Sophistication	How simple or user-friendly the network is from a user view
Speed	The amount of time required to move data from one point in a network to another point
Stability	To what degree a network can run without breakdowns—minor and major
Time	The interval between the start and finish of an operation
User friendliness	To what degree a user can work without getting frustrated
Wiring infrastructure	The wiring structure that connects all the net components

Chapter 18

Modeling an Enterprise Network

A model is only a perception of reality.

*T*his chapter reviews three types of modeling. The modeling types considered here are:

➤ Statistical
➤ Simulation
➤ Extrapolation

The chapter does not cover in detail how to do modeling but rather the place of modeling in integrating your enterprise network. Because of a number of new networking paradigms as well as changes to almost if not all aspects of corporate IT, the world of modeling is likewise changing. However, there still are basic fundamentals as to what a model can or cannot do.

Modeling has to be considered in the light of these paradigms:

➤ Switching network
➤ Client/server network
➤ Object-oriented network
➤ Intranet-Internet network

These paradigms should not be considered as separate entities but as interactive entities. These four paradigms have to be considered in any enterprise network model you do. A switching network is a conversion for a single-user-at-one-time to multiple-users-outside-of-time. More briefly stated, this is parallel processing. A client/server network has a focus on mainstreaming application data in a global environment in less time but with more transaction volumes than in prior networks. In an object-oriented network, the client can be a server, and a server can be a client. In an intranet-Internet network, the notion of boundaries ceases and "trusted" users become a thing of the past.

As discussed elsewhere, the components of your enterprise network can be either concrete (hosts, applications) or abstract (speed, time); an enterprise network as an entity cannot be viewed as a single type of infrastructure. Thus, the complexity of modeling has moved up a notch or two.

Below are some additional random thoughts on impacts that should be considered in doing modeling.

➤ Much of today's hardware was not designed to handle some of the technological changes. For example, most bridges and routers cannot handle the heavy traffic loads generated by new client/server applications.

➤ Much of today's software was not designed with 32-bit graphics or 32-bit processing in mind.

➤ Users are more in number and in a remote access environment, and they have more experience and have the intense desire to push the envelope of applications, such as using e-mail heavily.

➤ Two core network principles—simplicity and scalability—are rapidly going down the drain. They are being or have already been replaced by complexity and segmentation.

Statistical Modeling

Statistical modeling uses mathematical distributions to define traffic streams. You develop a set of simultaneous equations that are solved by using a computer. The results are bandwidth and latencies. You can determine such things as optimal performance configurations, performance breakpoints, and minimal resource requirements. Honestly, a statistical model is complex and may be more than a bit confusing.

To build a model you need to have an extensive amount of historical statistical data available:

➤ Bandwidth used
➤ Circuit
  ➤ Availability in percentage
  ➤ Busy number (average, maximum)
  ➤ Failures (average, maximum)

➤ Use in percentage
➤ Number of calls (real, virtual)
  ➤ Attempted
  ➤ Blocked (failure, traffic)
  ➤ Completed
  ➤ Disconnected
  ➤ Preempted
  ➤ Queued
➤ Number of packets
  ➤ Blocked
  ➤ Delivered
  ➤ Processed
  ➤ Transmitted
➤ Call queue
  ➤ Probability
  ➤ Size
  ➤ Time
➤ Averages
  ➤ Buffer use
  ➤ Call length
  ➤ Message delay
  ➤ Packet delay
  ➤ Packet queue time

There are more items that could be added to the list. This list is given to assist you in selecting a tool that could do a custom-designed simulation model.

Note: A weakness in the model is you may have numbers, but you do not necessarily have the why.

Simulation Modeling

Simulation is a process to imitate the physical components of your enterprise network. Simulation has a counterpart—emulation. *Emulation* is a process to imitate the physical components and the infrastructure. The infrastructure includes software and traffic. Emulation is not discussed here because of its complexity. A vendor usually uses emulation to validate the performance of its product.

Simulation uses prior historical performance data or performance data from a system similar to your own (a highly unlikely event). Simulation modeling comes in two flavors—discrete and state-change.

The discrete model uses mathematical distributions (raw or massaged) in a step-by-step series of equations. The result is bandwidth and latency predictions. The discrete model is used with production processes. Definable items such as network device counts, traffic counts, and throughputs are used in this simulation model. An advantage of a discrete model is that equilibrium of user input values can be established quickly.

The state-change model is concerned with conditions and events that can change the state of your enterprise network. Example states that might be considered are bridge online or offline, traffic low or high, or amount of application usage. This model is commonly the realm of statisticians. This model is good for determining possible configurations.

Note: A disadvantage of the state-change model is the requirement to include <u>all</u> conditions to get a realistic result.

In both models the device models can be either deterministic or statistically random (technically stochastic). Deterministic processes are basically extrapolated and linear. A view of reality shows that your enterprise network does not work linearly—traffic does not flow smoothly; it flows in bursts.

Extrapolation Modeling

Extrapolation modeling is the theoretical process of extending historical data. The extension can be either linear or nonlinear. An example of linear extension is using the bandwidth of a given set of users and their average percentage of utilization and then changing the average utilization percent and calculating the number of new users. An example of nonlinear extension is the plotting of your traffic loads.

Extrapolation modeling is not reliable. Very few events, if any, move in a linear fashion. It is not good for predicting bandwidth utilization or latency.

Conclusion

After reading the above, you may have concluded that modeling is an unnecessary activity. Wrong! New modeling tools are being introduced each day. As an enterprise network administrator, you need to evaluate these tools and determine their value in assisting you in integrating and implementing your enterprise network. It has been expressed that there is a new networking world or worlds—paradigms—that can have an impact on your perception and your users' perceptions of reality. What is important for you is to find the language, whether it be that of server/client or DCOM or something else, so that you can focus your users' expectations of the enterprise network.

III

Part

Chapter 19

Using Management and Performance Tools

A good tool can be like a sturdy stool.

This chapter reviews two types of system tools. The tool types considered here are:

➤ Management
➤ Performance

The chapter does not cover in detail how to use these tools but rather the <u>significance</u> of management and performance tools in integrating your enterprise network. Because almost if not all aspects of corporate IT are changing—methodologies, plans, practices, technologies, and skills—the tools have to be in the forefront of change. However, there still are basic fundamentals as to what a tool can or cannot do.

Tools have to be considered in the light of:

➤ Global access environment
➤ Manageable (intranet) and unmanageable (Internet)
➤ "Switching" technology
➤ Structured (intranet) and unstructured (Internet)

Tools have been developed that look at events in a "closed" environment—network (LAN or WAN) and an intranet. With the introduction of the Internet as a backbone for an enterprise, there has to be a new paradigm established for looking at remote access. This is discussed in another chapter.

The use of management tools of the intranet component of your enterprise network is discussed in this chapter. Also discussed is to what extent management tools can be used with the Internet.

The switching technology is based on telephony switching. The basic principle is either something is connected or is not connected, or something is on or it is off. In its extreme, switching means any node can be a segment with dedicated access to a high-performance work group and backbone systems.

Switching is a group of technologies for use in a virtual network. An enterprise network can be considered one in a very broad sense, maybe even in a narrow sense. The four switching types are cell, configuration, frame, and frame-to-cell.

Very briefly, the key characteristics of *cell switching* (ATM) are:

➤ A universal unit of information

➤ Multiple, logical work group support, independent of the physical attachment's location

➤ Destination address processed by nearest cell switch, resulting in point-to-point links

➤ Mixed-application services support

The key characteristics of *configuration switching*, also referred to as *port switching*, are:

➤ Remotely associates an intelligent hub host module with any internal hub segment using network management

➤ Uses an "intelligent patch panel"

Frame switching is also called *LAN switching*. Its key characteristics are:

➤ Uses native Ethernet or Token Ring frames as the informational units switched across the network

➤ Processes destination address by the nearest frame switch, resulting in point-to-point links

Frame-to-cell switching solves the problem of translating user devices without ATM adapter cards to communicate directly with ATM-linked devices on the same network. Like the other three switching types, frame-to-cell switching is called by another name, *LAN emulation*.

While you cannot have complete control of the enterprise network because of the Internet component, a new technology is being developed that gives you a foundation for data transmission management. This technology is an "overlay" of switching; it is structured networking.

Structured networking logically extends the "wired closet" concept. The core of structured networking is the network center. A network center serves as a wired closet and control where the bridges, routers, servers, etc., reside. Termination is at switching hub ports rather than at router ports.

Like any new technology there must be either management or performance tools or both. This technology does have network analyzers.

Management Tools

As the complexity of networking technologies grows, so do the types of management tools. As seen above, a part of the development of the new technology of switching and structured networking has to be the development of management tools—network analyzers. In fact, the marketplace demands that any new technology have a counterpart management tool.

You can take from the lists of components given in Chapter 17, "Defining Components," and generate a list of single items you need to manage or sets of items that have to be managed in tandem. These items, however, can be grouped into management functions. The list given below is of that nature.

- ➤ Configuration management
  - ➤ Change control
  - ➤ Infrastructure
  - ➤ Routing
  - ➤ Security (authentication and authorization)
- ➤ Operations management
  - ➤ Accounting
  - ➤ Auditing
  - ➤ Capacity

> ➤ Scheduling
> ➤ Troubleshooting
➤ Software management
> ➤ License
> ➤ Software (version control)
➤ Storage management
> ➤ Archival administration
> ➤ Backup and recovery
> ➤ Database administration
> ➤ Tape library

Performance Tools

Just as with management tools, the complexity of networking technologies has created a growth in performance tools. In fact, the marketplace demands that any new technology have not only a management tool but also a performance tool.

You can take from the lists of components given in Chapter 17, "Defining Components," and generate a list of items you need to determine their levels of performance. These items, however, can be grouped into types of performance tools required. The list given below is of that nature.

➤ Blueprints
> ➤ Equipment location
> ➤ Geographic perspective
> ➤ Logical structure
> ➤ Process flows
> ➤ Wiring routes
➤ Code profilers
➤ Configuration
➤ Disk defragmentation programs

➤ Inventories
  ➤ Equipment
  ➤ Software
➤ Network infrastructure
➤ Policy statements
➤ Protocol analyzers
➤ Traffic
  ➤ Analysis
  ➤ Statistics
➤ Tuning tools

Conclusion

There is usually a management or performance tool for any occasion. The danger is only having familiarity of a tool rather than expertise. It is important to know how, when, where, and why you are using a tool. However, the most important thing to know is what you are trying to manage or what type of performance is being evaluated. The first question to ask a vendor of their tool is "What are the tool's limitations?"

Management and performance tools can be used to bring in parallel two intranets in an enterprise network. You can determine bottlenecks and differences in performance. There needs to be tandem work done on both intranets, their access to the Internet, and their throughput result across the Internet.

It has been briefly alluded to that the new switching technology with its network analyzers can assist you in integrating your enterprise network. Before evolution, use your present management and performance tools to determine where you want to go in the context of your users' expectations.

Part

Chapter 20

Working with Protocols

*Correctly working with protocols
is like using good manners.*

This chapter looks at working with some key protocols that are a part
of an enterprise network. The protocols considered here are:

➤ HyperText Transfer Protocol (HTTP)
➤ Multipurpose Internet Mail Extensions (MIME)
➤ Network News Transfer Protocol (NNTP)
➤ Post Office Protocol (POP)
➤ Point-to-Point Protocol (PPP)
➤ Point-to-Point Tunneling Protocol (PPTP)
➤ Reverse Address Resolution Protocol (RARP)
➤ Serial Line Internet Protocol (SLIP)
➤ Simple Mail Transfer Protocol (SMTP)
➤ Transmission Control Protocol/Internet Protocol (TCP/IP)

   ➤ Address Resolution Protocol (ARP)
   ➤ File Transfer Protocol (FTP)
   ➤ Internet Control Message Protocol (ICMP)
   ➤ Internet Protocol (IP)
   ➤ Transmission Control Protocol (TCP)
   ➤ User Datagram Protocol (UDP)

Included in this chapter are also brief discussions on:

➤ Language of protocols
➤ Protocol analysis
➤ Domain Name Service (DNS)

➤ Network File System (NFS)

➤ Managing TCP/IP

➤ Troubleshooting TCP/IP

At the end of this chapter are brief definitions of the protocols discussed in this chapter and a short list of the many (about 2,000, many obsolete) Request for Comments (RFCs). An RFC is a document that defines aspects of protocols, management, and other tidbits about the Internet.

Note: When an RFC is updated or revised it gets a new RFC number, not a new version number. This means if an RFC has been revised five times, there are six numbers associated with the original document.

There are many ways to get RFCs electronically. One way is:

ftp://nic.ddn.mil/rfc/rfcNNNN.txt

NNNN is the number of the RFC.

The "quotation" given at the top of this chapter implicitly expresses the importance of protocols. It was the introduction of these protocols into private networks that laid the foundation for the private intranet. The next step, which is the focus of this book, is the integration of one or more private intranets with the Internet as an access and transmission backbone that results in an enterprise network using DCOM architecture and its supporting technologies.

Language of Protocols

What is a protocol? A *protocol* is a set of rules of exchange. To better understand this definition, perhaps a standard needs to be defined. A *standard* is a set of rules for defining a playing field where the exchange can take place. As an example, a standard for cards would include:

➤ Card is a single unit.

➤ Deck is a set of 52 cards.

➤ Suit is a set of 13 cards.

➤ Suit types are spade, heart, diamond, and club.

➤ Joker is an optional card that can be used as a substitute for any suit type.

A protocol is how these cards would be exchanged within a game. The protocol for the game of Hearts is:

➤ There are four players.

➤ Each player plays for self.

➤ The dealer deals 13 cards to each player one at a time, beginning from the dealer's left.

➤ There is an exchange of three cards at the beginning of each round with a cycle of left, right, across, and hold.

➤ The player with the two of clubs begins the round.

➤ Winner of first round selects a card from any suit except hearts, unless the remaining 12 cards are hearts.

➤ Players must follow suit, but when out of a suit a player can play any card of choice.

➤ Player that wins the round (the highest card of the suit of the originally played card for the round) plays the next card.

➤ Point cards are hearts (one point each) and the queen of spades (13 points).

➤ The winner is the player with the least number of points when another player reaches 100 or greater.

Many rules were surely left out of either list. This example does give an idea of the complexity of developing electronic transmission protocols and standards.

At the beginning of this chapter a list of 16 protocols was given, while in reality there are thousands of protocols (optimistic view). This discussion focuses on the TCP/IP protocol suite and the Open Systems Interconnection Reference Model (OSI Reference Model). The protocol language of TCP/IP evolved out of the language of the OSI model. The playing field is the open system architecture. A set of rules for playing on this field is TCP/IP.

The protocol language is formal. It works from the abstract—data transfer—to the concrete—data in the machine. The language is actually mathematically based. You know $a + b = c$ (abstract) becomes 1 apple + 2 apples = 3 apples (concrete). The language must be independent of:

➤ Application

➤ Hardware

➤ Operating system

➤ Software

All communication is defined in three steps—connection establishment, data transfer, and connection disconnection. Everything else is commentary. Communication is discussed in terms of how a layer (application, etc.) of different machines interact or how different layers (application and presentation, etc.) interact with each other. Also, another form of communication is defined in the model—can the sender and receiver identify each other? If the answer is yes, the relationship is referred to as *connection-mode* communication. If the answer is no, the relationship is referred to as *connectionless-mode*. A service data packet sent in the connectionless-node is called a *datagram*. This is important because when you read the name of a standard or a protocol and it includes the word "datagram" you know the mode of communication.

Why is the above discussion important to you in integrating your enterprise network? If you are working with an open system architecture, and you probably are, you must understand the language of the model and the associated standards and protocols to implement enterprise network integration. The brief example given above reflects there are different issues for connection-mode communications and connectionless-mode communications.

A general rule for working with protocols is that every term has a reverse term—similar to male and female, high and low, day and night, etc. This is important to you in your integration process because for every connection there is a disconnection. Below is a short list of key antonyms, or "counterterms":

➤ Segmentation—Reassemble

➤ Blocking—Unblocking

➤ Concatenation—Separation

➤ Multiplexing—Demultiplexing

➤ Splitting—Recombining

A later chapter discusses the language of standards. While the writers of the OSI and TCP/IP seek to provide a single consistent word definition, the user community as a whole after many years has been slow to adopt the terminology. The result is confusion. To successfully integrate an enterprise network you need to understand the language of the components, whether that of the OSI Reference Model or TCP/IP.

Protocol Analysis

The bad news is you cannot do infrastructure protocol analysis because traffic is generated locally and dispersed to other network segments. The good news is that if you can capture cross-product traffic, you then can develop an infrastructure perspective.

The minimum statistics you want to collect are bandwidth usage, error rates, latency, and traffic data. Out of these minimum statistics you may desire to collect such data as:

➤ Alarm history
➤ Collisions
➤ Event statistics
➤ Host data
➤ Number of packets
➤ Packet sizes
➤ Trends

There are a number of ways protocol analysis can assist you in integrating your enterprise network. Here is just a very short list of ten:

➤ Determination of excessive bandwidth usage
➤ Determination of excessive collisions (Ethernet)
➤ Identification of duplicate addresses
➤ Identification of incomplete file transfers
➤ Isolation of line and burst errors
➤ Isolation of unbootable nodes
➤ Location of ring error sources
➤ Data on dropped sessions
➤ Tracing paths of lost e-mail deliveries
➤ Tracking inaccessible resources

Each of the protocols discussed below may require their own protocol analyzer. Because of the dynamic changes in this area of technology, as these words are being written some vendor has developed or is developing a protocol analyzer that may further your enterprise network integration down the road. An important protocol analyzer is one that analyzes the key service server software as a group. The important action for you as the enterprise network administrator is to use whatever data analysis you do use in an integrated process, not segmented.

Protocols

This section details key protocols for working with an enterprise network.

HyperText Transfer Protocol (HTTP)

HTTP is the basic protocol developed at the CERN (Centre European Researche Nucleare, or European Laboratory for Particle Physics, or Conseil Européen pour la Recherche Nucléaire) that led to the creation of the World Wide Web. The principle of word linkage is used rather than file linkage.

Multipurpose Internet Mail Extensions (MIME)

MIME sends non-ASCII data over the Internet using text-based protocols, such as SMTP (see Simple Mail Transfer Protocol) and POP (see Post Office Protocol).

Network News Transfer Protocol (NNTP)

NNTP transmits USENET messages across the Internet.

Post Office Protocol (POP)

This protocol enables mail programs to interact with virtual mailboxes where mail can wait until either sent or retrieved. See Simple Mail Transfer Protocol (SMTP). This acronym (POP) can also refer to point of presence, which is a regional hub used by an Internet service provider to access the Internet.

POP uses port 110. For a complete list of port assignments, see RFC1700, "Assigned Numbers."

Point-to-Point Protocol (PPP)

PPP establishes dial-up connections to the Internet. PPP is more powerful than SLIP (see Serial Line Internet Protocol). PPP handles direct transmissions between two points.

To configure PPP you need:

➤ Source IP address

➤ Destination IP address

➤ Serial port identifier with its interrupt vector

➤ Correct baud rate configuration

➤ A netmask setting as with SLIP

➤ An undedicated line (SLIP requires a dedicated line)

When using a UNIX system the netconfig utility prompts are used to define the above information. This is done when a PPP chain is added.

Point-to-Point Tunneling Protocol (PPTP)

PPTP is an enhanced version of PPP that permits TCP/IP data to be transmitted over non-TCP/IP networks. It permits intranets viewed as "virtual internets" to be connected using the Internet as a go-between. See Point-to-Point Protocol (PPP).

Reverse Address Resolution Protocol (RARP)

This protocol permits an Ethernet address (physical network address) to be converted into an IP address. This conversion requires an RARP server. It is used to correct the ARP flaw that when a device does not know its own IP address, there is no process to generate requests and replies.

Serial Line Internet Protocol (SLIP)

SLIP is a very basic packet-framing protocol that has been highly enhanced by PPP (see Point-to-Point Protocol). It has basically been replaced by PPP.

Simple Mail Transfer Protocol (SMTP)

This text-based TCP/IP protocol exchanges mail messages on the Internet. It defines the format and content of transmissions between mail servers. See Multipurpose Internet Mail Extensions (MIME) and Post Office Protocol (POP). This is a user-friendly protocol. Most users are usually unaware of its existence.

SMTP uses port 25.

To diagnose SMTP, one utility you can use is snmpwatch. It monitors SMTP variable changes.

Transmission Control Protocol/Internet Protocol (TCP/IP)

TCP/IP is a suite of over 100 protocols that handles data transmissions over the Internet. Some of the protocols are ARP, FTP, ICMP, IP, RARP, TCP, and UDP.[1]

TCP/IP provides services, handles transmissions, and manages communications. Here are just a few particulars that are discussed under individual protocols:

➤ Controls transmissions using predetermined status signals

➤ Handles remote file transfers

➤ Handles transmission errors

➤ Manages the routing and delivery of data

➤ Provides electronic mail

➤ Provides remote logins

Address Resolution Protocol (ARP)

ARP is a member of the TCP/IP (see TCP/IP) suite that translates IP (see IP) addresses into physical network addresses.

The ARP Cache is the table that holds the IP addresses and their corresponding physical addresses. The table has a row for each device and four columns for data for each device—interface index, physical address, IP address, and type.

A flaw with ARP is when a device does not know its IP address, there is no way to generate requests and replies. The solution to getting around this flaw is to use RARP.

The arp utility or its equivalent can be used to add, delete, or modify the ARP Cache. There are many different implementations of this utility so you need to see the appropriate operating system documentation.

---

[1] While TCP/IP is an open protocol, vendors have made modifications for their products. You need to ask how a vendor's product varies from TCP/IP.

File Transfer Protocol (FTP)

FTP is a member of the TCP/IP (see TCP/IP) suite used to transfer files from one computer to another. Internet users can use FTP to download data from FTP servers. FTP uses ports 20 (data) and 21 (control). Telnet uses port 23.

Internet Control Message Protocol (ICMP)

ICMP is a member of the TCP/IP (see TCP/IP) suite that sends control and error messages back to senders for IP transmissions. An example message type is "Time to Live Exceeded." ICMP messages are treated as any datagram. This protocol must be a part of any TCP/IP implementation.

Internet Protocol (IP)

IP is the essential right side of the TCP/IP (see TCP/IP) suite that handles transmissions of data packets over the Internet and routes them to the correct destinations. It is similar to the address on an envelope and plays the part of the mail carrier too.

Internet as used in the protocol's title means "across networks" and was developed prior to "the Internet." It manages datagram addressing and fragmentation across any network.[2] IP "guesses" at the best route; however, it may not be the most efficient or even the fastest.

IP is connectionless. This means the receiver does not know the sender and vice versa.

Like most protocols IP is evolving and can be referred to by version or IPng (IP Next Generation). For more information on IPng, see RFC 1726 (cited in the RFC list at the end of this chapter).

IP is prone to trouble. Here are a few actions to take to keep trouble to a minimum:

➤ Scrupulously follow configuration rules—rule number one.
➤ Check bridges and routers to ensure synchronization with network changes.

Part III

---

2   There are proprietary protocols that have similar functions.

➤ Check for duplicate IP addresses.

➤ Check for faulty server tables if DNS is active.

➤ Check for packet fragmentation.

➤ Check hardware mapping.

➤ Check machine connectivity.

Transmission Control Protocol (TCP)

TCP is the essential left side of the TCP/IP (see TCP/IP) suite that handles the stream delivery services to Internet applications. It is reliable and complex because it retransmits corrupted and lost data packets, and it ensures transmitted data-bit order at the receiving end. See Internet Protocol (IP) and User Datagram Protocol (UDP).

TCP is not a piece of software, but a communications and connection-oriented protocol. It can be considered a "corrective" force to IP.

TCP enables applications to be designed without concern for message reliability or flow control. This is possible because TCP service management is a single layer.

TCP keeps up with all of its connections through a connection table. It is organized by row (a connection) and five columns—connection state (closed, waiting, etc.), local IP address, local port number, remote device's IP address, and the remote port number of the connection.

For a list of TCP designated ports, see RFC 1700, "Assigned Numbers."

The "biggie" in TCP troubleshooting is you need to check the configuration files and the settings.

User Datagram Protocol (UDP)

This protocol allows data packets to be sent from one Internet application to another. Two important characteristics are UDP is connectionless and unreliable. UDP does require the sender and the receiver to be connected. It does guarantee transmitted data-bit order at the receiving end. See Transmission Control Protocol (TCP).

The operating system documentation should be consulted for troubleshooting UDP. UDP can be affected by the same problems as TCP; however, it does have two problems that TCP does not have—lack of timeout values and too many transmissions.

When you troubleshoot UDP, begin with its configuration files and settings.

Domain Name Service (DNS)

DNS converts the common local name of a computer into a unique physical address. The Network Information Center (NIC) keeps a list of network names and their gateway address. The DNS has evolved from an IP address of four decimal numbers (from 000.000.000.000 to 255.255.255.255). The original IP address was a 32-bit binary number.

DNS uses a hierarchical naming architecture. The general structure is:

➤ Server name (www, ftp, etc.)

➤ Server subname(s)

➤ Server type (com for commercial, gov for government, country code, etc.)

➤ Main domain name

The DNS is the "front end" to a URL (Uniform Resource Locator). A URL also includes a file path, filename, and perhaps an internal anchor.

There are a number of RFCs that describe and explain domain names. One of the latest is RFC 1876, "A Means for Expressing Location Information in the Domain System."

DNS at the local level uses a name server and a name resolver to establish and track domain names. This activity involves the interworking of a number of protocols.

The set of machines managed by a name server is called a *zone*. Name servers communicate with each other with a zone transfer protocol. Management of message transmissions between name servers is better handled by UDP than TCP because of its connectionless mode.

The DNS resolving path is:

➤ Application query

➤ Name resolver

➤ Name server

➤ Next level name server (can be either lower or higher)

III

Part

DNS prohibits going to a third server. It can go all the way down these four steps and then back up or resolve at step 2 or 3. An error message is generated if the operation is negative.

Only if the name resolver can resolve the name directly is a query sent forward to a name server. When a name resolver receives information from a name server, it stores it temporarily in a cache. The time of storage is configuration determined. The port number used is 53.

A UNIX DNS server requires the configuring of five files and databases. This usually is a one-time event per server. The UNIX files are:

➤ named.hosts
➤ named.rev
➤ named.local
➤ named.ca
➤ named.boot

These are the conventional names. If you have been using a UNIX system for some time, you may have changed the names.

For Windows 95, the DNS configuration procedure is:

➤ Control Panel
➤ Network
➤ TCP/IP
➤ Properties
➤ WINS configuration (not used on most networks)
➤ DNS configuration
➤ IP Address
➤ Gateway
➤ Bindings

Network File System (NFS)

NFS is a set of UNIX protocols developed by Sun Microsystems, Inc., to run on workstations from different vendors. It enables workstations to access transparently each other's directories. NFS is tied into TCP/IP.

NFS is based on the client/server model. It was designed also to work efficiently in a multitasking environment.

There are a number of RFCs dedicated to NFS. Below are three of the most recent:

➤ RFC 2055—"Web NFS Server Specification"

➤ RFC 2054—"Web NFS Client Specification"

➤ RFC 1813—"NFS Version 3 Protocol Specification"

Managing TCP/IP

This is an overview on some very basic ideas about TCP/IP management. There is included in this book a part on just the planning process for the integration of your enterprise network.

There seem to be two fundamental tasks for network management:

➤ Monitoring—watching network behavior and analyzing status reports

➤ Controlling—reconfiguring the network to improve performance or correcting ineffective functions

According to the ISO there are five management areas. The areas are referred to as Specific Management Functional Areas (SMFAs). These management areas are:

➤ Accounting

➤ Configuration

➤ Fault

➤ Performance

➤ Security

The Internet Architecture Board has also established a management process. The process involves the use of the Simple Network Management Protocol (SNMP) and the standard Common Management Information Services and Protocol over TCP/IP (CMOT). CMOT is based on the OSI network management standards Common Management Information Services (CMIS) and Common Management Information Protocol (CMIP).

SNMP is dynamic and in an evolutionary state. It has been integrated into a number of commercial products.

Like TCP/IP, SNMP is not a single protocol. While there are over 100 protocols in TCP/IP, SNTP has only three:

➤ Management Information Base (MIB)—a database

➤ Structure and Identification of Management Information (SMI)—the database specification

➤ Simple Network Management Protocol (SNMP)—the method of communicating

Troubleshooting TCP/IP

There are many products available to assist you in troubleshooting your enterprise network. There are products that also assist dynamically in system configuration. Again, this book does not discuss the exact how because of your legacy base and the many, many network interoperability variables. The best teacher is experience. This is no truer than in the area of troubleshooting. It has been pointed out under the various protocols discussed above some of their particular troubleshooting issues.

The secret to effective troubleshooting is scrupulously following configuration rules and orderly monitoring of system activities. The essence of good troubleshooting is an understanding of the limitations of your software and hardware products.

Protocol Definitions

Given below are brief definitions for each of the protocols discussed above.

Address Resolution Protocol (ARP)—A member of the TCP/IP (see TCP/IP) suite that translates IP (see IP) addresses into physical network addresses.

File Transfer Protocol (FTP)—A member of the TCP/IP (see TCP/IP) suite that is used to transfer files from one computer to another. Internet users can use FTP to download data from FTP servers.

HyperText Transfer Protocol (HTTP)—The basic protocol developed at the CERN that led to the creation of the World Wide Web. The principle of word linkage is used rather than file linkage.

Internet Control Message Protocol (ICMP)—A member of the TCP/IP (see TCP/IP) suite that sends control and error messages for IP transmissions. An example message is "Traffic is too heavy."

Internet Protocol (IP)—The right side of the TCP/IP (see TCP/IP) suite that handles transmissions of data packets over the Internet and routes them to the correct destinations. It is similar to the address on an envelope and plays the part of the mail carrier too.

Multipurpose Internet Mail Extensions (MIME)—The protocol that sends non-ASCII data over the Internet using text-based protocols, such as SMTP (see Simple Mail Transfer Protocol) and POP (see Post Office Protocol).

Network News Transfer Protocol (NNTP)—The protocol that transmits USENET messages across the Internet.

Post Office Protocol (POP)—Usually refers to POP3, but there is an unrelated POP2. This protocol enables mail programs to interact with virtual mailboxes where mail can wait until either sent or retrieved. See Simple Mail Transfer Protocol (SMTP). Can also refer to point of presence, which is a regional hub used by an Internet service provider to access the Internet.

Point-to-Point Protocol (PPP)—This protocol established dial-up connections to the Internet. PPP is more powerful that SLIP (see Serial Line Internet Protocol).

Point-to-Point Tunneling Protocol (PPTP)—An enhanced version of PPP that permits TCP/IP data to be transmitted over non-TCP/IP networks. It permits intranets viewed as "virtual internets" to be connected using the Internet as a go-between. See Point-to-Point (PPP).

Reverse Address Resolution Protocol (RARP)—This protocol permits an Ethernet address (physical network address) to be converted into an IP address. This conversion requires an RARP server.

Serial Line Internet Protocol (SLIP)—A very basic packet-framing protocol that has been highly enhanced by PPP. See Point-to-Point Protocol.

Simple Mail Transfer Protocol (SMTP)—The text-based TCP/IP protocol that exchanges mail messages on the Internet. It defines the format and content of transmissions between mail servers. See Multipurpose Internet Mail Extensions (MIME) and Post Office Protocol (POP).

Transmission Control Protocol (TCP)—The left side of the TCP/IP (see TCP/IP) suite that handles the stream delivery services to Internet applications. It is reliable because it retransmits corrupted and lost data packets, and it ensures transmitted data-bit order at the receiving end. See Internet Protocol (IP) and User Datagram Protocol (UDP).

Transmission Control Protocol/Internet Protocol (TCP/IP)—A suite of over 100 protocols that handles data transmissions over the Internet. Some of the protocols are ARP, ICMP, IP, RARP, TCP, and UDP.

User Datagram Protocol (UDP)—This protocol allows data packets to be sent from one Internet application to another. Two important characteristics are UDP is connectionless and unreliable. UDP does require the sender and the receiver to be connected. It does guarantee transmitted data-bit order at the receiving end. See Transmission Control Protocol (TCP).

Request for Comments (RFC)

An RFC is a document that defines aspects of protocols, management, and other tidbits about the Internet. An RFC is the first step in creating a new Internet standard. The steps are:

1. RFC draft
2. Internet draft (as many refinements as required)
3. Proposed standard (as many refinements as required; at least two implementations)
4. Draft standard (as many refinements as required; wide implementation)
5. Official standard

There are many ways to get RFCs electronically. One way is:

ftp://nic.ddn.mil/rfc/rfcNNNN.txt

NNNN is the number of the RFC.

 Caution: RFCs are being revised all the time. A revised RFC gets a new number, not a version number.

The list of RFCs given here is in numerical order.

RFC768	"User Datagram Protocol," Postel, J.; 1980
RFC791	"Internet Protocol," Postel, J.; 1981
RFC799	"Internet Name Domains," Mills, D.; 1981
RFC821	"Simple Mail Transfer Protocol," Postel, J.; 1982
RFC896	"Congestion Control in IP/TCP Internetworks," Nagle, J.; 1984

RFC903	"Reverse Address Resolution Protocol," Finlayson, R.; Mann, T.; Mogul, J.; Theimer, M.; 1984
RFC959	"File Transfer Protocol," Postel, J.; Reynolds, J. K.; 1985
RFC974	"Mail Routing and the Domain System," Partridge, C.; 1986
RFC1011	"Official Internet Protocols," Reynolds, J.; Postel, J.; 1987
RFC1027	"Using ARP to Implement Transparent Subnet Gateways," Carl-Mitchell, S.; Quarterman, J.; 1987
RFC1032	"Domain Administrators Guide," Stahl, M.; 1987
RFC1033	"Domain Administrators Operations Guide," Lottor, M.; 1987
RFC1036	"Standard for Interchange of USENET Messages," Adams, J.; 1987
RFC1074	"NSFNET Backbone SPF-Based Interior Gateway Protocol," Rekhter, J.; 1988
RFC1090	"SMTP on X.25," Ullmann, R.; 1989
RFC1104	"Models of Policy Based Routing," Braun, H.; 1989
RFC1124	"Policy Issues in Interconnecting Networks," Leiner, B.; 1989
RFC1157	"Simple Network Management Protocol (SNMP)," Schoffstall, M.; Fedor, M.; Davin, J., Case J.; 1990
RFC1173	"Responsibilities of Host and Network Managers: A Summary of the 'Oral Tradition' of the Internet," Van Bokkelen, J.; 1990
RFC1180	"TCP/IP Tutorial," Socolofsky, T.; Kale, C.; 1991
RFC1206	"FYI on Questions and Answers: Answers to Commonly Asked 'New Internet User' Questions," Malkin, G.; Marine, A.; 1991
RFC1207	"FYI on Questions and Answers: Answers to Commonly Asked 'Experienced Internet User' Questions," Malkin, G.; Marine, A.; Reynolds, J.; 1991
RFC1208	"Glossary of Networking Terms," Jacobsen, O.; Lynch, D.; 1991
RFC1214	"OSI Internet Management: Management Information Base," Labarre, L., ed.; 1991
RFC1234	"Tunneling IPX Traffic through IP Networks," Provan, D.; 1991

III

Part

RFC1241 "A Scheme for an Internet Encapsulation Protocol: Version 1," Mills, D.; Woodburn, R.; 1991

RFC1244 "Site Security Handbook," Holbrook, P.; Reynolds, J.; 1991

RFC1267 "A Border Gateway Protocol 3 (BGP-3)," Lougheed, K.; Rekhter, Y.; 1991

RFC1331 "Point-to-Point Protocol (PPP) for the Transmission of Multi-protocol Datagrams over Point-to-Point Links," Simpson, W.; 1992

RFC1332 "The PPP Internet Protocol Control Protocol (IPCP)," McGregor, G.; 1992

RFC1341 "MIME (Multipurpose Internet Mail Extensions) Mechanisms for Specifying and Describing the Format of Internet Message Bodies," Borenstein, N.; Freed, N.; 1992

RFC1421 "Privacy Enhancement for Internet Electronic Mail: Part I—Message Encryption and Authentication Procedures," Linn, J.; 1993

RFC1422 "Privacy Enhancement for Internet Electronic Mail: Part II—Certificate-Based Key Management," Kent, S.; 1993

RFC1497 "BOOTP Vendor Information Extensions," Reynolds, J.; 1993

RFC1513 "Token Ring Extension to the Remote Networking Monitoring," Waldbusser, S.; 1993

RFC1638 "PPP Bridging Control Protocol (BCP)," Baker, F., ed.; 1994

RFC1704 "On Internet Authentication," Haller, N.; Atkinson, R.; 1994

RFC1726 "Technical Criteria for Choosing IP: The Next Generation (Ipng)," Kastenholz, F.; Partridge, C.; 1994

RFC1731 "IMAP4 Authentication Mechanisms," Myers, J.; 1994

RFC1742 "Appletalk Management Information Base II," Waldbusser, S.; Frisa, K.; 1995

RFC1746 "Ways to Define User Expectations," Manning, B.; Perkins, D.; 1994

RFC1752 "The Recommendation for the IP Next Generation Protocol," Bradner, S.; Mankin, A.; 1995

RFC1757 "Remote Networking Monitoring Management Information Base," Waldbusser, S.; 1995

RFC1772	"Application of the Border Gateway Protocol," Rekhter, Y.; Gross, P.; 1995
RFC1774	"BGP-4 Protocol Analysis," Traina, P.; 1995
RFC1791	"TCP and UDP over IPX Networks with Fixed Path MTU," Sung, T.; 1995
RFC1792	"TCP/IPX Connection Mib Specification," Sung, T.; 1995
RFC1812	"Requirements for IP Version 4 Routers," Baker, F.; 1995
RFC1825	"Security Architecture for the Internet Protocol," Atkinson, R.; 1995
RFC1826	"IP Authentication Header," Atkinson, R.; 1995
RFC1827	"IP Encapsulating Security Payload (ESP)," Atkinson, R.; 1995
RFC1848	"MIME Object Security Services," Crocker, S.; Freed, N.; Galvin, S.; 1995
RFC1853	"IP in IP Tunneling," Simpson, W.; 1995
RFC1855	"Netiquette Guidelines," Hambridge, S.; 1995
RFC1939	"Post Office Protocol—Version 3," Myers, J.; Rose, M.; 1996
RFC1944	"Benchmarking Methodology for Network Interconnect Devices," Bradner, S.; McQuaid, J.; 1996
RFC1955	"New Scheme for Internet Routing and Addressing (ENCAPS) for IPN," Hinden, R.; 1996
RFC1957	"Some Observations on Implementations of the Post Office Protocol (POP3)," Nelson, R.; 1996
RFC1958	"Architectural Principles of the Internet," Carpenter, B.; 1996
RFC1963	"PPP Serial Data Transport Protocol (SDTP)," Schneider, K.; Venters, S.; 1996
RFC1968	"The PPP Encryption Control Protocol (ECP)," Meyer, G.; 1996
RFC1983	"Internet Users' Glossary," Malkin, G.; 1996
RFC1984	"IAB and IESG Statement on Cryptographic Technology and the Internet," Carpenter, B.; Baker, F.; 1996
RFC2002	"IP Mobility Support," Perkins, C.; 1996
RFC2007	"Catalogue of Network Training Materials," Foster, J.; Isaacs, M.; Prior, M.; 1996

III

Part

RFC2011	"SNMPv2 Management Information Base for the Internet Protocol using SMIv2," McCloghrie, K.; 1996
RFC2012	"SNMPv2 Management Information Base for the Transmission Control Protocol," McCloghrie, K.; 1996
RFC2013	"SNMPv2 Management Information Base for the User Datagram Protocol Using SMIv2," McCloghrie, K.; 1996
RFC2026	"The Internet Standards Process—Revision 3," Bradner, S.; 1996
RFC2030	"Simple Network Time Protocol (SNTP) Version 4 for Ipv4, Ipv6 and OSI," Mills, D.; 1996
RFC2033	"Local Mail Transfer Protocol," Myers, J.; 1996
RFC2057	"Source Directed Access Control on the Internet," Bradner, S.; 1996
RFC2063	"Traffic Flow Measurement: Architecture," Brownlee, N.; Mills, C.; Ruth, G.; 1997
RFC2064	"Traffic Flow Measurement: Meter MIB," Brownlee, N.; 1997
RFC2072	"Router Renumbering Guide," Berkowitz, H.; 1997
RFC2084	"Considerations for Web Translation Security," Bossert, G.; Cooper, S.; Drummond, W.; 1997
RFC2107	"Ascend Tunnel Management Protocol—ATMP," Hamzeh, K.; 1997
RFC2119	"Key Words for Use in RFCs to Indicate Requirement Levels," Bradner, S.; 1997
RFC2127	"ISDN Management Information Base," Roeck, G.; 1997
RFC2151	"A Primer on Internet and TCP/IP Tools and Utilities," Kessler, G.; Shepard, S.; 1997
RFC2136	"Dynamics Updates in the Domain Name System (DNS Update)," Vixie, P.; Thomson, S.; Rekhter, Y.; Bound, J.; 1997
RFC2137	"Secure Domain Name System Update," Eastlake, D.; 1997
RFC2200	"Internet Official Protocol Standards," Postel, J.; 1997

Chapter 21

Identifying Interconnectivity Issues

*The space between atoms connects
the universe as a whole.*

This chapter looks at certain key interconnectivity devices that have an impact on your enterprise network infrastructure. The key devices covered in this chapter are gateways, bridges, hubs, repeaters, routers, and switches.

The devices discussed here are intermediate nodes in contrast to clients and servers that are end nodes. Besides the interconnectivity devices discussed, other examples are network interface cards and wiring concentrators.

Interconnectivity issues vary from device to device and from vendor to vendor. However, there are common key performance issues that you should consider for any device. Below are ten issues:

➤ Bandwidth
➤ Communication latency
➤ Device configuration
➤ Network configuration
➤ Network segmentation
➤ Protocol implementation
➤ Protocol mix
➤ Traffic loads
➤ Transmission latency
➤ Wiring infrastructure

For any interconnectivity device from any vendor ensure that you understand the claims, and if necessary ask for validation to your satisfaction. Remember that the performance specifications given are based on a

Part

III

particular configuration, load, and protocol implementation, and to a specific level of enterprise network integration.

Gateways

A standard definition for a *gateway* is a server that performs protocol conversion between different types of networks and applications. For an enterprise network, consider a gateway the access server from an intranet to the Internet. Its counterpart would be the firewall that can be considered the entrance into your intranet from the Internet. Some of the functions or characteristics of a gateway are:

➤ Is bidirectional
➤ Can be a major bottleneck if not configured correctly
➤ Can have multiple ports
➤ Handles multiple protocol translation

Bridges

A *bridge* is a signal repeater that filters traffic between LAN segments. The segments can be different types; for example, one is an Ethernet and the other is a Token Ring. Some of the functions or characteristics of a bridge are:

➤ Is bidirectional
➤ Buffers packets
➤ Builds tables that indicate nodes by bridge port
➤ Can have multiple ports
➤ Can be slow on large networks with many nodes
➤ Can impact latency negatively
➤ Can use too much bandwidth
➤ Can impact Internet performance positively
➤ Has limited addresses
➤ Uses the same overhead for small and large packets

Hubs

A *hub*, or *concentrator*, concentrates multiple network connections into a manageable configuration. Some of the functions or characteristics of a hub are:

➤ Does not check packet address
➤ Functions as a passive wiring concentrator
➤ May have backplanes to increase bandwidth
➤ Has varying performance based on configuration
➤ Is useful for broadcasts and multicasts

Repeaters

A *repeater* replicates a decaying transmission signal to extend the signal's normal transmission length. Some of the functions or characteristics of a repeater are:

➤ Is bidirectional
➤ Boosts poor quality signals
➤ Drops simultaneously arriving packets
➤ Enforces protocol specification on excessive designed networks
➤ Enhances the chances for corrupt data
➤ Increases overall bandwidth utilization
➤ Operates bit by bit at the physical level
➤ Does not depend on a protocol

Part

Routers

A *router* is an interconnectivity device that forwards data packets from one LAN to another or from one WAN to another. A router differs from a bridge in that it processes protocols at the data and network layers of the OSI model. Some of the functions or characteristics of a router are:

➤ Is bidirectional
➤ Can act as a firewall for segmented traffic
➤ Can have multiple ports
➤ Can handle multiple protocols

➤ Can create broadcast storms

➤ Compacts protocol information to forward packets to their destinations

➤ May cause performance degradation because of a high potential for buggy software

➤ Is much slower than a bridge

➤ Provides traffic filtering, forwarding, and routing

➤ Is slower than a repeater

➤ Can be a source for transmission latency

➤ Is susceptible to network-level protocol translations

➤ Uses the same overhead for small or large packets

➤ Has a variety of protocols

Switches

A *switch* can come in at least two flavors—matrix, or network, and virtual. Because of the dynamic changes in this area there are many implementations. A *matrix*, or *network, switch* is basically a shared media technology that acts like a wiring concentrator. A *virtual switch* may be the ultimate in microsegmentation technology because it includes only nodes (source and destination) in a temporary (virtual) network. The virtual switch is based on telephony technology.

Chapter 22

Evaluating Service Servers

*Legacy is anything past
the given moment.*

A *server* can be defined as any device not on the client side of the network. Perhaps it can be narrowed to two functions—a service or an access. This is similar to defining the human race as women and men. This chapter focuses on the service servers and the next chapter discusses access servers.

There are five "basic" service servers that most users think of as the intranet or the Internet. These service servers are:

➤ Chat
➤ Directory
➤ E-mail
➤ News
➤ Search

A difficulty in defining a service server is there is no simple way to view a service. The basic services can be viewed from one or more of the following four perspectives:

➤ Application
➤ Communications
➤ Database
➤ Storage

The big issue, of course, is legacy software design and technology. There can be significant differences between software written in 1995 and in 1997 (upward compatibility, but not downward). There can even be configuration issues within a specific version of software. For example, a person uses Times New Roman 12-point font, while another person uses

Arial 10-point font. There are graphics in the document that have to appear in a particular position on a page. The correct positioning may not happen because of this one configuration difference.

As a person concerned with integration of an enterprise network, you have to resolve legacy and configuration issues in three environments—intranet "A," intranet "B," and the Internet.

This chapter discusses some of the concerns you may have about these five key service servers you probably use and the impact of legacy. This discussion is in the client/server format since that is where most of the technology is at present. However, there is another model or paradigm—object-oriented (DCOM and its supporting technologies, discussed in detail in Chapters 4 and 5).

When applicable, associated protocols to a given server are discussed:

➤ Chat servers use the Internet Relay Chat (IRC) protocol

➤ Directories use the Lightweight Directory Access Protocol (LDAP)

➤ E-mail servers use the Post Office Protocol (POP), Simple Mail Transfer Protocol (SMTP), and Internet Message Access Protocol (IMAP)

➤ News servers use the Network News Transfer Protocol (NNTP)

➤ Search engines are based on Z39.50 standard—Wide Area Information Server (WAIS)

Chat Servers

One of the earliest tools of online services was the ability to chat. The Internet Relay Chat (IRC) protocol is used.

Why is this important in an enterprise network? By setting up groups with special interests that are made up of people in diverse areas and locations, perhaps new ideas can be developed to improve corporate productivity. Also, there may be an increase of team sense across the corporation—an elimination of "them" and "us."

The technical issues involved are installation, maintenance, and available platforms. Above these issues are administration and control. A technological issue is amount of bandwidth required.

There have been significant technological changes in the chat environment. Among them is the development of a graphical interface. Changes that might come are Virtual Chat and the use of Java applets to enhance the system.

When determining the requirements for a chat system, these items should be in the mix:

➤ Sales support requirements

➤ Real-time support needs

➤ Desire for special-interest groups

➤ Policy for employee awareness on corporate direction and issues

The word is how well people should be able to communicate with each other as groups.

Directory Servers

The ideal directory server is to have a single entry point that controls all employee information. The system would have an access privilege procedure. Some people should be able to see a person's phone and department numbers. Only people in Human Resources should be able to retrieve full information.

Besides tracking employee information, a directory service should keep up with application resources, server configuration, server operation, and, of course, access data. Based on local requirements, this information should be available from any terminal.

The controlling protocol for directory services is Lightweight Directory Access Protocol (LDAP). It is a multiple platform and operating system protocol. Legacy data can be used to enhance the environment with the ability to use a single login.

E-Mail Servers

The secret success of e-mail service is not the sending of basic mail quickly and efficiently, but how well attachments can be sent. The big issue is whether you should use shareware or commercial products.

III

Part

Here are a few things you need to consider if you are new to e-mail service:

➤ Account administration
➤ Client tools
  ➤ Searching
  ➤ Spelling and grammar checking
  ➤ Uses POP3 (SMTP) or IMAP
➤ Directory (includes aliases)
➤ LAN and WAN server protocols
➤ Platform requirements
➤ Post Office Protocol (POP), Simple Mail Transfer Protocol (SMTP), and Internet Message Access Protocol (IMAP).
➤ Remote access
➤ Server options

News Servers

While you might be thinking of the already established newsgroups on the Internet, you may want to consider an internal news server using push technology. There is nothing better than home delivery.

News servers use the Network News Transfer Protocol (NNTP). This is the protocol used to distribute USENET (the Internet news forum) posts. A key concern is to have filters to eliminate redundancy and focus on the news service required for your users.

One tool you should consider is the installation of a newsreader as a supplement to the service. The major browsers have reading options.

There has to be a balance between service and administrative requirements. An impact area is your decision as to the availability of internal and external newsgroups.

Beware: There are few commercial newsgroup products available. This does not seem to be a growth area.

Search Servers

Because of technological advances in search engines, there is an expectation of users of your enterprise network that they also have such a utility available to them. One way to define the criteria for your search engine is to look at the many available on the Web. But in the reality of the virtual world, perhaps these are some of the bottom-line criteria you need to consider when buying:

➤ Price (per site, per individual, both)

➤ Index size to database comparison

➤ Maintenance, such as reindexing time

➤ Installation size (server and terminals)

➤ Platforms (Windows NT, UNIX, Solaris)

➤ Number of released versions and how often

A search engine usually has two major components—indexer and interrogator. A good indexer can handle your HTML, ASCII, and RTF files. The concern should be what impact the index algorithm has on memory requirements. The interrogator should have an excellent filtering algorithm so results are returned quickly and are ordered by significance.

Besides the basic short-term financial considerations and system requirements, there are long-term issues and functions that also need to be considered. They may not appear to affect your budget today; however, they not only can affect the budget year after year, but also how users see and use the system. A short list includes:

➤ Access controls

➤ Configuration requirements

➤ Cross-intranet searches

➤ Directory requirements

➤ Hardware interoperability

➤ HTML conversion time

➤ Installation time

➤ Programming requirements

➤ Scalability (Small networks become large—will software still function?)

Part III

> ➤ Search (Boolean) logic
> ➤ Software interoperability
> ➤ Support time and requirements
> ➤ Updating software
> ➤ User-friendliness

Issues

Some of the implementation issues for an enterprise network and its services caused by software design and technology are:

> ➤ Shareware versus commercial application versions
> ➤ Software version
> ➤ Software configuration
> ➤ Different implementations of the same service
> ➤ Different service protocols
> ➤ Single servers versus server clusters

While the remarks here use e-mail for examples, they are applicable in principle to any service. These items can seem to be unimportant, but they may be the items that keep you awake at night.

You may select shareware because it is free or very inexpensive. The hidden cost is that you may need a very knowledgeable and experienced programmer of the service to do local requirements. How do you spell the programmer's name? DOLLARS!

One should consider the importance of the software version issue given above. For example, there can be significant differences between software written in 1995 and in 1997 (upward compatibility, but not downward). A user has written a document using a word processor in the latest version and sends the document to another user with an earlier version for review. A result is an unsatisfactory (clean word) printing with the reviewer unhappy (another clean word) with the writer. You might get back a comment like, "Have you tried printing this?" There are now two unhappy users wondering why there is not one version of the word processor (read "any application").

There can even be configuration issues within a specific version of software. For example, a person uses Times New Roman 12-point font, while another person uses Arial 10-point font. There are graphics in the document that have to appear in a particular position on a page. This positioning may not happen because of this one configuration difference. The best way to understand this is to take a document with the first font type and change it to the second. This can catch you in e-mail attachments and with the problem described above.

Two implementations of a service may be distinctly different. One implementation may use a text command such as Print, while the other one uses a printer icon. It can get more sophisticated when new types of icons or drop-down menus are used in implementing functions. There are a number of e-mail servers and they probably all handle attachments differently.

The use of different protocols is tricky, especially in e-mail. It is not just the use of the protocols given in the introduction, but special LAN and WAN protocols that have to be considered.

The last issue to be considered here is a recent manifestation. The first step was to have a server for a single application or service. The next step was to put two or more services on one server. There is the joy of ensuring that the installation of one service does not change the system configuration of an already installed service. The third step and the present one is to have server clusters.

What is a *server cluster*? It is the configuration of two or more servers so they appear as one to both the users and the client applications. This idea strives to eliminate fault tolerance, to increase availability time, and to enhance scalability.

There is no discussion here of server clusters because this is a changing technology. You do need to know what the basic architectures or models are if approached by a vendor on this subject. The three architectures are:

➤ No share
➤ Share disk
➤ Share memory

Chapter 23

Evaluating Access Servers

*An access can be a right of passage
or a barrier to the wrong.*

As mentioned in the last chapter, a *server* can be defined as any device not on the client side of the network. This chapter focuses on the access servers, as the last chapter discussed service servers. The word "access" implies a "going into"; however, access servers can involve throughput, input, output, and checking or verification.

There are at least six "basic" access servers in the domain of the network administrator. Access servers usually take their name from the key function they perform. These key access servers are:

➤ Certification
➤ Firewalls
➤ Gateways
➤ Proxies
➤ Routers
➤ Web server (DCOM)

There are three major issues involved in the implementation of access servers in an enterprise network. They are:

➤ Legacy
➤ Optimization
➤ Security

This chapter discusses some of the implementation and maintenance concerns you may have about these six key access servers you probably use. This chapter also discusses optimization. Legacy is discussed throughout this book. Security, with an emphasis on basic Java security, has its own separate chapter.

Certification Servers

Certification servers become most important in an enterprise network because this is a developing environment where more people who want to make mischief can. *Certification* is a technique where all parties involved in data exchange can "trust" each other. The basic principle of certification is to have an intermediary party trusted by at least two parties certify that a public key can be shared by them so there can be secure data exchange.

As the size of the parties grows there has to be a certification authority. This authority signs a public key that acts as proof of trust. As the concept of certification has evolved, so has a protocol. An application has been developed that supports the Secure Socket Layer (SSL) protocol. The trend is to use digital certificates for two-way authentication. This type of authentication has been around for a time in Lotus Notes.

Beyond the SSL protocol there is the use of the X.500 directory services and the X.509 specification of the International Telecommunications Union (ITU). Digital certificates are stored in an X.500-based directory. The fields of an X.509, version 3, are:

➤ Version
➤ Serial number
➤ Algorithm identifier
➤ Issuer
➤ Period of validity
➤ Subject
➤ Subject's public key
➤ Signature

The driving force behind X.509 is RFC 1244, "Site Security Handbook." This area is rapidly changing because of the need for new requirements. It is highly recommended you check both the specification and the RFC for updated information.

Firewalls

A *firewall server* is a fortified gateway. A certification server can be a support component of your security system in conjunction with a firewall.

To keep the evildoers out, most firewalls perform the same functions, but the implementation can vary from vendor to vendor. The four key functions are:

➤ Fortified operating systems

➤ Internet Protocol (IP) filtering

➤ Isolating strategies

➤ Proxy servers

Implementing a firewall may require at least a security consultant, significant expenditures, and a minimum of two pieces of hardware with associated hardware. The hardware requirements are:

➤ Bastion host (guards the intranet structure)

➤ Screen router (does packet filtering)

You may actually have the requirement for a series of firewalls. This is based on your decision as to level of system security. You need at least an external firewall between the intranet and the Internet. This means one on each intranet in your enterprise network. Also, you may need one or more firewalls to protect proprietary resources such as financial data.

Where do you look for further ideas on the use of firewalls in your enterprise network?

➤ Application layer of the TCP/IP protocol suite

➤ Network tunneling

➤ Secure Socket Layer (SSL) protocol

➤ X.500 standard

Part III

Gateways

The term "gateway" has been around for a long time. It probably was used first to convey the functions of a router. It is a point of access—to the Internet or to an intranet.

A *gateway* performs bidirectional protocol conversions between heterogeneous (unlike) networks. The integration or implementation issues revolve around which layers of the OSI Reference Model are required for protocol conversions and where these conversions take place. To add to the confusion, a gateway operation can take place at any layer. There is one last confusion; gateways come in both hardware and software flavors.

There is a key question you need to ask vendors about their gateways—What networking protocols do you use? If they start discussing connections to a particular operating system or to an environment, they do not have a gateway.

What should you consider in a gateway? There are three general functions:

➤ File transfers
➤ Management support
➤ Remote logon

Proxies

A *proxy* is a separate storage facility (database) to handle frequently used applications or data. It is a substitute for the real thing. When a proxy supports a set of multiple IP address identities, it is sometimes referred to as a virtual Web server.

A proxy server can have many different functions:

➤ Assist in security processing within a firewall
➤ Increase a server's responsiveness
➤ Increase a server's security architecture
➤ Distribute processing workload
➤ Forward a browser's request

Here is a simple example of when you might use a proxy in your enterprise network:

➤ User launches browser.
➤ User enters a URL.
➤ Request goes to proxy server.
➤ Request goes to Internet.

This process should be transparent to the user. The user thinks it is a direct connection to the Internet. This gives you a firewall and a way to control where a user may get to on the Internet. If configured correctly, you can eliminate users going to their favorite sport site or other non-productivity sites.

What are some of the criteria you might consider in buying a commercial proxy server product?

➤ Ability to reduce traffic flow

➤ Access restriction options for users

➤ Caching scheme

➤ Data distribution process

➤ Dependability

➤ ISP requirements

➤ Maintenance

➤ Resource management

➤ Security

➤ Service control

➤ Speed

Routers

They are many different routers, but the one that should be included in any discussion of firewalls, gateways, and security is the screening router. The functions of a screen router are based on the network (IP protocol) and the transport (TCP protocol) layers of the OSI (Open Systems Interconnection) Reference Model (1978) of the International Organization for Standardization (ISO).

A *screening router* acts as a controller of traffic on network segments. This activity in turns controls the service types on each of these segments. If there is a service compromise, the result is thus limited.

Screening routers are also known as packet filter routers. This secondary name comes from the capability to discriminate between packets. Packet filtering is based on the protocol criteria from the OSI Reference Model. Packet filtering is based on the following:

➤ Source port number

➤ Destination port number

➤ TCP flags (usually ACK and SYN)

Web Servers (DCOM)

For a detailed discussion on DCOM, see Chapter 4. The discussion below focuses on a DCOM Web server model.

You would want a DCOM Web server for the same reasons you use the DCOM model:

➤ Code reuse

➤ Configuration management

➤ Enhanced security

➤ Fault tolerance

The DCOM architecture allows for the removal of certain barriers in current technologies for implementing distributed systems. It does this by permitting distributed objects to act like local objects.

What can you get from a DCOM Web server?

➤ Checking for Internet security requirements

➤ Maintaining of state information

➤ Server location transparent to users

➤ Object-oriented

➤ "Unlimited" connections

Optimization and Access Servers

Each network has its own unique optimization issues because of legacy software configurations and hardware architectures. Here are ten common optimization issues that should be considered in the implementation and maintenance of your enterprise network:

➤ Cache size

➤ Control file locations

➤ Disk fragmentation

➤ Hard disk seek and access times

➤ Improper allocation of resources

➤ Load balance

➤ Memory fragmentation

➤ Partitioning

➤ Processing priorities

➤ Processing scalability

Chapter 24

Evaluating Browsers

Using a browser is like
using a looking glass.

*T*his is probably the most dynamic area of change in all of Internet technology. It is the introduction of a user-friendly graphical user interface and the associated technologies that set the groundwork for the rapid growth of intranets. This chapter looks at evaluating this core software technology and the implications of the use of browsers in your enterprise network.

A basic definition of a *browser* is it is a graphical user interface (GUI) that enables you to look at data on the Internet and at data on your enterprise network. The browser concept has evolved so that it should also be a user-friendly interface to user services—e-mail, chat, news, search, and directory. The browser definition is now at the desktop stage.

There are really two browsers against which every other browser is evaluated. Perhaps the two big ones also need to be evaluated more closely by you, in particular in the implementation of Java applets. The section below discusses evaluation criteria. The other section in this chapter discusses alternative browsers. For example, have you considered the question "Do your users' desktops have the memory to handle one of the big two?"

Browser Evaluation Criteria

This section does not have a goal of defining the best browser, but giving an evaluation process for selecting one or more browsers. While functionality between browsers may be very similar, the functions may be handled differently. A simple test is to run an HTML document with a variety of tags and font types and sizes using two or more browsers. Notice the

III

Part

227

differences in appearance and other modes of presentation. One of the "little" things may be the fonts. Just to add to the confusion, select various font configurations within one browser and see how the HTML document outcome changes.

Before giving the evaluation criteria, here are a few suggestions for using the criteria. Draw a matrix such as the one below and use the numbers from 1 to 4 to indicate ratings.

➤ 1 = unsatisfactory

➤ 2 = poor

➤ 3 = satisfactory

➤ 4 = good

When you finish the evaluation, total each column and see how the browsers compare.

Also, you can give weight to each criteria. For example:

➤ 0 = not required

➤ 1 = nice to have

➤ 2 = required

Any kind of scheme is fine; just try to make the scheme be unbiased. There is much emotional baggage involved when selecting one of the big two.

Here is a basic matrix:

	Browser A	Browser B	Browser C
Criteria 1			
Criteria 2			
Criteria 3			
Criteria 4			

The following criteria are in an alphabetical list. You should establish the priority as recommended above.

➤ Availability

➤ Conferencing

➤ Disk size requirements

➤ Display capabilities

   ➤ Color

- ➤ Forms
- ➤ Frames
- ➤ Tables
- ➤ Documentation
- ➤ E-mail client support
- ➤ Font controls
- ➤ Foreign language support
- ➤ General performance
- ➤ Graphic handling
- ➤ Help capabilities
- ➤ HTML support
- ➤ Java support
- ➤ Load time
- ➤ News support
- ➤ Platform requirements
- ➤ Platform support differences
- ➤ Plug-in capability
- ➤ Printing capabilities
- ➤ RAM requirements
- ➤ Scripting support
- ➤ Security
- ➤ Stability
- ➤ Usability
- ➤ User-friendliness
- ➤ Vendor support
- ➤ Video capabilities

Some of these 30 evaluation criteria are far more important than others. The key criteria may be disk and memory size requirements, platform capabilities, HTML handling, and user-friendliness. As you look over the list, the same criteria appear as those for almost any application you have on your enterprise network.

Why Alternative Browsers

At first glance it may appear to be easy to have just one browser since the focus in this book is DCOM and its supporting technologies. It all changes when you consider the platforms for remote access and, of course, your legacy hardware. Again, it is important to weight each of the criteria for its implications in your having a balanced enterprise network.

There are browsers available that are very good for site development but not for general uses. Some browsers may work better on one platform than another.

As a part of your network structure, you may need to consider organizational groups and how they interact with other groups or what special needs they may have.

Are you going to use a browser's e-mail capabilities or use one of the many e-mail applications available?

These are just some of the issues you need to consider when implementing your browser policy. There may be many more questions you can ask, but if you use the 30 criteria above and acknowledge perhaps the need for more than one browser, you are far down the road to success in this area.

Chapter 25

Developing Integration Standards

A standard is a common playing field.

*T*his chapter looks at the importance of standards for implementing your enterprise network. The first action is to have a working definition of "standard." For the purpose of the following discussion, *standard* is defined as a property that can be defined, represented, or recorded under specified conditions. It was stated in an earlier chapter that a standard is a set of rules for defining a playing field where an exchange can take place, an exchange being, of course, one of data.

In an earlier chapter, modeling was discussed. A search for a standard for software resulted in the development of the concept "open system or architecture." To represent this concept, the Open Systems Interconnection Reference Model (OSI Reference Model) was adopted as a standard. Like most things in life there is evolution in how the standard can be changed to reflect technological changes. The next evolutionary steps were the Client/Server Model and the Object Management Architecture Reference Model (OMA Reference Model). Currently the step is the Object-Oriented Paradigm (OOP) and DCOM architecture. Because your legacy hardware and software were designed on pre-OOP models, you can use these models in some form to develop your integration standard for your enterprise network, but make new definitions in the context of the OOP and DCOM. Life is a series of compromises that can lead to success.

It is not the intention to discuss these models in detail in this chapter, only to highlight some basic principles or ideas used in these models. Each of us has his or her own set of experiences, but out of these experiences we establish a common ground for communications. You, the enterprise network administrator, have a fundamental duty to assist your users in defining their expectations as to services. You have to act as a translator. While most of your users do not have the technical knowledge of any given model, many of them have heard the concepts as defined in these three models. For example, it is very easy to misunderstand the concept "open." Some may think it means I can go anywhere, anytime I want on the system. You have to explain it means that when you use a given application on one platform, the data generated is readable and usable on a different platform. This is a long way around saying that this leads to an integration standard. You must configure the protocols so this does happen.

Your intranets may be LANs or WANs, but an enterprise network is a global area network (GAN). Recognize that the Internet, while it is to be the backbone of your enterprise network, is really a WAN.

Types of enterprise networks were discussed earlier in this book. In any of these types you must have at least two protocols functioning to be an enterprise network as discussed in this book—HTTP and TCP/IP.

Standards Organizations

There are many national standards groups; however, probably the most important group is the International Organization for Standardization (ISO). Some of the important ISO members are:

➤ USA: The American National Standards Institute (ANSI)

➤ France: Association Francaise du Normalization (AFNOR)

➤ Germany: Deutsches Institut fur Normung (DIN)

➤ UK: British Standards Institute (BSI)

The ISO tries to set standards worldwide. These standards are in many areas, not just computers. The language of definition of the ISO is English. The semantic and syntactical issues are incredible—how to abstractly describe systems. A standard used to assist in the writing of standards is ISO's Abstract Syntax Notation One (ASN.1). It provides the language, for instance, to describe all aspects of TCP/IP.

There is a standards group for the Internet. It is the Internet Architecture Board (IAB, 1992), earlier known as the Internet Activities Board (1983). The IAB in its earliest form was the Internet Configuration Control Board (ICCB, 1980). The ICCB was the standards group formed by the Defense Advanced Research Projects Agency (DARPA).

The IAB in 1986 created two task forces. The Internet Engineering Task Force (IETF) works on the refinement of standards. One of IETF's interests is the RFCs that were discussed in an earlier chapter. The other task force, which is interested in long-term research, is the Internet Research Task Force (IRTF).

There is a defined process for creating a new Internet standard.[1] The process begins with a Request for Comment (RFC). The steps are:

1. RFC draft
2. Internet draft (as many refinements as required)
3. Proposed standard (as many refinements as required; at least two implementations)
4. Draft standard (as many refinements as required; wide implementation)
5. Official standard

OSI Reference Model

The OSI Reference Model was generated out of the frustrations of every hardware and software vendor having their own proprietary method for making their product(s) work. The products were all incompatible with each other. The call was for platforms that use more than one vendor.

Without going into a discussion of the layers of the OSI Reference Model, let us look at the key principles that the seven layers represent. These principles are basic to the successful operation of any computer system. These principles are:

➤ Application data must be received and transmitted from one user to another.
➤ Data must be presented to a user as sent by another.
➤ Data exchange must be organized and synchronized between application processes.
➤ Data must be transported transparently from one user to another.
➤ The data path must have a physical routing.
➤ The data link must be controlled for error detection.
➤ Data transmission can be by mechanical, electronic, functional, and procedural means.

---

1   For further details, see RFC 1602, "The Internet Standards Process" by A. Chapin (1992).

On the basis of these seven principles you can begin to get answers from your vendors and your support team to be successful in the integration of your enterprise network. You should ask application vendors how their products work in tandem with other products. Do Java and Visual J++ applications function in the same manner? This is a metaphorical question. This book, or any other, cannot give you "the answer." You have to ask the questions, but a book like this one can assist in the interrogation process.

Chapter 26

Developing Technical Policies

A policy is good insurance.

This chapter looks at the importance of technical policies to give direction to your enterprise network. The first action is to have a working definition of "policy." For the purpose of the following discussion, *policy* is defined as a plan or course of action. While a standard is a set of rules for defining a playing field where an exchange can take place, a policy defines the boundaries of the field. Any policy has three players:

➤ The enforcer—enterprise network administrator

➤ The implementers—technicians

➤ The users

It is critical to the technical policy development process that all three players are represented. If all three players are not involved, the policy may not work. Perhaps this statement should be stronger—A policy will not work if not all the players are involved in its development.

The chapter on security has a discussion on security policies. It may seem strange, but if there is not a buy-in on such things as "Do not use 'sex' or death and birth dates as passwords," a security policy fails. If this is true, what about complex issues such as application configurations defined in a technical policy?

Technical Policy Attributes

What are ten key attributes of a technical policy?

➤ There should be a statement up front that says, "If an action is not stated as permitted, then it is prohibited."

➤ Define the justifications.

- ➤ Technology
- ➤ Corporate
- ➤ Social
- ➤ Legal
- ➤ Define the expectations.
  - ➤ Organizational overview
  - ➤ Component particulars
- ➤ Reference the standards.
- ➤ Reference any relevant benchmarks.
- ➤ Define consequences.
- ➤ State implementation procedures.
- ➤ State enforcement procedures.
- ➤ State how users are to follow the policy.
- ➤ State any special considerations.
  - ➤ Corporate customers
  - ➤ Vendors

Reasons for a Technical Policy

There should be a general corporate technical policy, but there should be specific technical policies also. What are some of the reasons for having a specific technical policy?

- ➤ Access procedures
- ➤ Application residence
- ➤ Benchmark definitions
- ➤ Configuration definitions
- ➤ Interoperability criteria
- ➤ Maintenance and upgrade schedules
- ➤ Network optimization
- ➤ Performance standards
- ➤ Processing procedures
- ➤ Tool responsibilities

Policy as a Management Backbone

Policy is the backbone to good enterprise network management. The difference between a network technical policy and an enterprise network technical policy is the requirement that both the Internet and an intranet be considered in tandem. The goals need to be realistic. Here are ten general needs that you should make specific to your organization:

➤ Adequate access for all users

➤ Adequate data delivery

➤ Design and development improvement

➤ Improved awareness among users

➤ Increased productivity

➤ Minimum downtime

➤ Reduction in maintenance costs

➤ Reliable backup procedures

➤ Resource organization

➤ User satisfaction

Developing technical policies enables you to manage assets, resources, and people. Having technical policies probably helps reduce significantly the cause of ill will between network management and users—lack of awareness.

Policy for Policies

What should these policies have to assist in good enterprise network management? Here are seven examples from Management 101:

➤ Belief in the professionalism of the users

➤ Change management

➤ Emphasis on exploration

➤ Minimum restrictions

➤ Open-door policy

➤ Reasonable monitoring of resource usage

➤ User-defined boundaries

Part IV
Resolving the Big Issues

*T*his part of the book looks at two issues that seem to overpower everything else. First, there seems to be a trend towards telecommuting, which leads to issues such as remote access control and management. The remote access interface has to be user-friendly and data transmission has to be as reliable as the Rock of Gibraltar and as fast as a speeding bullet. Actually, the speed should be a bit faster than the speed of light. Second, since there is a potential global environment, how can the user terminal be secure?

Thus, the big issues covered here are:

➤ Remote access
➤ Security

Chapter 27

Remote Access

The remote door is the front door,
just farther away.

Remote access, while a key aspect of any discussion of security, requires a separate discussion because of the additional issues that are generated. Your enterprise network with remote access is not a wide area network, but a global area network (*cyberagora*). Your users expect to be able to access an enterprise network anytime and from anywhere in the world.

Remember that the questions and comments made about what you have to do behind the firewall are even more valid in the remote access world. Without discussing the technical implications, there are three things that should be discussed about remote access. These items are:

➤ Key issues
➤ Remote access management
➤ Box of the future

Key Issues

The remote access issues are the same as from any workstation. However, they seem to take on a dynamic life unique to the environment. Here are some of the key issues:

➤ Access speed
➤ Control standards
➤ Cost
➤ Customer service
➤ Application distribution

➤ Privacy

➤ Security

➤ Transaction reliability

➤ Workstation (read "desktop") capabilities

Remote Access Management

There are two key documents you need to be aware of to get a handle on remote accessing. The first document is Simple Network Management Protocol (SNMP). The second is Management Information Base (MIB). MIB defines how data is stored so SNMP can manage it.

The key issue of SNMP is if your network management data falls into hands that, shall we say, are unclean, you do have an insecure situation. There is now arriving on the market authentication utilities to assist in this area. Using SNMP means managed devices can:

➤ Be rebooted after being powered down

➤ Have routing tables reconfigured

➤ Be queried for traffic from the last reboot

➤ Provide traffic data such as protocol data

Perhaps the key to good remote access management is to have a comprehensive and usable policy for audit trails and system logs. It has to be emphasized to all users that they are the best firewalls if they follow security guidelines.

The basic principle of remote access management is always how you answer the question, "What kind of door or doors do I have to my house (enterprise network)?" Rather than have a local and a somewhat controllable environment behind the firewall, it is a global and a random environment that you have to try to manage. The thought is you have to try!

Box of the Future

Finding solutions to the key remote access issues is a growth area. Major time is devoted at intranet and Internet conferences, and in magazine and newspaper articles. One of the best places to see the future is to look at the business section of any major newspaper. Check for who is making alliances, mergers, or partnerships in the "Web world." This world includes software developers, computer builders, cable companies, and telephone companies. As this was written, there was a newspaper article of the deals happening on set-top boxes among Telecommunications Inc., General Instruments, Sun Microsystems, and Microsoft.

While these developments are to make money for these corporations and others like them, you as an enterprise network administrator need to be aware of the various technological implications. This technological concept (application) seeks to resolve most, if not all, of the key remote access issues.

For every bright cloud, there is a dark cloud. The dark cloud is the people who are comfortable with the remote access environment are the same people who also want to have their own computers and their own applications that they can configure the way they want it. This individualism, of course, is the doorway to insecurity and transaction unreliability.

The future is a closed box where a remote user can access the enterprise network and get the application components required using Java applets to do data manipulation. The access bandwidth is at least a cable modem. An intranet can be accessed from the set-top box perhaps in ways yet to be determined. Just think—your users can access their favorite movies with the same box. What about an infomercial for your users (salespeople to the company's customers)?

What does this trend mean to you? You have to think about design, development, and implementation when you use a set-top box. What are the new control and access standards? What are the costs for the hardware? What are the hidden costs such as corporate usage versus private usage through some cable company? How does this differ from the use of an ISP? Who wants to be there yesterday?

Chapter 28

Security

Security is as good as the weakest link.

There is a basic contrast between established network systems and Internet technologies as to security implementation. Many mainframe systems have a password control system. The controls are at a minimum:

➤ Users must change their password every *x* days.

➤ Users cannot use the same password within a year.

➤ Users' accounts are disabled with three invalid login attempts.

Unfortunately, the solution that many database vendors take is to graft security onto their Internet database middleware and achieve these results. Future solutions may be based on the new object technologies such as DCOM (see Chapter 4) and the use of Kerberos authentication. Also, Java and ActiveX tools could be used to access your present password control system.

However, the big perceived issue of data transmission security may not be behind the firewalls on your intranet(s), but in front of your firewall on the Internet. Users fear giving out credit card information or any other sensitive financial or personal information. The hidden issue is that it has been demonstrated more than once that "crackers" (hackers with a bad attitude) do not fear password controls.

Certain minimal steps are required to integrate a security system into your enterprise network:

➤ Determine the level of security required for the system as a whole and then for certain types of information such as financial and personal.

➤ Determine how effective present security controls are and whether they should be integrated into your enterprise network.

> ➤ Develop a security policy.
> ➤ Enforce the security policy.

This chapter briefly looks at these security subjects:

➤ Crackers and spoofing

➤ Standards

➤ Policies

➤ Firewalls

➤ Kerberos authentication

➤ Java security highlights

➤ Common access control holes

➤ Basis for a Java applet network security policy

Crackers and Spoofing

Before taking up some security solutions, crackers and spoofing should be discussed. There has been a long-time fear of *hackers*, people who have fun getting into computer systems and may do potential damage. Out of the hacker environment has grown a new breed that is malign, the *cracker* who wants to get into a system and do grave damage or get information that can do damage to your company or your customers. Crackers use the usual techniques of hackers, but have also developed new techniques. Among them is spoofing.

Spoofing is the technique of creating a false world and getting you to act as though it was a real world. The results are the spoofer can see and control the victim's (your) activities on the Internet or intranet or enterprise network. An environment or context or situation is created so the victim (you) gives out relevant security information—passwords, social security number, account numbers, etc.

The spoofer can send you misinformation or information in your name. You could have items from your inventory misrouted or one of your customers charged for items they did not receive. Beyond the standard theft, there is, of course, the possibility of the cracker getting into your financial database or other databases and wreaking havoc.

You cannot think of one place as the point to focus your security process. You must look at the whole system—your intranet(s) and the Internet, the backbone for transporting data. You have to think in terms of both hardware and software security. How many of your users do not have passwords for their workstations? Have you considered the security impacts of the browser(s) that your users have?

Spoofers take advantage of contextual cues that Web designers use—such things as colors, symbols, logos, pop-up screen (menus), etc. Active Web users unconsciously use these cues like car drivers think about stop or railroad signs (speed limit signs are not a good example). Speed limit signs establish false contexts for drivers—if I drive within the speed limit, I am safe. A spoofer is a person who drives outside the speed limit and makes the highway unsafe, but wants you to believe it is safe.

One last thought on spoofing. Spoofing comes from the ideas developed on URL rewriting techniques. The goal of the developers of these ideas was to provide useful services. Others, the spoofers, used these ideas to develop security attacks through hiding clues to origination.

Ideas on Security Standards

You can and should develop your own set of security standards; however, why reinvent the wheel? The Department of Defense has many standards, one being the "C2 Principles." The C comes from Division C of the DOD Red Book for networks. This division is concerned with *discretionary access control* (DAC). This really means there should be a protection method with fundamental criteria. The 2 is a level of finely grained (1 could be considered grained) discretionary access control.

There are four fundamental requirements in this standard. They are, in alphabetical order:

➤ Accountability
➤ Assurance
➤ Documentation
➤ Security policy

Accountability is an audit system for proper identification and authentication. Details are found in the DOD Orange Book. The key principle is to have a log system that is tamper proof. One of the "thou-shall-haves" is a password system. A question to ask any vendor of an access control product is "How does the product implement this standard?"

Assurance is the enforcement system. An assurance system should be an enforcement mechanism that assures the principles outlined in accountability, documentation, and security policy. The two major components of assurance are system architecture and system integrity. Ensure you get a clear definition of how a vendor handles assurance because unfortunately this section does have a fuzzy concept or two.

Documentation has four criteria:

➤ Security features user's guide
➤ Trusted facility manual
➤ Test documentation
➤ Design documentation

Three are of common use; however, the Trusted Facility Manual is directed to the concerns of a secure site. But one should consider it equally with the other three because it concerns a disaster recovery plan. The requirements are not extensive; for example, the user's guide can be a single summary.

While discussed last here, the first principle of C2 is a *security policy*. The principle is "There shall be an explicit and well-defined security policy enforced by the system." A document that follows this principle is RFC 1244, "The Site Security Handbook." Section Two of this handbook deals with security policies. The basic ideas from that are discussed in the following section.

Thoughts on Security Policies

The key areas of a security policy are:

➤ Risk assessment
➤ Policy issues
➤ Policy violations
➤ Protection policy
➤ Policy interpretation
➤ Policy publication

RFC 1244, "The Site Security Handbook," has been a living document through the dedication of the Site Security Policy Handbook Working Group (SSPHWG). It is not a specific standard but an information source for the Internet community.

Rather than discuss the RFC in detail, here are key policy issues raised in Section 2.3:

➤ Who is allowed to use the resources?

➤ What is the proper use of the resources?

➤ Who is authorized to grant access and approve usage?

➤ Who may have system administration privileges?

➤ What are the user's rights and responsibilities?

➤ What are the rights and responsibilities of the system administrator versus those of the user?

➤ What do you do with sensitive information?

Firewalls

A *firewall* is a restrictive barrier that controls traffic on and off the Internet. Like any wall, it is not absolute. Like the original concept of a barrier to block fires, the electronic firewall should be able to stop ordinary fires—intrusions—but watch for the blaze or bonfire. A firewall is designed to meet a specific level of security.

Firewall software and hardware has to be chosen carefully, and just as carefully be configured and maintained. Firewalls can be defined by the techniques used. Four categories of firewalls are:

➤ Application gateways

➤ Circuit-level gateways

➤ Packet filters

➤ Passive

The best solution is not to use a single technique. Depending on your security requirements and network configuration, a blending of these techniques is necessary. Remember: You can never be completely secure.

As the firewall business is a growth industry, no particular solution is given here. However, there are ten key thoughts for considering a firewall, whether it be today or tomorrow:

➤ A firewall should be adaptable.

➤ Firewall protocol should be verifiable.

➤ A firewall should be easily maintained.

➤ Routers were not designed to be firewalls.

➤ Firewall security is as good as your mistrust.

➤ Firewall protocol is as good as its foundation.

➤ Firewalls should deny any access not explicitly permitted.

➤ Packet filtering is fragile and, to say the least, difficult to use.

➤ Firewall structure must change as the rest of the system changes.

➤ Firewalls should support your security policy, not be the originator of it.

Kerberos Authentication

Kerberos is a part of the Open Software Foundation (OSF) that is used in a Distributed Computing Environment (DCE). Users are required to log into a security server first; the server then controls usage.

Kerberos takes its name from the three-headed dog that was guardian of Hades' gateway. Kerberos, the software, has three parts:

➤ Database

➤ Authentication server

➤ "Ticket-granting" server

In a physical sense, all three of these parts are on one physical server. This server should, of course, be in a secured area. Read this as "locked away from general public usage."

Kerberos exchanges are encrypted. The encryption does make traffic analysis difficult. This can be a partial solution to some spoofing.

While Kerberos is a very strong application, it does have its weak spots. Some of these are:

➤ Network overhead

➤ Each network application has to be modified to work with Kerberos (this does take a programmer some time for each application)

➤ Subject to "dictionary attacks" (a disassembling of encrypted passwords that are in the form of ordinary or dictionary words)

Kerberos and Windows NT 5.0

When the Kerberos security provider is used in Windows NT 5.0, delegation-level impersonation is supported. However, running a component as the launching user component is not recommended. Any client access attempt creates a new window station and loads a new component instance. There would be load overload of a large number of users connected to the same component at the same time. The use of the REGCLS_MULTIPLEUSE flag does not resolve this issue.

Kerberos API and MS-Windows

On MS-Windows, the standard Kerberos API is available. These standard routines are implemented in a dynamic-link library called kerberos.dll. Due to the standard DLL calling conventions, all pointers passed to or returned from the MS-Windows Kerberos implementation are FAR pointers. The interface file kerberos.h, which is included by the usual krb.h include file, provides function prototypes that cause any pointer's arguments to be converted to FAR pointers. Any values that are pointers are to be handled as FAR pointers. Values that are specified as int are 16-bit numbers using MS-Windows compilers.

The kerberos.dll can be installed anywhere on the search path. Use the driver to #include krb.h in all source modules that call Kerberos routines. Ensure the program calls krb_start_session before calling any other Kerberos routines. Link the code with the keberos.lib to call kerberos.dll.

Java Security Highlights

This section is not an accounting of the successes or failures of Java security. The improvements in the security component of Java seem to change daily. When you read an article on this subject, the information given is determined by the writer's perspective on Java, the writer's meaning of security, and the writer's experiences. One should not look for glories or damnations, but rather the questions and solutions for the use of any software, Java being just one component.

Before all other things, the key thing to remember about Java security is it is as good as the programmer.

Java is intended to be used for both standalone applications and applets that are executed by Java-enabled Web browsers. Java security is really a discussion of the intended use of the Java language as a mechanism for providing executable content.

Java provides executable content to Web browsers with an embedded interpreter and runtime library. These Web browsers can download Java

IV

Part

programs called applets, and have the Java interpreter execute the program. The security of the system fundamentally depends on the security of three layers:

➤ Java language itself

➤ Java libraries

➤ Web browser itself

Java is an object-oriented language. The important features from a security standpoint are:

➤ Safety of the type system

➤ Lack of pointers as a language data type

➤ Use of packages with distinct namespaces

➤ Access control for variables and methods within classes

➤ Use of garbage collection (automatic memory allocation)

It is necessary to check if there are adequate methods of controlling resources in an analysis of the effectiveness of Java security:

➤ Access to the network is well protected.

➤ Access to the file system is well protected.

➤ Access to control of threads is fairly limited.

➤ Access to environment variables is protected by security checks.

➤ Protection of memory is done by the language specification itself.

➤ Protection provided for output devices is that any applet window can be forced to have a special marking noting that it is unsafe.

➤ An applet can only access the keystrokes or mouse clicks of the user when the applet's window has been selected.

➤ Any attempted system calls, including attempts to exit, are checked.

Common Access Control Holes

There can be many security holes in a system. One set is access controls:

➤ Retained system passwords from original configuration

➤ Retained passwords when employees change jobs

➤ No standards for password structure—get rid of the common passwords such as "god," "sex," birth dates, close family names, etc.

➤ Passwords written down where others can view them

➤ Shared passwords

➤ Trust of dial-up system

➤ Security laxness

Applet Network Security Policy

Here is a summary on the use of java.net.Socket or java.net.URLConnection. Because java.applet.AppletContext.showDocument() does not have any security restrictions, it is not discussed here.

Applications can connect anywhere they like, unless you use a security manager, which limits connections. Therefore, this summary is limited to applets running in a browser.

Applets are divided into two categories: trusted and untrusted. *Trusted applets* are not subject to any security restrictions and can therefore open connections to any host. *Untrusted applets* have the opposite abilities.

For an applet to be considered trusted, the requested name must be in the classpath. The procedure is when an applet is loaded, a check is first made to see if the requested *applet name* exists in the classpath (if none is set, then the internal default classpath is used). If the applet is found in the classpath, it is loaded. Note the *applet name* is the value of the CODE attribute in the APPLET tag.

An applet still can load if there is no requested name or classpath. It is loaded from the location specified by the combination of URLs used to load the page containing the applet and in the CODEBASE attribute. This applet is untrusted.

A trusted applet does not impose a security concern. The rest of the discussion is about the untrusted applet. It is where an applet is loaded from that plays a central role in determining which host(s) it can connect to. The host that served the applet is referred to hence as the *originating host*.

Below are security restrictions imposed on untrusted applets for Appletviewer, Internet Explorer, and Netscape.

Appletviewer (JDK)

The default security mode only allows connections to the originating host. This mode is modified using either the Applet|Properties menu or by setting the property appletviewer.security.mode=xxx in ~/.hotjava/

properties directly, where *xxx* is set for unrestricted access, *host* for the default behavior, or *none* to disallow all network connections. The menu item sets this property automatically.

To enable the proxy under JDK 1.0.2, you need to set the property proxy-Set to true, set the proxyHost property to point to the proxy server, and set the proxyPort property to the correct port. In the Appletviewer these can also be set using the Applet|Properties menu. For JDK 1.1 you must set http.proxyHost to the correct host and http.proxyPort to the correct port; setting http.proxyHost to null disables the proxy.

Microsoft Internet Explorer

The information is dependent on the version of IE in use. Check the latest documentation for details. One issue is how to use java.net.Socket on a proxy server. A problem is the support for a proxy is part of the protocol used above TCP/IP (such as HTTP, FTP, Gopher, etc.); it is not possible to encapsulate the proxy-specific information at the socket layer. Another problem is most firewalls do not allow TCP connections out; that is, the only way out is through the proxy server (usually for HTTP and FTP, perhaps Gopher).

This issue can be improved by using the java.net.URLConnection class. This implementation shields that a proxy is being used, checks the true destination of the request against the applet's origin, and allows such connections through the proxy. Using URLConnection works even behind a firewall and an HTTP proxy is used to get out.

Netscape

The security is similar to the default mode of Appletviewer. The exception is java.net.URLConnection and the protocol must also match. If an applet is loaded using the HTTP protocol from a secure server, then only use https:URLs (it is https, not http) for the URLConnection to be used. Netscape seems to ignore when an applet is loaded using the file protocol or the Open File... menu. At this time, there is no supported way for changing the network security policy.

Part V
Final Thoughts

*T*here is an expectation that a complex problem can be solved in ten words or less. These last two chapters do not achieve that goal. These last two chapters are a brief summary of the issues and project and technical management processes given throughout the prior chapters, and an overview of how Java, DCOM, and DCOM's supporting technologies can be synthesized.

But just to satisfy the need for simple solutions, here are the key ideas given in the book:

➤ The ability to find an answer is more important than the ability to know the answer.

➤ Common sense is a very rare sense.

➤ Networking is a team effort of people, hardware, and software.

➤ Relationships vary as weeds in the garden.

➤ A paradigm is a twisted view of reality.

➤ A baby, a child, a teenager, an adult, and a senior citizen are labels for any one human being.

➤ A parameter has two sides: internal and external.

➤ Any activity has its own hidden agenda.

➤ A sequence may be a bit forward and a bit backwards.

➤ Because I know one word in a language, does that mean I have the skill to speak it?

➤ Resistance is a serious folly.

➤ Shakespeare would not have been able to write a play if Caesar had read the message.

➤ Time is both benign and malign.

➤ One name for a timely <u>commitment</u> is a schedule.

➤ A risk can be a victory or a loss.

➤ Bad cost estimates impact the budget, the financial plan.

➤ A budget is a financial plan that is impacted by wayward cost estimates.

➤ Components are visible and invisible, but all are important.

➤ A model is only a perception of reality.

➤ A good tool can be like a sturdy stool.

➤ Correctly working with protocols is like using good manners.

➤ The space between atoms connects the universe as a whole.

➤ Legacy is anything past the given moment.

➤ An access can be a right of passage or a barrier to the wrong.

➤ Using a browser is like using a looking glass.

➤ A standard is a common playing field.

➤ A policy is good insurance.

➤ The remote door is the front door, just farther away.

➤ Security is as good as the weakest link.

➤ A metaidea is an idea that is part of the beginnings.

➤ Good documentation is like a good building foundation.

Note these ideas can be found at the beginning of each chapter.

Chapter 29

DCOM and Metaconcepts

*A metaidea is an idea that is
part of the beginnings.*

This chapter briefly considers a notation of high-level and fundamental model designing for the synthesis of DCOM and Java internetworking, metalanguages. This notation is valid for the synthesis of components and objects in an objected-oriented paradigm. Two relevant metalanguages are Microsoft's Interface Definition Language and Rational Software Corporation's Unified Modeling Language. They present two environments for developing a synthesis for an enterprise network with DCOM architecture and Java internetworking. This chapter does not give detailed explanations because of legacy environments. These are high-level interpretations based on earlier developments of metaconcepts in the schools of analytical, conceptual, and linguistical philosophies.

Note: A *metalanguage* is the highest level of a language environment. For example, in this book "architecture" could be a concept in a metalanguage.

This is a very dynamic area of development. What is true today may not be true tomorrow. Basic overviews of DCOM and Java and Visual J++ with a focus on networking are in Chapters 4 and 5. Parts II and III cover the administrative and technical methodologies for integration at the design level for the implementation of an enterprise network with DCOM architecture and Java internetworking.

V

Part

For the latest technical details and specifications, refer to these Microsoft Web sites:

www.microsoft.com/java/
www.microsoft.com/visualj/
www.microsoft.com/visualj/support/
www.microsoft.com/

Search on IDL, MIDL, and Interface Definition Language.

For information on the Unified Modeling Language, refer to Rational Software Corporation's site:

http://www.rational.com/uml/index.shtml

Why is this important to you, the network or system administrator? These metalanguages help to resolve issues or questions such as:

➤ What is a component?

➤ What is an object?

➤ Can an object be a component?

➤ When do I use a method and when do I use a property?

➤ What is a proper enumeration name?

➤ What is inheritance?

➤ What is the place of a dynamic-link library in an object-oriented network?

➤ When is an interface an interface?

➤ What is a parameter?

➤ What is a pointer?

To develop a synthesis between architecture and a language that reflects the attributes of the architecture, a series of *metaconcepts* must be stated to reflect the synthesizing. *Meta* comes from the Greek for "after," as in "later or higher level" of, as in this case, concept. *Concept* is a general idea or notion. The obvious result is a "high-level notion." The key metaconcepts that are relevant here are:

➤ Metalanguage

    ➤ Unified Modeling Language (UML)

    ➤ Interface Definition Language (IDL)

➤ Metamodel (Object Model)

➤ Metasystem (System Model)

Metalanguage

The metalanguage of all specialized metalanguages is, of course, ordinary language. Here are two very simplistic definitions to explain the difference between a language and a metalanguage. A *language* is a series of words put together according to syntactical rules. A *metalanguage* groups words into singular notions using certain types of rules. Examples of these rule types are philosophic, linguistic, scientific, or, as is relevant here, system modeling and defining. Two important specialized and technical metalanguages for synthesizing DCOM architecture and Java hierarchy are Unified Modeling Language and Interface Definition Language.

Unified Modeling Language (UML)

Unified Modeling Language (UML) is a tool that assists in creating an object-oriented design. Rational Software Corporation, along with a number of partners including Microsoft, Hewlett-Packard, IBM, and Oracle, developed UML for this activity. Use the site references on the previous page for further information.

UML is a language that seeks to use the best engineering practices for developing large and complex system models. It can be used in both software and non-software environments. This means you can model a client either as software or as hardware. It is used for specifying, visualizing, constructing, and documenting a system's infrastructure (see Chapters 17, "Defining Components," and 18, "Modeling an Enterprise Network").

The notion of a metamodel is discussed later in this chapter. But there is a very important business reason for having a model that the use of UML can give—the model is like a building blueprint. It aids in system definition, system visualization, and system construction. UML assists you in designing an object-oriented system network.

According to the documentation, there are key UML functions. For details, refer to that documentation. A summary of these goals is:

➤ Provides an expressive way to see the objects in the model

➤ Provides flexibility within a core concepts (four in number) environment

➤ Provides software independence

➤ Provides a formal definitional structure for a basis for common modeling understanding

➤ Provides holistic support for high-level development concepts such as components and patterns

➤ Provides a best of practice environment

Besides not being a process, UML is not a programming language. Its name says UML is a modeling language. It is also not a tool interface, but a semantic metamodel (see a later section on the metaconcept of meta-model).

There are many ways to approach the design of a Java application with UML. The goal of the design is to have an application that can be easily changed and extended. The design should have two separate parts: application logic and technical logic. Here is a brief set of possible design steps:

1. Identify end user requirements.
2. Do an analysis that captures system requirements.
3. Do a usage analysis (may be considered a part of step 2).

   ➤ Who or what uses (actors).

   ➤ Who or what is used (use cases).

4. Create a design model.
5. Write the Java code.
6. Test the code.
7. Return to step 5 as necessary.
8. Implement the application.

There are many good rules for writing Java code for an application. In fact, a book probably could be written on the subject if there is not one already. Here are ten core design-coding rules:

➤ Do a visual model of the use cases and associated actors of the application.

➤ Do a domain class structure.

➤ Do a sequence diagram to represent each of the use case paths or scenarios.

➤ Do an architectural overview that shows application packages and dependencies.

➤ Do a detailed objects design structure.

➤ Do any state diagrams as required.

➤ Do a functions class diagram model.

➤ Do a component diagram showing dependencies.

➤ Do coding based on models.

➤ Do testing based on expectations based on models.

Note: This list is not comprehensive. It represents just some of the activities in the design process when one uses UML.

An example of a domain class structure is to have a series of three-part boxes: class names, class attributes, and class methods. The boxes are linked with lined arrows that represent associations of the classes. The lines should be labeled with type of association.

A detailed objects design structure looks similar to the domain class structure. The design of the various classes of the objects package is specified here. Further specifications can be written as to interfaces and data types for attributes.

It is most likely that any application will be a collaborative effort. As in any project effort there is a communication process that establishes a place for feedback and the ability to change the model based on this. This feedback is not a change to the model because someone wants to have a change. There needs to be a requirement for change based on the model definition.

Interface Definition Language (IDL)

IDL is a metalanguage because at a high level it fully defines an interface and fully specifies each operation's parameters. IDL concepts are mapped to a programming language such as Java. The basic principles of IDL are to be non-platform specific and to be an implementing environment, not a programming environment.

Microsoft Interface Definition Language (MIDL) is an implementation of IDL. Since its introduction, MIDL has been under enhancement and evaluation by Microsoft as a part of its ongoing program of tighter integration with Java. The discussion here is important to understand the principles or guidelines of MIDL rather than the how-to-do.

The fundamental notations of IDL may not change, but the bundling or implementing will. For example, as this chapter is written one computer magazine editor writes his belief that Microsoft Transaction Server (MTS) may no longer be a distinctive technology because of the first COM+

release. Only the users of MTS will know the actual answer. This is a reason for a network administrator to understand the guiding principles of network design and development over techniques.

The requirement to use MIDL to write interface for DCOM is not absolute, as is the use of IDL to write CORBA interfaces. IDL is preferred because it was designed to support distributed services. It is based on the OSF DCE standard. MIDL lets you describe interfaces, member functions, and attributes of the functions.

> **Note:** OSF is the Open Software Foundation. DCE is the Distributed Computing Environment. For further information, see **www.opengroup.org**.

Recognize the MIDL environment is dynamic as Microsoft pursues its vision of an object-oriented network. When working with Visual J++, this knowledge is nice to know. The ActiveX Wizard handles the conversion activity. Here are five basic steps for defining an interface:

1. Write the interface to include:
   - ➤ Data types
   - ➤ Member functions
   - ➤ Contract information

   The contract information is between the client application and the server component (object). There are three parts:

   - ➤ Programming mode definition (language)
   - ➤ Interface interoperation (application)
   - ➤ Remote server access (network)

2. Compile the interface to build proxy and stub interfaces.
3. Use the interfaces from step 2 to construct the dynamic-link libraries (.DLLs).
4. Distribute the proxy .DLL to appropriate client applications.
5. Distribute the stub .DLL to appropriate server components (objects).

There are a number of concepts associated with IDL. Here are eight:

Attributes	Keywords that specify data characteristics in remote procedure calls (RPCs) and the interface's characteristics.
Header	Contains interface attributes and a body with other interface definitions.
Body	Contains data types used in RPCs and remotely executed function prototypes.
uuid	A unique 132-bit number that specifies the interface identifier (IID).
IUnknown	Source for all interfaces.
Directional parameters	Specifies direction of data pass: [in], [out], and [in, out].
Array	See Appendix C for a list of types.
Pointers	See Appendix C for a list of types.

Metamodel

Metamodel is the highest level result relative to a modeling language. It is the goal for all phases of modeling; the logical, epistemological, methodological, and eventually the ontological side as well. Metamodel is the inclusive term for these notions: model of, model in, model from, model with, and model for.

➤ A model of consists of an examination of a model object, in the analysis of its kinds of problems, of its methods, of its techniques, of its logical structure, of its semantical organization, and of its general results.

➤ A model in is a study of the implications of object model, the examinations of the universal categories and hypotheses underlying modeling theories, taking part in modeling research, or emerging in the synthesis of its results.

➤ A model from implies a starting from or standing on position (the observable, the repeatable).

> ➤ A model <u>with</u> denotes an accompanying position, not leading the way through new doors.

> ➤ A model <u>for</u> brings to mind the idea of a clarifier for the structure and function of modeling systems and procedures.

Metamodel is more comprehensive than any single one of the above notions.

The UML model has a unique set of names for its graphical diagrams. They may be referred to by other names; however, the names given here are the correct ones. The four basic graphical diagrams are:

> ➤ Use case diagram
> ➤ Class diagram
> ➤ Behavior diagrams
> ➤ Implementation diagrams

Note: Behavior and implementation diagrams have further subdiagrams.

UML uses model extension stereotypes. Because of this, UML can be used to model any business system. The major stereotypes are use case (model, system, and package), object (model and system), organization unit, work unit, worker (case and internal), and entity. The object stereotype is important in that an *object model* (metamodel) is the things internal to a business infrastructure. An *object system* (metasystem) is the organization and work units and their relationships.

Metasystem

Metasystem is the highest level result relative to a system language. It is the goal for all phases of system modeling; the logical, epistemological, methodological, and eventually the ontological side as well. Metasystem is the inclusive term for these notions: system <u>of</u>, system <u>in</u>, system <u>from</u>, system <u>with</u>, and system <u>for</u>.

> ➤ A system <u>of</u> consists of an examination of a system infrastructure, in the analysis of its kinds of problems, of its methods, of its techniques, of its logical structure, of its semantical organization, and of its general results.

➤ A system <u>in</u> is a study of the implications of system infrastructure model, the examinations of the universal categories and hypotheses underlying modeling theories, taking part in modeling research, or emerging in the synthesis of its results.

➤ A system <u>from</u> implies a starting from or standing on position (the observable, the repeatable).

➤ A system <u>with</u> denotes an accompanying position, not leading the way through new doors.

➤ A system <u>for</u> brings to mind the idea of a clarifier for the structure and function of modeling systems and procedures.

As with a metamodel, a metasystem is more comprehensive than any single one of the above notions. In the context of UML, a metasystem is known as an *object system*, which is the organization and work units and their relationships. See Chapter 17, "Defining Components," for further information on the concrete and abstract components of a network infrastructure that can be used for the development of a metasystem.

Chapter 30

Project Management Synthesis

*Good documentation is like
a good building foundation.*

This chapter uses documentation as the synthesizing methodology to demonstrate the project and technical management processes discussed throughout the earlier chapters (see Chapter 7, "Identifying Killer Acts," for details on project management documentation). A completed documentation set is a statement of administrative and technical network goals and expectations; software and hardware legacy; market realities; and, finally, costs, skills, resources, and time constraints. There are not two sets of documents but one. This chapter is a look at the types of documentation rather than the specific documents.

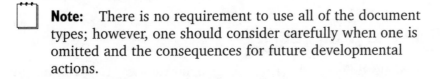 **Note:** There is no requirement to use all of the document types; however, one should consider carefully when one is omitted and the consequences for future developmental actions.

In summary, the administrative project documentation details at a minimum:

➤ Business plan and justification
➤ Network integration goals and objectives
➤ People involved (organizational chart)
➤ Milestones
➤ Cost and budgetary parameters
➤ Skill levels
➤ Risk management criteria

Part V

> ➤ Impact of the use of outside resources
> ➤ Quality control and verification process
> ➤ Training requirements

In summary, the technical project documentation details at a minimum:

> ➤ Scope definitions for
>> ➤ DCOM components (Web server, interfaces in IDL, etc.)
>> ➤ DCOM internetworking (URL, server, client interface, applications, etc.) definitions
> ➤ Model definitions
> ➤ Configuration requirements (software and hardware)
> ➤ Technical policies
> ➤ System security requirements
> ➤ Browser analysis
> ➤ Standards implementation requirements
> ➤ Interconnectivity analysis
> ➤ Performance tools requirements

Note: The fundamental principle of any project and technical management process is document what you will do and then how you have done it. Do not forget the why, when, or where.

Business Plan and Justification

These document and verify market opportunities. They can be global in nature or segmented to localized conditions. These reports should be an agreement of the viability of enterprise network integration using DCOM architecture and its supporting technologies. These reports should include how your enterprise network is to be introduced into the marketplace.

These reports justify the features, services, and applications for enterprise network integration. This input can be based on such things as customer needs, market opportunities, competition, new governmental regulations, product surveys, and (inferred) commitments for special functionality. These reports should include adequate descriptions to make design decisions. The report should also include revenue gains. The counter to this is a statement on revenue losses if this activity is not taken.

These documents include a general rationale for making the financial investment. The justification may include:

➤ Market need
➤ Concept (as compared to definition)
➤ Required functions and characteristics
➤ Impact on products
➤ Distribution strategy
➤ Competition data
➤ Return on Investment (ROI)
➤ Market window

Network Integration Goals and Objectives

The specifications give adequate requirement and limitation data for the design and development group(s). There should be design flexibility to achieve expectations. The specifications describe the expected "what" for enterprise network integration.

The specifications describe in <u>detail</u> the enterprise network integration requirements and the targeted market. The key to a successful network would include these administrative items:

➤ Market historical background
➤ Application of the enterprise network
➤ Market life cycle
➤ Portfolio information
➤ Success administrative criteria for the enterprise network
➤ Administrative design constraints
➤ Usage standards
➤ Customer participation

People Involvement

There should be an organizational chart of the team with a description of major project responsibilities. There must be a detailed statement of the network administrator's responsibilities. All other responsibility statements should be linked to this description. The format of the chart is optional or in accordance with corporate policy.

To ensure adequate people involvement, a communications document includes as a minimum:

➤ People doing the reporting

➤ People receiving the reports

➤ Types of reports to be sent

➤ When reports are sent (specific dates or after an event occurs)

➤ How reports are sent

The communications document has a "global" component as well as "local" communications processes.

Technical Network Proposal

The proposal details the technical side of the project. This includes the key goals for the new enterprise network such as:

➤ Minimal change to the legacy software and hardware in the identified intranets

➤ Internet backbone interconnectivity

➤ DCOM architecture rather than client/server architecture

➤ DCOM supporting technologies for maximum interoperability, portability, and reusability

➤ Implementation date

➤ Compliant to marketing specifications unless otherwise noted

The following information can be discussed as required:

➤ Definition of preliminary functions

➤ Hardware requirements

➤ Installation requirements

➤ Maintenance requirements

> Software strategy
> Target costs based on preliminary development definition
> Software requirements
> Summary of commercial information
> Testing requirements
> Verification requirements

Network Specification

This specification is a technical formal response to the administrative specification that defines the requirements for an enterprise network.

This specification may include the following types of information:

> Updates to the network proposal
> Enterprise network definition from a user and external viewpoint
> Enterprise network definition from a technology (hardware and software) element point
> Enterprise network estimated costs
> Enterprise network introduction strategy
> Enterprise network operational description
> Specific testing requirements
> Standards requirements

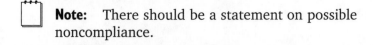

Note: There should be a statement on possible noncompliance.

Milestones and Support Requirements

These milestones and requirements include the following:

> Start and end dates for completion of the enterprise network integration
> Software features and requirements (maintenance and support)
> Hardware requirements (availability status)
> End user support

Part

V

The schedule (milestones defined within the context of time) can be as elaborate as required to implement your enterprise network. It should be usable. An example of a schedule is a flow chart with milestones and times. There could also be links to key players and groups and their responsibilities to the implementation of the enterprise network integration. A schedule should include the quality control milestones and the verification milestones.

Technical Design and Development Documents

This plan captures all major design and development deliverables and milestones for management tracking and reporting. The document may include the following items (if applicable):

➤ Enterprise network goals

➤ Enterprise network definition

➤ Enterprise network software structure description

➤ Enterprise network hardware structure description

➤ Enterprise network user definition

➤ Enterprise network market (summary from enterprise network specification)

➤ Risk assessment

➤ Responsibilities defined

➤ Resources defined

➤ Enterprise network milestones

➤ Verification dates

Cost and Budget Parameters

These two parameters can be simply defined. *Cost* is the informal financial definition. *Budget* is the formal financial definition. A cost in a budget is referred to as an expense. Costs are defined in a budget or budgets as to who is going to pay and when, usually monthly. These parameters include expected development costs, administrative costs, and estimates for direct labor as well as capital and expense requirements. Remember that the indirect costs should be considered as important as direct costs.

The documentation for these parameters includes the monitoring and reporting costs at each major phase of implementation. There should be comparisons to the original funding document used to establish financial targets and expected milestones and deliverables. The concern is how the costs (actual expenditures) and revenues go into the budget (the financial plan).

Quality Control and Verification Process

Documentation defines the role of quality control in <u>all</u> phases of the enterprise network integration process. It also defines the deliverables, functions, and specific activities required of quality control to ensure the successful completion.

This documentation includes the verification process that is a set of quality metrics that defines the various measures by which the quality of a new application is measured, attained, and controlled. The verification process is a part of the initial network design.

Note: A verification plan written after the design only looks at the "design done," not at the "design expected."

The documentation summarizes the staff, resources, and equipment required by quality control to perform and to support specific activities.

This documentation identifies the strategy for managing the software and hardware elements in the enterprise network that are a part of the trial, and the trial's location. Also, the when and by whom should be included in the strategy. This provides a clear identification of the testing requirements plus the extent of the resources and capabilities to trial.

Customer Oriented Documentation

This documentation considers such events as how the customers become users of the enterprise network. This documentation also includes a process for customer support. A strategic document provides how timely and quality enterprise network documentation becomes available.

V

Part

Training documentation has two components: internal requirements and customer requirements (external). This documentation shows how training is to be designed, developed, implemented, and verified. The emphasis is on the customer's needs and expectations.

Risk Documentation

It is important that any Risk Assessment consider both threats and opportunities. The Risk Assessment should be reviewed by all the components of the team. The review should, at the least, include representatives from each component (your group, marketing, and enterprise network users). A Risk Assessment should be done at least at every major phase of integration.

The assessment should be against established thresholds. An example of a threshold is that no action is taken until a certain number of errors are found.

Business Affiliation Documents

There is a strong possibility that outside services will be required because of the dynamic technological changes going on with DCOM and its supporting technologies. Documentation provides information when the enterprise network is to be developed by a third-party developer, such as a DCOM vendor or developer. The plan as a minimum consists of the following:

➤ Explanation for the need for a third-party developer
➤ How the third party doing the development qualifies
➤ What part the third party plays in the marketing program

There should also be a document that provides how the enterprise network is to be serviced by a third-party developer. The question is, "Will the third party do customer service?"

Using Microsoft IDL

A component can be created without using Microsoft Interface Definition Language (MIDL). However, it is important to recognize the importance of MIDL to the design of COM's programming model. There is a key principle about MIDL that one should be aware of—it is for defining interfaces and is <u>not</u> for implementing applications. This principle ensures language independence. A server could be written in Java and the client could be written in C++. This adheres to a basic characteristic of DCOM—portability, or the capability to run across a variety of platforms.

Up-front design considerations are important. It is always difficult to give a set of design principles without examples and exceptions to the rule. This is not specifically a code design book, but a process book for network administrators to be aware of core guidelines for doing internetworking. Here are ten key principles for interface design:

➤ An interface should be designed to support distributed networking.

➤ A DCOM interface must directly or indirectly derive from the IUnknown interface.

➤ The interface contract associated with a particular interface identifier (IID) cannot change.

➤ The interface should have complete documented information that describes the contract represented by the interface (programmer's responsibility).

➤ The interface should include a descriptive, human-readable, and unique name. (The IID is actually the only relevant name.)

➤ The number of methods per interface should be limited.

➤ The number of parameters per method should be limited.

➤ The method syntax of the interface should not have more than two unions.

➤ The interface's semantics should be as specific as possible.

➤ When a new version of an interface is created, use the current versional standards.

Java Internetworking Definitions

There are a number of items that have to be considered in developing Java internetworking. The first of these is the building of Java applets; this leads to the creating of Java servers, Java clients, and Java applications. The basic steps in the building process are:

1. Plan what action is to happen.

2. Assemble the required parts (sounds, images, links, etc.).

V

Part

3. Assign actions (link actions with events).
4. Test the applet.
5. Compile code or build script.
6. Implement (put on server classes, HTML code, and content elements).
7. View with Java-enabled browser.

The next level of concern is the interconnectivity between a server and the clients. The basic example is connecting the client to an instance of the server that is already running. More details on this idea are in Appendix C, "Java Internetworking Code." Because of browser handling of the restrictions on IP addressing that affect applet connections (security concerns), the client/server connections need to be built as applications.

While the development of business applications using Java is a fast-growth industry, there are three key issues:

➤ Programmers have not yet had time to develop expertise.
➤ Java is not robust.
➤ Design tools are limited.

The actualities of the above three issues are rapidly changing. For the latest in Java business applications and tools development, go to these Microsoft Web sites:

> **http://www.microsoft.com/java/**
> **http://www.microsoft.com/visualj/**
> **http://www.microsoft.com/visualj/support/**

A major impact of Java is in application version control. Easy deployment of applications across the network environment is possible. This means everyone uses the same versions of word processor, spreadsheet, etc. Individual applications need not be deployed on individual workstations. The key to this possibility is that the enterprise network or an intranet has to have an appearance of being a Web environment. In other words, the network has to use Web enabling protocols.

A part of the solution for Java business application development is to have a clearly defined high standard (quality) end goal. Part II of this book speaks to the administrative planning process for enterprise network integration; however, this same planning process is applicable to any Java business application development and design project. Part III speaks to the technical planning side of the design process. Both run in parallel with each other.

Application development productivity can increase two to five times over traditional programming development. The development is implemented by an instant rollout over a Web server.

An important component in the development of Java internetworking is having the right tools. Java tools can be divided into at least four categories:

➤ Authoring and animation
  ➤ Animating objects
  ➤ Scrolling banners
  ➤ "Wizarding"
➤ Database connectivity (end-to-end, server-based database solutions)
➤ Developer
  ➤ DCOM
  ➤ Visual J++
  ➤ Microsoft Java Virtual Machine
➤ Miscellaneous
  ➤ Security
  ➤ Services

Selection of the right development tool for the right situation and the right person is very important. There are three key selection criteria:

➤ Experience or skill level of developer
➤ Type of application
➤ Development platform

Skill level can range from a professional object-oriented programmer to an HTML developer to a person with initiative but no practical experience.

Believe it or not, there are development tools available for each of these levels.

Model Definitions (UML)

In an objected-oriented system design analysis, there are three major goals. The goals are:

➤ Define the system requirements.

➤ Identify the possible system classes.

➤ Map the system requirements to class attributes and operations.

The result should be a *class diagram* that integrates the system classes into a coherent model. There is a tool that assists in creating an object-oriented design. Rational Software Corporation developed Unified Modeling Language (UML) for this activity. For the latest information on UML, go to Rational's Web site:

http://www.rational.com/uml/index.shtml

What is a class diagram? Sometimes referred to incorrectly as an object diagram or object model, the class diagram describes classes and their static relationships to other classes in the system. An example of a dynamic relationship is when an object invokes the services of another object.

Here is a very brief table of key modeling concepts:

Construction model	A model that describes how services are defined. See implementation.
Execution model	A model that describes how services are performed. See method.
Implementation	A definition that provides the information needed to create an object and to allow the object to participate in providing an appropriate set of services. See construction model.
Inheritance	The construction that passes the methods of the implementing class from the interface class.
Method	Code that performs a service. It is an implementation of an operation. See execution model.
Object	An entity that provides one or more services that can be requested by a client.
Object model	A presentation that gives organization to a set of object concepts and terminology.
Object system	An object collection that isolates the service requestors from the service providers within an interface.

Configuration Requirements

Anyone who is named as a system administrator has experienced this problem on an individual scale and greater. It is critical to the integration of an enterprise network that there be configuration standards. These requirements include at a minimum:

➤ Operating systems
➤ Platforms (even number of display colors)
➤ Service applications
➤ Operational applications

The big reason for this is performance and interoperability. Here is a simple example: Representatives from 12 different functions within a corporation have been asked to give presentations on a common problem to the CEO. There are no standards for the presentation. Each representative uses a different font or many different fonts, or different colors to signify the same idea, while some use only text or only graphics, etc. What is the impact of these presentations on the CEO? The customer will probably draw the correct conclusion—there need to be standards even in the simplest of situations.

Technical Policies

For the purpose of this discussion, *policy* is defined as a plan or course of action. While a standard is a set of rules for defining a playing field where an exchange can take place, a policy defines the boundaries of the field and the players. Any policy has three players:

➤ The enforcer—enterprise network administrator
➤ The implementers—technicians
➤ The users

It is critical to the technical policy development process that all three players are represented. If all three players are not involved, the policy may not work. Perhaps this statement should be stronger: A policy will not work if not all the players are involved in its development.

There are ten steps in creating a technical policy:

1. State up front that "If an action is not stated as permitted, then it is prohibited."
2. Define the justifications.
   ➤ Technology
   ➤ Corporate
   ➤ Social
   ➤ Legal
3. Define the expectations
   ➤ Organizational overview
   ➤ Component particulars
4. Reference the standards.
5. Reference any relevant benchmarks.
6. Define consequences.
7. State implementation procedures.
8. State enforcement procedures.
9. State how users are to follow the policy.
10. State any special considerations.
    ➤ Corporate customers
    ➤ Vendors

Policy is the backbone to good enterprise network management. The difference between a network technical policy and an enterprise network technical policy is the requirement that both the Internet and an intranet be considered in tandem. The goals need to be realistic. Here are ten general needs that you should make specific to your organization:

➤ Adequate access for all users
➤ Adequate data delivery
➤ Design and development improvement
➤ Improved awareness among users
➤ Increased productivity
➤ Minimum downtime
➤ Reduction in maintenance costs
➤ Reliable backup procedures

➤ Resource organization
➤ User satisfaction

Security System Requirements

Security requirements are a consideration of a number of things such as levels of enforcement, types of enforcement, "bad guys," policy, etc. Chapter 28, "Security," details this area.

Certain minimal steps are required to integrate a security system into your enterprise network:

➤ Determine the level of security required for the system as a whole and then for certain types of information such as financial and personal.
➤ Determine how effective present security controls are and whether they should be integrated into your enterprise network.
➤ Develop a security policy.
➤ Enforce the security policy.

The key areas of a security policy are:

➤ Risk assessment
➤ Policy issues
➤ Policy violations
➤ Protection policy
➤ Policy interpretation
➤ Policy publication

RFC 1244, "The Site Security Handbook," is a living document through the dedication of the Site Security Policy Handbook Working Group (SSPHWG). It is not a specific standard but an information source for the Internet community.

Rather than discuss the RFC in detail, here are key policy issues raised in Section 2.3:

➤ Who is allowed to use the resources?
➤ What is the proper use of the resources?
➤ Who is authorized to grant access and approve usage?

➤ Who may have system administration privileges?

➤ What are the user's rights and responsibilities?

➤ What are the rights and responsibilities of the system administrator versus those of the user?

➤ What do you do with sensitive information?

One of the security requirements is the defining and creating of at least one software and hardware firewall. A *firewall* is a restrictive barrier that controls traffic on and off the Internet. Like any wall, it is not absolute. Like the original concept of a barrier to block fires, the electronic firewall should be able to stop ordinary fires—intrusions—but watch for the blaze or bonfire. A firewall is designed to meet a specific level of security.

Firewall software and hardware has to be chosen carefully, and just as carefully be configured and maintained. Firewalls can be defined by the techniques used. Four categories of firewalls are:

➤ Application gateways

➤ Circuit-level gateways

➤ Packet filters

➤ Passive

One of the security requirements is, of course, the one that revolves around Java.

Java provides executable content to Web browsers with an embedded interpreter and runtime library. These Web browsers can download Java programs called applets, and have the Java interpreter execute the program. The security of the system fundamentally depends on the security of three layers:

➤ Java language itself

➤ Java libraries

➤ Web browser itself

Java is an object-oriented language. The important features from a security standpoint are:

➤ Safety of the type system

➤ Lack of pointers as a language data type

➤ Use of packages with distinct namespaces

➤ Access control for variables and methods within classes

➤ Use of garbage collection (automatic memory allocation)

Browser Analysis

There are really two browsers against which every other browser is evaluated. Perhaps the two big ones also need to be evaluated more closely, in particular in the implementation of the use of Java applets.

Here is a list of functions and attributes by which the browsers can be evaluated. Chapter 24, "Evaluating Browsers," gives a method for using this list in an "objective" manner.

The following criteria are in an alphabetical list. You should establish the priority as needed.

➤ Availability
➤ Conferencing
➤ Disk size requirements
➤ Display capabilities
   ➤ Color
   ➤ Forms
   ➤ Frames
   ➤ Tables
➤ Documentation
➤ E-mail client support
➤ Font controls
➤ Foreign language support
➤ General performance
➤ Graphic handling
➤ Help capabilities
➤ HTML support
➤ Java support
➤ Load time
➤ News support
➤ Platform requirements
➤ Platform support differences
➤ Plug-in capability
➤ Printing capabilities
➤ RAM requirements

> ➤ Scripting support
> ➤ Security
> ➤ Stability
> ➤ Usability
> ➤ User-friendliness
> ➤ Vendor support
> ➤ Video capabilities

Standards Implementation Requirements

This book is a cry in the wilderness for standards. There are needs for standards in:

> ➤ Software to achieve interoperability and interconnectivity
> ➤ Hardware to achieve portability
> ➤ Security to achieve peace of mind
> ➤ Tools to achieve performance and efficiency
> ➤ Application configurations for effective communications
> ➤ Object definitions to accomplish unity
> ➤ System architecture to fulfill customer expectations

Interconnectivity Analysis

Interconnectivity issues vary from device to device and from vendor to vendor. However, there are common key performance issues that you should consider for any device. Below are ten issues:

> ➤ Bandwidth
> ➤ Communication latency
> ➤ Device configuration
> ➤ Network configuration
> ➤ Network segmentation
> ➤ Protocol implementation
> ➤ Protocol mix
> ➤ Traffic loads

> Transmission latency
> Wiring infrastructure

For any interconnectivity device from any vendor, ensure that you understand the claims, and if necessary ask for validation to your satisfaction. Remember that the performance specifications given are based on a particular configuration, load, and protocol implementation, and to a specific level of enterprise network integration.

Performance Tools Requirements

You can take from the lists of components given in the chapter on defining components, Chapter 17, and generate a list of items you need to determine their levels of performance. These items, however, can be grouped into types of performance tools required. The list given below is of that nature.

> Blueprints
>> Equipment location
>> Geographic perspective
>> Logical structure
>> Process flows
>> Wiring routes
> Code profilers
> Configuration
> Disk defragmentation programs
> Inventories
>> Equipment
>> Software
> Network infrastructure
> Policy statements
> Protocol analyzers
> Traffic
>> Analysis
>> Statistics
> Tuning tools

Software Terms and Definitions

Terms	Definitions
access control	The capability to control who accesses what on the network.
address	Every piece of data or software has one so the operating system can use it.
Address Resolution Protocol (ARP)	A member of the TCP/IP suite that translates IP addresses into physical network address. See TCP/IP and IP.
American National Standards Institute (ANSI)	A voluntary organization whose purpose is to coordinate national (public and private) standards in the U.S.
analog line	A transmission that has a continuously variable quantity (state). The most common example is voice grade for telephones. See binary line.
authentication	The act of verifying a user logging in or the integrity of a transmitted message.
Asymmetric Digital Subscriber Line (ADSL)	This line type is AT&T's asymmetric alternative to ISDN. (See Integrated Services Digital Network.) It uses ordinary copper telephone wires with uplink speeds of 64 Kbps, but with downlink speeds of 6 Mbps.
backbone	The portion of the network that carries the majority of the traffic. In an enterprise network this is the Internet.
bandwidth	Range of transmission frequencies that a network can use. Bandwidth is measured for digital signals in bits per second (bps) or for analog signals in hertz (Hz).
binary line	A transmission that is in either an off (0) or an on (1) state. The most common example is data grade telephone lines. See analog line.
bridge	The device that connects two LANs. The LANs do not have to be of the same type, for example, Token Ring or Ethernet.
CERN	The Centre European Researche Nucleare, or European Laboratory for Particle Physics in Geneva, Switzerland. Responsible for the development of HTTP (see HyperText Transfer Protocol) and the creation of the World Wide Web (WWW). All addresses that begin with http:// are part of the WWW.

Terms	Definitions
client/server network	A network model that views access computers as clients and resource computers as servers. Clients are also known as workstations.
Common Gateway Interface (CGI)	Handles information transfer between forms used on Web pages and programs or scripts found on Web servers. A major use is database inquiries.
Domain Name Service (DNS)	The readable name for an IP address, for example, mysite.com. This is in comparison to *nnn.nnn.nnn.nnn*, where *nnn* can be 000 to 255. See Uniform Resource Locator.
Frequently Asked Questions (FAQs)	A list of the most common questions on a given subject. They are found at many locations over the Web. The first question is usually "What is 'x'?"
File Transfer Protocol (FTP)	A member of the TCP/IP suite used to transfer files from one computer to another. Internet users can use FTP to download data from FTP servers. See TCP/IP.
firewall	Server software that controls access from the Internet. The outgoing access can be referred to as a gateway.
gateway	Server software that controls access to the Internet. The incoming access can be referred to as a firewall.
gopher	An early Internet protocol developed at the University of Minnesota (hence the name) for file access and transfer.
home page	The first page of a Web site.
host	Any computer system or device connected to the Internet.
hub	The network device used to concentrate multiple connections into one location. A hub is also referred to as a concentrator.
HyperText Markup Language (HTML)	A programming language that uses tags to describe textual formats. It is commonly used to develop Web pages. Its graphic counterpart is VRML. See Virtual Reality Modeling Language.
HyperText Transfer Protocol (HTTP)	The basic protocol developed at the CERN that led to the creation of the World Wide Web. The principle of word linkage is used rather than file linkage.
Integrated Services Digital Network (ISDN)	The telephony protocol to handle digital form data rather than analog form data. See Asymmetric Digital Subscriber Line.
International Organization for Standardization (ISO)	The international organization whose members represent national standards groups; seeks international standards compliance. Mistakenly referred to as the International Standards Organization.
Internet	Literally means "between nets (networks)." The global network based on TCP/IP.
Internet Architecture Board (IAB)	This board coordinates the work of the Internet Engineering Task Force (IETF) and the Internet Research Task Force (IRTF).

Terms	Definitions
Internet Control Message Protocol (ICMP)	A member of the TCP/IP suite that sends control and error messages for IP transmissions. An example message is "Traffic is too heavy." See Transmission Control Protocol/Internet Protocol.
Internet Engineering Task Force (IETF)	The international group that focuses on protocol engineering and development for the Internet.
Internet Group Management Protocol (IGMP)	A member of the TCP/IP suite that permits broadcasting messages to groups of computers. This is the basis for spamming (trash mail) and push technology. See Transmission Control Protocol/Internet Protocol.
Internet Network Information Center (InterNIC)	This group is responsible for RFCs. See Request for Comments.
Internet Protocol (IP)	The right side of the TCP/IP suite that handles transmissions of data packets over the Internet and routes them to the correct destinations. It is similar to the address on an envelope and plays the part of the mail carrier too. See Transmission Control Protocol/Internet Protocol.
Internet Relay Chat (IRC)	A protocol used for computer conferencing over the Internet.
Internet Research Task Force (IRTF)	The international group that focuses on long-term research related to the Internet.
Internet service provider (ISP)	A company that provides access to the Internet for a fee.
intranet	Literally means "within the net (network)." It is a private network that uses Internet technologies (TCP/IP, HTTP, browsers, etc.).
local area network (LAN)	A network that covers a distance of less than one mile. See wide area network.
Multipurpose Internet Mail Extensions (MIME)	The protocol that sends non-ASCII data over the Internet using the text-based protocols, such as SMTP (see Simple Mail Transfer Protocol) and POP (see Post Office Protocol).
network architecture	The network standards that define how signals are sent and how traffic is regulated over that network. There can be a model or one unique to a particular network. Unique ones are usually developed based on a model.
network management	It is human, the enterprise network administrator and staff; and electronic, the management. Its object is to keep the network working efficiently and effectively.
Network News Transfer Protocol (NNTP)	The protocol that transmits USENET messages across the Internet.
newsgroups	Online forums where information can be exchanged.
packet-switching	The data transmission technology that enabled the Internet to be developed. Messages are broken up into small addressable groups (packets) and then put back together at the destination point.

Terms	Definitions
Post Office Protocol (POP)	Usually refers to POP3, but there is an unrelated POP2. This protocol enables mail programs to interact with virtual mailboxes where mail can wait until either sent or retrieved. See Simple Mail Transfer Protocol (SMTP). Can also refer to point of presence, which is a regional hub used by an Internet service provider to access the Internet.
Point-to-Point Protocol (PPP)	This protocol establishes dial-up connections to the Internet. PPP is more powerful that SLIP. See Serial Line Internet Protocol.
Point-to-Point Tunneling Protocol (PPTP)	An enhanced version of PPP that permits TCP/IP data to be transmitted over non-TCP/IP networks. It permits intranets viewed as "virtual internets" to be connected using the Internet as a go-between. See Point-to-Point Protocol (PPP).
protocol	A set of rules, methods, procedures, or conventions used to define data transmission. See standard.
Reverse Address Resolution Protocol (RARP)	This protocol permits an Ethernet address (physical network address) to be converted into an IP address. This conversion requires an RARP server.
Request for Comments (RFCs)	Online documentation that permits review for new and enhanced protocols, and new and enhanced standards by all interested parties. InterNIC is responsible for the documentation management. See Internet Network Information Center.
router	A network device to direct (route) data packets between LANs or WANs or between a LAN and a WAN.
scalability	The amount of expansion (growth) without changing or with minimal change in procedures.
Serial Line Internet Protocol (SLIP)	A very basic packet-framing protocol that has been highly enhanced by PPP. See Point-to-Point Protocol.
server	A computer that distributes services or resources. There are many types of servers such as HTTP, SMTP, Gopher, RARP, etc. A given computer can house many different types of server software. The system architecture is dependent on the goals of the enterprise network and level of security required.
Simple Mail Transfer Protocol (SMTP)	The text-based TCP/IP protocol that exchanges mail messages on the Internet. It defines the format and content of transmissions between mail servers. See Multipurpose Internet Mail Extensions (MIME) and Post Office Protocol (POP).
standard	A standard is a set of rules for defining the playing field where exchange of data can take place. The play is defined by a protocol. See protocol.
Telnet	A terminal emulation protocol for remote logon to the Internet.

Terms	Definitions
Transmission Control Protocol (TCP)	The left side of the TCP/IP suite that handles the stream delivery services to Internet applications. It is reliable because it retransmits corrupted and lost data packets, and it ensures transmitted data-bit order at the receiving end. See Internet Protocol (IP), User Datagram Protocol (UDP), and Transmission Control Protocol/ Internet Protocol (TCP/IP).
Transmission Control Protocol/Internet Protocol (TCP/IP)	A suite of over 100 protocols that handles data transmissions over the Internet. Some of the protocols are ARP, ICMP, IP, RARP, TCP, and UDP.
Uniform Resource Locator (URL)	A human-readable format that identifies a resource location on the Internet. One key component is the DNS. See Domain Name Service.
USENET	It provides user access to news and e-mail on the Internet.
User Datagram Protocol (UDP)	This protocol allows data packets to be sent from one Internet application to another. Two important characteristics are UDP is connectionless and unreliable. UDP requires the sender and the receiver to be connected. It does guarantee transmitted data-bit order at the receiving end. See Transmission Control Protocol (TCP).
Virtual Reality Modeling Language (VRML)	A markup language developed to enhance HTML as to graphic handling and transmissions. It permits 3-D scenes. See HyperText Markup Language.
wide area network (WAN)	A network that extends over a distance greater than one mile. See local area network.
World Wide Web (WWW)	The virtual network that uses HTTP servers. See HyperText Transfer Protocol. Commonly mistaken by many as the Internet. Its creation in 1994 is the means by which the Internet came into popular use.

Hardware Terms and Definitions

This is supplemental information for Chapter 17, "Defining Components," and Chapter 21, "Identifying Interconnectivity Issues." This glossary has eight sections:

- ➤ ATM (Asynchronous Transfer Mode) Forum
- ➤ Cabling and fiber
- ➤ Hardware/software devices
- ➤ IEEE 802 Group
- ➤ Network types
- ➤ Protocols
- ➤ Standards
- ➤ Vendor groups

ATM Forum

Terms	Definitions
155 Mbps UNI Standard	In two versions: multimode and shielded twisted-pair. The multimode version is incompatible with STS-3c (Synchronous Transport Signal) UNI. This version is for private networks only.
51 Mbps UNI Standard	ATM Forum 51 Mbps User-Network Interface for Category 3 Unshielded Twisted Pair (UTP). The transmission convergence layer (framing) conforms to the STS-1 SONET standard.
ATM	Asynchronous Transfer Mode. A method for switching fixed-size packets (cells). It runs at different speeds over different media, including T3 and E3 as well as 51 Mbps, 100 Mbps, 155 Mbps, and 622 Mbps UNI standards.
ATM Forum	Nonprofit international industry consortium whose charter is to accelerate ATM acceptance and interoperability.
STS-3c UNI	SONET format for Synchronous Transport Signal level 3 concatenated (155.52 Mbps).

Terms	Definitions
TM	Traffic Management. It has eight functions to manage and control traffic: Connection Admission Control, Feedback Control, Usage Parameter Control, Priority Control, Traffic Shaping, Network Resource Management, Frame Discard, and ABR Flow Control.
UNI	User Network Interface. This is the standard for connections between stations or users and switches.

Cabling and Fiber

Terms	Definitions
100 Mbps Copper UNI Standard	ATM Forum UNI specification for 100 Mbps over copper cable.
100 Mbps UNI Standard	ATM Forum 100 Mbps multimode fiber private UNI specification. Borrows optical characteristics and basic encoding of FDDI.
AUI	Attachment Unit Interface. It is the Ethernet/IEEE 802.3 interface between a media attachment unit (MAU) and a station network interface card (NIC).
BNC Connector	Bayonet Neill-Concelman Connector. A standard connector that uses 10Base2 coaxial cable to a MAU.
Category 3 Unshielded Twisted Pair	Standard for unshielded twisted-pair cable for voice use. Some data communications standards such as 10BaseT can use it.
Category 4 Unshielded Twisted Pair	Standard for unshielded twisted-pair cable in Token Ring networks.
Category 5 Unshielded Twisted Pair	Standard for unshielded twisted-pair cable for data up to 100 Mbps.
CDDI	Copper Data Distribution Interface. Implementation of FDDI protocols over STP and UTP cables.
coaxial cable	Any electrical communications cable with a design so one conductor is in the center and the second conductor forms a ring around it.
fiber optic cable	A very long, narrow, flexible medium for conducting modulated light transmissions. Used for high-speed communications.
MAU	Media Attachment Unit. It is an IEEE 802.3 or Ethernet device, which attaches a station to the cable. Popular name is transceiver.
multimode fiber	A type of fiber mostly used for short distances. It can carry up to 100 Mbps for typical short distances; the actual maximum speed (given the right electronics) depends upon the actual distance.

Terms	Definitions
STP	Shielded Twisted Pair. A type of twisted-pair cable with a metallic shield around the twisted conductors. The shield reduces the noise from the cable and reduces the effects of noise on the communications in the cable, but changes the electrical characteristics of the cable so some equipment optimized to non-shielded cable runs worse on shielded cable.
single mode fiber	A type of fiber optic cable used for longer distances and higher speeds, for example, for long-distance telephone lines.
twisted-pair	Type of wire used by a telephone company to wire telephones—at least over distances like between your location and the central office. It has two conductors, which are twisted. The twists are important: They give it electrical characteristics, which allow some kinds of communications otherwise not possible. Ordinary telephone cables are not shielded.
UTP	Unshielded Twisted-Pair. A type of twisted-pair cable without a shield around the twisted conductors. The wiring does not require fixed spacing.

Hardware/Software Devices

Terms	Definitions
bridge	A device that connects and passes packets between two network segments that use the same communications protocol.
concentrator	A device that allows a number of stations to be connected to a LAN with a star topology. In the case of Ethernet, it is simply a multiport repeater or a hub.
dial-up modem	A modem that uses ordinary dial-up telephone lines as opposed to private or leased lines.
firewall router	A router that blocks traffic according to various criteria for security. An example is a router that allows no telnet to any host through one of its interfaces but allows FTP to a list of authorized hosts through the same interface.
gateway	Originally referred to as a router. Currently refers to a protocol conversion device.
hub	A device that usually refers to a multiport repeater or concentrator consisting of a chassis with slots to be populated by cards. It allows for a configuration with various numbers and combinations of LAN ports. Various types of devices can be referred to as a hub such as terminal servers, bridges, routers, gateways, etc.

Terms	Definitions
relay	A device that interconnects LANs. A data link relay is a bridge, but a network link relay is a router.
repeater	A device that regenerates and cleans up signals, but does no buffering of data packets between network segments. It can extend an Ethernet by strengthening signals, but timing limitations on Ethernets still limit size.
router	A network device that determines the optimal path for network traffic.
terminal server	A communication processor device that allows a number of asynchronous devices such as terminals and printers to be attached to a LAN. It permits remote logins across the LAN.

IEEE 802 Group

Terms	Definitions
10BaseF Standard	Three Ethernet specification variants (10BaseFB, 10BaseFP, and 10BaseFL) of IEEE 802.3 Specification over multimode fiber-optic cabling.
10BaseFB	Part of the 10BaseF Standard for a 10 Mbps synchronous Ethernet using a fiber-optic signaling backbone.
10BaseFL	Part of the 10BaseF Standard of a 10 Mbps multimode fiber Ethernet that attaches a pair of devices (each being either a host or a repeater) as a link segment. It was designed to replace FOIRL. 10BaseFL transceivers can operate with FOIRL transceivers. Its description is found in IEEE 802.3 Section 18.
10BaseFP	Part of the 10BaseF Standard for a passive (without repeaters) star fiber Ethernet. Its description is found in IEEE 802.3 Section 16.
10BaseT	A variant of IEEE 802.3 that uses two pairs of twisted-pair cable between stations.
100BaseT	IEEE 802.3 standards for 100 Mbps Ethernet, 100BaseTX, and 100BaseT4. They are the specifications for STP wiring.
100BaseT4	Ethernet specification for using four pairs of Category 3, 4, or 5 UTP wiring. Wiring length should not exceed 100 meters.
100BaseTX	Ethernet specification for using two pairs of either UTP or STP wiring. Wiring length should not exceed 100 meters.
IEEE	Institute of Electrical and Electronics Engineers. This is the world's largest technical professional society with the focus on advancing theory and practice of electrical electronics, and computer engineering and science.
IEEE 802 Standards	The set of IEEE standards for the definition of LAN protocols.
IEEE 802 Group	Group that standardizes LAN technologies.

Terms	Definitions
IEEE 802.1	The standard for network management and network bridging that describes an algorithm that prevents bridging loops.
IEEE 802.12	The standard for the use of the demand priority media access scheme at 100 Mbps.
IEEE 802.2	The standard for the LAN data-link protocols that handle errors, flow control, and the network layer.
IEEE 802.3	The standard for LANs that use CSMA/CD access at a variety of speeds over a variety of physical media.
IEEE 802.4	A standard for Token Bus LANs. Basically standardizes MAP, a protocol that operates a Token Bus protocol on broadband.
IEEE 802.5	A standard for token passing (4 Mbps and 16 Mbps) on LANs.
IEEE 802.6	A standard for metropolitan area networks (MANs) to support data rates from 1.5 Mbps to 155 Mbps.
IEEE 802.7 Group	Technical advisory body on broadband.
IEEE 802.8 Group	Technical advisory body on FDDI and fiber optics.
IEEE 802.9 Group	Technical advisory body on integrated data and voice networks.
SQE	Signal Quality Error is an IEEE 802.3 transmission function that tests the transceiver back to the controller.
ThickWire	ThickWire Ethernet or IEEE 802.3 10Base5.
ThinWire	ThinWire Ethernet or IEEE 802.3 10Base2.

Network Types

Terms	Definitions
backbone	A part of the network that is the primary traffic path that interconnects other parts of the network. In an enterprise network, the Internet can be considered the backbone.
collapsed backbone	A non-distributed network backbone is where all network segments are interconnected through a single internetworking device such as a router or multiport bridge.
Counterrotating Ring	A methodology that uses two ring networks going in opposite directions to provide redundancy. The network interfaces can change the path of the ring that the data flow around.
DECNet	This is the trade name of Digital Equipment Corporation for some of its networking products. It is a network built out of Digital Equipment Corporation's own networking protocols (with some standard protocols also used).

Terms	Definitions
FDSE	Full-Duplex Switched Ethernet. A variant of Switched Ethernet, which does not use CSMA/CD but uses slightly modified network interface cards to send and receive packets simultaneously.
Full-Duplex Token Ring	IBM design to add switching to token ring hubs that allows full-duplex linking to individual computers using modified token ring adapters. Has the same wiring characteristics as token ring.
Ring	A connection of two or more nodes in a logically circular topology with the data flow sequential.
Token Ring	Usually, a token ring is a type of LAN that has stations wired in a ring, where each station constantly passes a special message, a token, on to the next. Any station that has the token can send a message.

Protocols

Terms	Definitions
CMIP	Common Management Information Protocol is an OSI protocol for management of network equipment. See SNMP.
CMOT	CMIP OVER TCP/IP provides for the control and management of data between a manager and a remote network element.
Ethernet	This LAN data-link protocol was invented by the Xerox Corporation and was developed by a vendor consortium. It was later standardized as IEEE 802.3 with a few modifications.
FDDI	Fiber Data Distribution Interface. LAN data-link protocol designed to run on multimode fiber. Raw data transmission rate is 100 Mbps. Developed by ANSI.
FDDI-2	It has the same speed, same fiber, and same basic protocol as FDDI. FDDI-2 adds a layer, which allows for the allocation of fixed bandwidth to any application.
IPX	Novell's protocol used by Netware. A router with IPX routing that interconnects LANs so that Novell Netware clients and servers can talk through the router.
MIB	Management Information Base is the set of parameters an SNMP management station can query or set in an SNMP agent such as a router. Standard, minimal MIB has two definitions (MIB I, MIB II), and vendors often have custom entries.
OSI	Open Systems Interconnection. An ISO standard for communication between computer equipment and networks.

Terms	Definitions

OSI Reference Model	An ISO model for communication between computer equipment and networks, which maps out seven protocol layers. This model explains what each layer does. The model is often used to explain any protocol (not just OSI).
	Top layer: layer number 7: application layer
	                  layer number 6: presentation layer
	                  layer number 5: session layer
	                  layer number 4: transport layer
	                  layer number 3: network layer
	                  layer number 2: data-link layer (e.g., IEEE 802.x)
	Bottom layer: layer number 1: physical layer (wire and electricity)

protocol	The rules by which two network elements trade information in order to communicate.
routing protocol	A protocol sent between routers to exchange information on how to route to various parts of the network.
SDH	Synchronous Digital Hierarchy. Similar to SONET, but used outside North America. Some of the SDH and SONET standards are identical. Standardized by the CCITT.
SNMP	Simple Network Management Protocol. Manages IP-based network equipment like routers and bridges; also includes wiring hubs, workstations, etc.
tunneling	The taking of some protocol family's ability to move packets from user to user, or to open virtual circuits between users, and use this as if it were a data-link protocol to run another protocol family's upper layers (or even the same protocol family's upper layers). For example, running TCP/IP over AppleTalk instead of something like Ethernet.

Standards

Terms	Definitions
ANSI	American National Standards Institute is a definer of hardware and software standards.
ANSI X3	ANSI group developing standards for information processing.
ANSI X3T9	ANSI group within X3 developing standards for I/O interfaces.
ANSI X3T9.3 Committee	ANSI group within X3T9 that standardizes HIPPI.
ANSI X3T9.5 Committee	ANSI group within X3T9 that standardizes FDDI, PMD, and SMF-PMD, and is standardizing TP-PMD and LCF-PMD.
Fiber Channel	An ANSI standard to replace HIPPI. It uses optical fiber instead of copper cables. Speeds are up to roughly 1 Gbps.

Terms	Definitions
FOIRL	Fiber Optic Inter-Repeater Link. A standard for running IEEE 802.3 over fiber, linking two devices (each either a host or a repeater) as a link segment. 10BaseFL has replaced it.
GOSIP	Government Open Systems Interconnection Profile. A subset of OSI standards specific to U.S. government procurements that maximizes interoperability in areas where plain OSI standards are ambiguous or allow options.
HIPPI	High-Performance Parallel Interface. Used to connect supercomputer to peripherals.
HSSI	High Speed Serial Interface. A data terminal (DTE) and circuit terminating (DCE) equipment interface for high-speed (52 Mbps) communication over WAN links.
SONET	Synchronous Optical Network. A set of standard fiber optic-based serial standards used with ATM in North America. Developed by Bellcore. Different types of SONET run at different speeds (OC1 runs at 51 Mbps, OC3 runs at 155 Mbps, OC12 runs at about 600 Mbps, OC48 runs at over 2 Gbps). SONET uses different types of fiber. (OC3 has several variants for use with different fibers and different distances; there are versions for both single mode and multimode fiber.)
T1	A phone company standard for running 24 digitized voice circuits through one 1.5 Mbps digital channel.

Vendor Groups

Terms	Definitions
Fast Ethernet Alliance	A group of vendors that works on a 100 Mbps version of IEEE 802.3.
Fiber Channel Systems Initiative	A group of vendors that works to accelerate Fiber Channel acceptance and interoperability. Members include HP, IBM, and Sun.
Full Duplex Switched Ethernet Consortium	A group of vendors that works on the details of FDSE.

Java Internetworking Code

Because Microsoft has a dynamic software development environment, the comments in this appendix may only express a historical instance. Things do not necessarily change, but their labels will. Microsoft is seeking a tighter integration with Java. This appendix emphasizes process over detail.

This appendix looks at six areas for which one would have need for creating Java internetworking code and a support newsgroup, Java Networking. The six areas are:

➤ Sockets
➤ Applets and Servlets
➤ Uniform Resource Locator (URL)
➤ Microsoft Interface Definition Language (MIDL)
➤ Remote Procedure Calls (RPC)
➤ Java Database Connectivity (JDBC)

This appendix closes with three miscellaneous coding examples.

Sockets

The key idea to remember is that Java sockets are <u>always</u> TCP sockets. A *socket* is an addressable point. It consists of an IP address and a TCP or UDP port number. There can also be a third parameter, a Boolean value. This value indicates whether the socket is a stream or a datagram. A socket provides an application access to the TCP/IP protocols.

Note: Because of the unreliability of datagram sockets, programmers almost exclusively use stream sockets.

TCP/IP API has a characteristic that is common to Java, portability. It works across operating systems and hardware that support TCP/IP. It uses numbers to uniquely identify a communications endpoint.

TCP is a connection-oriented protocol. Its counterpoint is User Datagram Protocol (UDP) which is a connectionless service, a datagram.

There are a number of ways to categorize sockets. Categories are usually language view dependent. A Java view is:

➤ Socket (TCP endpoint, a "thing")
➤ ServerSocket (TCP endpoint, a "person")
➤ DatagramSocket (UDP endpoint, a "mailbox")
➤ DatagramPacket (UDP endpoint, a "letter")
➤ URL (Uniform Resource Locator, an "address")
➤ URLConnection (Web object connection, a CGI-bin script)

Writing a socket can be an easy process. Below is a four-step process for writing a socket for TCP/IP port 7, Echo:

1. Read a keyboard input.
2. Write it to a socket connected to TCP port 7.
3. Read the reply from the socket connection.
4. Print the input from the socket to the screen.

Selected TCP port numbers are:

➤ 13   DAYTIME
➤ 21   FTP
➤ 23   Telnet
➤ 25   SMTP (Simple Mail Transfer Protocol)
➤ 37   TIME
➤ 42   NAMESERV (Host Name Server)
➤ 110   POP3 (Post Office Protocol v3)
➤ 161   SNMP (Simple Network Management Protocol)

The Socket class has three key methods:

➤ close   Closes the connector
➤ getInputStream   Gets the input stream for the socket
➤ getOutputStream Gets the output stream for the socket

To connect directly to a server and to do direct protocol handling, use Java's Socket classes. Creating the object makes the connection.

```
Socket comm = Socket("www.yourplace.com, 80);
```

The ServerSocket class is all you need to write Java code for servers. It has the constructors and all the various methods required.

A server's life cycle is basically six steps:

1. A ServerSocket is created on a port using a ServerSocket() constructor.
2. ServerSocket waits for an incoming attempt using its accept() method.
3. Either the socket's getInputStream or its getOutputStream method is called to get data streams that communicate with the client.
4. There is interaction between the server and client based on the protocol used.
5. The connection closes.
6. Server returns to step 2.

Handling Applets and Servlets

Java API supports applet cooperation with two explicit methods: getApplet and getApplets. There are three key problems for handling APIs:

➤ Application implementation is without a standard.
➤ They return "accessible" applets; however, there is no standard for the meaning of "accessible."
     ➤ Could be applets on the same page
     ➤ Could be applets from the same site
     ➤ Could be browser dependent
➤ They only show fully loaded and initialized applets.

Basic code is:

```
Applet myapt = getAppletContext().getApplet ("Myapt");
```

The myapt variable sets to an applet instance of an applet called "Myapt."

An applet such as "Myapt" is specified in HTML, not Java. For example, to find an animator applet the HTML might look as follows:

```
<applet code ="Animator.class" width=15 height=20 name="Myapt">
<!-- parameters here -->
</applet>
```

The getApplets method differs from getApplet in that it returns an enumeration. An enumeration enables one to query an applet's characteristics, such as name. Here is basic code using getApplets:

```
Applet myapt;

for (    Enumeration n = getAppletContext().getApplets();
            n.hasMoreElements();
              ) {
        try {
        Applet t = (Applet) n.nextElement();
        if ("Myapt" equals (t.getParameter("name"))) {
                myapt = t;
                break;
          }
        }
        catch (ClassCastException n) {
        }
}
```

Servlets are server-side applets. Applets are client-side oriented. Servlets are defined as either trusted or untrusted. A *trusted servlet* is loaded from a local or identified site. An *untrusted servlet* is loaded from an unknown Internet location.

Handling Uniform Resource Locators (URLs)

The core Java library has built-in classes for working with the Internet and the Web. One important class is URL. This makes a fetch of a document very easy. A high-level document type can be among other types:

➤ Text

➤ Image

➤ Video

- Audio
- HTML
- VRML
- Java class file

The core code using URL is:

```
URL home = new URL("http://www.myplace.com/");
Object page = home.getContent();
```

There are various ways to create a new URL object. The most common way, and perhaps the simplest, is (URL string spec). A URL string is a single parameter.

```
URL doc = new URL("http://www.myplace.com/~doc1/");
```

URLConnection does much of the handling of URLs. Some methods for handling information return are:

- getContentEncoding   Data encoding for transport
- getContentLength   Document byte length
- getContentType   Document MIME media type
- getExpiration   Document expiration date
- getLastModified   Get latest version of document

Using the java.net package, you may get a URLConnection object and manipulate it. There are provisions for:

- Opening the connection
- Guessing the content type using the filename
- Setting the correct content handler to get a file
- Getting content length, type, and date
- Determining type of stream available

The life cycle or states of a given URLConnection are:

- created   Options set
- connected   Connection opened and initialized
- output   Optional: Data written
- input   Data read
- disconnected   Connection closed

Microsoft Interface Definition Language (MIDL)

When doing Java internetworking with DCOM architecture, the use of Microsoft Interface Definition Language (MIDL) is a way for a programmer to define interfaces. MIDL describes the interfaces that client objects call and object implementation provides. An IDL interface defines an interface and specifies an operation's parameters.

MIDL plays an important role in DCOM programming. In fact, all DCOM programming should begin with MIDL to define the interfaces. The ISUM interface would be as follows:

```
import "unknwn.idl";
[ object, uuid(4000004-0000-0000-1942-00000000001)  ]
interface ISUM : IUnknown
{
        HRESULT Sum[in] int x, [in] int y, [out, retval] int* retval);
};
```

The universally unique identifier (UUID) assigned to the interfaces makes it unique. The ISUM interface's uuid is derived from IUnknown. IUnknown is imported from the unknwn.idl file.

The resulting Java for ISUM would look as follows:

```
public interface ISum extends com.ms.com.IUnknown
{
     public abstract int Sum(int x, int y);
}
```

Note: DCOM uses a 128-bit interface identifier. Even with the algorithm used to create a *global* unique identifier, there will be enough to last until there is a new generation or two of software. The practical usage is infinite even though the number is not infinite.

MIDL-Java Mapping

The following list gives the mapping for basic MIDL types to Java types. Since there are no unsigned types in Java, there is a requirement to convert to a larger type if applicable.

➤ boolean   boolean
➤ char   char (8-bit unsigned character data item)
➤ wchar_t   char (16-bit wide character type)
➤ octet   byte
➤ string   java.lang.String
➤ wstring   java.lang.String
➤ short   short (16-bit integer)
➤ unsigned short   short (16-bit integer)
➤ long   int (32-bit integer)
➤ unsigned long   int (32-bit integer)
➤ long long   long (32-bit integer)
➤ float   float (32-bit floating-point number)
➤ double   double (64-bit floating-point number)
➤ fixed   java.math.BigDecimal

Directional Attributes

MIDL has three directional attributes: [in], [out], and [in, out]. The default is that parameters are passed into the server, or [in], as a part of the request message that invokes a method. These three directional attributes assist in the goal of limiting network traffic generated by remote calls.

The [out] attribute is used for directing data to the client. Data is sent in the response message when the function call is completed. The freeing of memory is the client's responsibility.

The [in, out] attribute is used to pass data as specified by a pointer parameter. It must pass to a server as part of a request message and return to the client using a request message. Again, it is the client that frees memory.

Arrays

MIDL can handle a number of array types. The rule of thumb is the directional attribute.

Here are six array types:

➤ Character   Handles string parameters

➤ Conformant   Determines at run time the number of elements transmitted to the server

➤ Fixed   Determines if an argument points to a single item or to multiple items

➤ Multidimensional Handles level of indirection

➤ Open   Handles the attributes of both conformant and varying arrays

➤ Varying   Handles the problem when a server returns less than the full number of elements

Pointers

MIDL can handle a number of pointer types. The pointer type is determined by the pointer_default attribute. The default is unique.

Here are four pointer types:

➤ Full   Handles the code distribution that was executed within a single process

➤ Interface   Handles when one interface has to point to another

➤ Reference   Points to a valid memory address

➤ Unique   Functions like a full pointer except it cannot handle aliases

Remote Procedure Calls (RPC)

The concept of RPC is one of the items being impacted by the way Microsoft views its integration with Java. It is, according to its name, a technique to handle objects that are not local.

RPC addresses the issue of the number of errors that can occur when applications seek to communicate with each other over a network. It provides a facility to build distributed systems based on the legacy procedural model, Local Procedure Call (LPC). This is done through the use of Microsoft Interface Definition Language (MIDL). See the discussion above on MIDL.

Java Database Connectivity (JDBC)

While Open Database Connectivity (ODBC) is probably a de facto standard for database access, Sun wrote the first platform-independent database Java driver. The driver is a low-level interface to an ODBC driver. If your version of Visual J++ does not have the base Java class java.sql.*, it can be downloaded from Microsoft. Expect, as you read this, there have been toolkits developed that include dynamic mapping of tables to Java classes and embedded SQL.

JDBC was created to directly access databases from within a Java object. JDBC's core is the DriverManager. It provides a common interface to a JDBC Driver object. The Driver creates and implements for a specific database these objects:

➤ Connection
➤ Statement
➤ ResultSet

The DriverManager then acquires these three objects for itself.

JDBC connects Java Beans to a relational database through a JDBC driver. It allows these beans to save their state to legacy data stores. The API is implemented in the java.sql package. This package defines the interfaces for the driver. Vendors have implemented database-specific JDBC drivers.

The JDBC API defines classes from the java.sql package so an applet or an application connects to a database. The applet usually remotely links through the Internet or an intranet to a relational database. The drivers are a group of Java classes that include java.sql.CallableStatement, java.sql.Connection, java.sql.PreparedStatement, and java.sql.Statement. It is java.sql.DriverManager that does the loading and unloading of the correct driver.

There are four types of drivers. Each has its programming trade-off. The driver types are:

➤ JDBC-to-ODBC
➤ native API, partial Java
➤ net protocol, all Java
➤ native protocol, all Java

The first is complex. The second is as complex as the first with the requirement to access ODBC. The third is the most flexible but requires additional security support. The fourth is commonly used for intranet access but requires a vendor solution.

Newsgroup: Java Networking

A very interesting newsgroup is Java Networking. To subscribe, send an e-mail to java-networking-request@cdt.luth.se and put in the body Subscribe.

To get a feel for the subjects discussed during a month's period, here is a listing in alphabetical order:

➤ Archie connection using sockets

➤ Auto-executing class files

➤ Capturing TAB in AWT

➤ Closing half a socket

➤ Closing a URLConnection

➤ Dynamic reloading of servlet classes

➤ Extending FilterInputStream

➤ Getting URL of a frame

➤ How to redirect a Web page

➤ Is it possible for me to control my server's actions?

➤ Java C Interface

➤ Java Debugger

➤ Java Plug-in Security

➤ Java Socket Programming

➤ NullPointerException in sun.net

➤ Ping!

➤ Programming with JNI

➤ Question about multiple connections to a socket

➤ Question on DatagramPacket from vector

➤ Reading URL using openStream

➤ RSVP implementations

➤ Running servlets from a Jar

➤ Select

➤ SNMP Support

➤ Socket Input and OutputStreams

➤ Sockets

➤ Sockets and try{ blocks

➤ SSL for HP-UX

➤ TCP versus UDP

The responses came from all over the world. Most of the original e-mails got quick replies with straightforward support. The range of experience was from little to significant.

The writer of the Ping! e-mail asked, "How would one perform a ping operation in Java?" One person responded, "Sigh. Native method." However, others did respond with other possible answers.

Miscellaneous Java Internetworking Code

This section looks at short pieces of code to give ideas. This is not a comprehensive tutorial on writing Java code for internetworking since this book's focus is for a network manager to become aware of a process used by an important member of his development team, the Java programmer.

There are a few books out on this subject. It is also recommended you see articles in the many Java-oriented magazines or journals.

Note: It is common to use an *e* as a variable name in Java coding; however, to show other possibilities, other variables are used in the examples.

InetAddress Object and getByName

This program has two parts: creating an InetAddress object and using UnknownHost Exception.

```
import java.net.*;

class company  {

    public static void main (String args[])     {
```

```
        try   {
            InetAddress address = InetAddress.getByName("www.
company.com");
            System.out.println(address);
        }
         catch (UnknownHostException u)   {
             System.out.println("Cannot find www. company.com");
         }
      }
   }
```

InetAddress Object and getLocalHost

This example shows how to get your own IP address and the difference between print and println. A new line character is printed with println. The result is message plus address plus a period and then a new line.

```
import java.net.*;

class myIP   {

    public static void main (String args[])     {

        try   {
            InetAddress mycomputer = InetAddress.getLocalHost();
            byte[] address = mycomputer.getAddress();
            System.out.print(My IP Address is ");
            for (int i = 0; i < address.length; i++)    {
                int unsignedByte = address[i] < 0 ? address[i] + 256 :
address[i];
                System.out.print(unsignedByte + ".");
            }
            System.out.println();
            }
        catch (UnknownHostException u)   {
            System.out.println("Cannot find IP address.");
        }
      }
   }
```

Note: A programming historical point: The variable *i* has been commonly used for a variable name for an integer since the inception of COBOL.

Method: getImage

This method is found in the java.applet package. This method retrieves image information based on a URL parameter, path, and filename (a string). This function makes a return immediately, but the image is not retrieved until the Image object is needed. The basic syntax is:

```
public image getImage(URL path, filename);
```

The four examples show that one image can be retrieved in many ways, depending on its location.

```
// Uses a URL to find images directory
// Uses a string filename parameter to get image file
Image logo1 = getImage(new URL("http://www.mycompany.com/"),
"logo1.gif");


// Uses getCodeBase()
// Applet on many Web servers
// Image only in one directory
Image logo1 = getImage(getCodeBase(), "logo1.gif"));


// Uses getDocumentBase()
// Applet on one Web server
// Applet embedded in many Web pages that load different images
Image logo1 = getImage(getDocumentBase(), "logo1.gif"));


// Uses getDocumentBase()
// Directory called graphics
// Directory graphics and HTML page in a common directory
Image logo1 = getImage(getDocumentBase(), "graphics/logo1.gif"));
```

Note: Downloading sounds uses syntax similar to the four examples above.

Index

Other books by George Doss

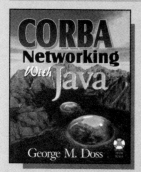

CORBA Network-ing with Java
George M. Doss

This Doss title focuses on a ten-step process of project management for a collaborative effort in the development of an enterprise network with CORBA architecture and Java internetworking. The emphasis is on practical solutions. This title is targeted for experienced object-oriented programmers in identifying key programming design issues. Included on the CD are computer-based training courses highlighting intranet fundamentals. The book emphasizes two key networking issues—remote access and security.

350 pp. • 7½ x 9¼ • December 20, 1998 • ⬥ includes CD
1-55622-654-3 • $36.95 US
$70.95 AUS. • $57.95 CAN.

level: intermediate/advanced
category: networking/CORBA/Java/project management

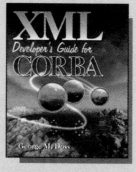

XML Developer's Guide to CORBA
George M. Doss

Experienced programmers and developers who have worked with Java, SGML, and especially HTML in a networking environment are ideally suited for this book. The title is also targeted for those programmers and developers who have considerable experience with the CORBA network architecture. The key feature of this innovative title is the development of XML applications based on Common Object Request Broker Architecture (CORBA). Included with the CD is a training course on XML 1.0 recommendations for the official specification for the language.

350 pp. • 7½ x 9¼ • June 20, 1999 • ⬥ includes CD
1-55622-668-3 • $39.95 US
$75.95 AUS. • $61.95 CAN.

level: intermediate/advanced XML and CORBA programmers and developers
category: XML/CORBA/object-oriented networking/Java

Other related books

Practical Guide to SGML/XML Filters
Norman E. Smith, CDP

Practical Guide to SGML/XML Filters presents techniques for processing Standardized General Markup Language (SGML) and EXtensible Markup Language (XML) data and documents. The techniques described in this book also apply to HTML. SGML and XML documents are very structured, which allows programs, also called filters, to easily convert the information to other forms such as Ventura or TeX for typesetting, to HTML or Windows Help for online access, or to CD-ROM for distribution. The book presents seven programming languages commonly used for creating SGML and XML filter programs: AWK, BALISE, C, Perl, OmniMark, SGMLC, and S-Engine. Ten case studies, with working code, of common SGML and XML filter programs are included. The programmer or web master who has to convert documents and data between different formats will find this book useful.

550 pp. • 7½ x 9¼ • ⬥ includes CD
1-55622-587-3 • $59.95 US
$113.95 AUS. • $89.95 CAN.

level: advanced
category: SGML/XML/HTML programming

Practical Guide to XML
Norman E. Smith

Practical Guide to XML provides a framework for programmers and developers to develop XML, or Extensible Markup Language, applications. The book reviews the differences between SGML and XML, and identifies current XML applications. Readily available XML tools are identified including tools written by the author and specifically enhanced for this book. The inclusion of case studies of real-world applications reinforces the practical emphasis of the title. Examples are provided in multiple programming languages. The example code and a selection of XML-capable software are included on the CD-ROM.
Norman E. Smith has written twelve computer books for Wordware Publishing, including *Practical Guide to SGML/XML Filters* (1-55622-587-3) and *Developer's Guide to HP Printers* (1-55622-603-9).

350 pages • 7½ x 9¼ • January 20, 1998 • ⬥ includes CD
1-55622-635-7 • $29.95 US
$56.95 AUS. • $44.95 CAN.

level: intermediate/advanced
category: Internet programming/ XML programming

  Visit our web site at **www.wordware.com**

Top Sellers

Collaborative Computing with Delphi 3

James Callan

854 pp. • 7½ x 9¼ • includes CD
1-55622-554-7 • **$59.95** US
$113.95 AUS. • $89.95 CAN.

level: advanced
category: Delphi programming

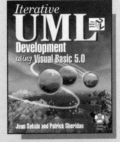

Iterative UML Development Using Visual Basic 5.0

Jean M. Sekula and Patrick W. Sheridan

296 pages • 7½ x 9¼ • includes CD
1-55622-638-1 • **$42.95** US
$81.95 AUS. • $64.95 CAN.

level: introductory to intermediate
category: object-oriented prog./Visual Basic 5.0

Developing Enterprise Applications with Power-Builder 6.0

Blair Taylor

704 pp. • 7½ x 9¼ • includes CD
1-55622-609-8 • **$49.95** US
$94.95 AUS. • $74.95 CAN.

level: intermediate to advanced
category: client-server development

Learn ActiveX Scripting with Microsoft Internet Explorer 4.0

Nathan Wallace

688 pp. • 7½ x 9¼ • includes CD
1-55622-611-X • **$44.95** US
$85.95 AUS. • $67.95 CAN.

level: introductory to intermediate
category: ActiveX/Internet Explorer 4.0

Digital Imaging in C and the World Wide Web

W. David Schwaderer

402 pp. • 7½ x 9¼ • includes CD
1-55622-602-0 • **$39.95** US
$75.95 AUS. • $59.95 CAN.

level: intermediate to advanced
category: Internet/digital imaging/C programming

Learn AutoCAD LT 97 for Windows 95/NT

Ralph Grabowski

280 pp. • 7½ x 9¼ • includes CD
1-55622-597-0 • **$24.95** US
$47.95 AUS. • $37.95 CAN.

level: introductory to intermediate
category: CAD/graphics

Learn Personal Oracle 8.0 with Power Objects 2.0

Jose Ramalho

456 pp. • 7½ x 9¼
1-55622-546-6 • **$39.95** US
$75.95 AUS. • $59.95 CAN.

level: introductory to advanced
category: database programming/Oracle

Learn Visio 5.0 for the Advanced User

Ralph Grabowski

376 pp. • 7½ x 9¼ • includes CD
1-55622-595-4 • **$34.95** US
$66.95 AUS. • $52.95 CAN.

level: intermediate to advanced
category: business graphics/Windows applications

The Tomes of Delphi 3: Win32 Graphical API

Ayres, Bowden, Diehl, Dorcas, Harrison, Mathes, Reza, and Tobin

930 pp. • 7½ x 9¼ • includes CD
1-55622-610-1 • **$54.95** US
$104.95 AUS. • $82.95 CAN.

level: intermediate to advanced
category: Delphi 3/Win32 programming

Learn Visio 5.0

Ralph Grabowski

408 pp. • 7½ x 9¼
1-55622-568-7 • **$29.95** US
$56.95 AUS. • $44.95 CAN.

level: introductory to intermediate
category: CAD/drawing/business graphics

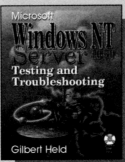

Companion CD

This CD-ROM contains two computer-based training courses:

➤ Fundamentals of an Intranet

➤ Developing a Project Plan

1. Minimum monitor requirements:
   a. 640 x 480 pixels
   b. High color (16-bit)
2. To see Fundamentals of an Intranet, either copy Intranet.exe to your hard drive and run or click on Intranet.exe.
3. To see Developing a Project Plan, either copy Project.exe to your hard drive and run or click on Project.exe.

 Notice: Opening the CD package makes this book nonreturnable.